Comparative Constitutional Review

Comparative Constitutional Review

Cases and Materials

Michael Louis Corrado

ARCH T. ALLEN PROFESSOR OF LAW
AND PROFESSOR OF PHILOSOPHY
UNIVERSITY OF NORTH CAROLINA
AT CHAPEL HILL

CAROLINA ACADEMIC PRESS
Durham, North Carolina

Library of Congress Cataloging in Publication Data

Corrado, Michael Louis, 1940–
Comparative Constitutional Law: Cases and Materials / by Michael Louis
Corrado.
   p. cm.
   Includes bibliographical references and index.
   ISBN 0-89089-710-7
   1. Judicial review—Europe—Cases. 2. Constitutional law—Europe—
Cases 3. Judicial review—United States—Cases 4. Constitutional law—
United States I. Title

   K3175.C67 2004
   342--dc22

2004004189

Carolina Academic Press
700 Kent Street
Durham, North Carolina 27701
Telephone (919) 489-7486
Fax (919) 493-5668
www.cap-press.com

for Crispin and Gian

Contents

Preface

A casebook is a collection of bits and pieces of cases, statutes, constitutional provisions, articles, and books, assembled by an editor. The successful casebook tells the story of a certain body of law—or rather, it sets down material upon which the reader should be able to construct a story fitting a certain body of law.

This particular casebook is a result of a project I undertook some five or six years ago. At that time I had been teaching comparative law for some years, and I had come to the conclusion that what the field needed was more casebooks: not bigger and better, but smaller casebooks. The problem is that comparative law teachers have very different ideas of what ought to be taught, and how it ought to be taught, and none of the few large casebooks out there really answers the needs of the teacher trying to put her course together in her way.

My idea was to begin a collection of much smaller casebooks devoted to particular areas of comparative law. Each one would contain cases and materials, but would be small enough (and inexpensive enough) so that the comparative law teacher might, instead of having her students buy one large casebook, construct her course out of a number of these smaller "case-booklets." Happily Carolina Academic Press also thought such a series was a good idea, and we soon had five titles under contract. Two of the titles have already been published: one an introduction to comparative law, the other on comparative criminal procedure.

A book on comparative constitutional review was one that seemed especially appropriate for the series. It could be the basis for a unit on judicial review in any comparative law course; but it might also be useful as the basic text in a seminar on comparative judicial review. Outside the field of comparative law it could well fit into a general course on constitutional law, an advanced course on judicial review, or even an introduction to law course. I undertook that part of the project myself, and the present volume is the result.

If the book has a theme it is the moving nature of the subject matter. Chapter One begins in the French Revolution, with a rationale for parliamentary supremacy. It seems to me that a full understanding of constitutional review of legislation requires a background understanding of what the world would be like without it, and why some might prefer a world of that sort.

The book is intended not only for American students, but for students abroad as well, and consequently it contains, in Chapter Two, a brief survey of the American notion of constitutional review, starting out (again) from the late eighteenth century and the American Revolution. Chapter Three takes up the development of the independent constitutional court, starting with Kelsen and Austria between the two World Wars and tracing the development of such courts in Italy, Germany and France after the second of those wars. The difference between constitutional review in American courts and constitutional review in much of the rest of the world is that in the United States such review takes place in the ordinary courts, and elsewhere it is restricted to the specialized constitutional courts. The ordinary courts have no role whatever, except in some places to pass questions of constitutionality on to the constitutional courts.

The significance of the developments described in the final chapter can best be understood against the background of this traditional constitutional impotence of the ordinary courts. The development in the last half of the twentieth century of a supranational government in Europe with its own courts and legislature has brought to the ordinary courts of Europe the power of judicial review of legislation. Conversely the willingness of the ordinary courts to use that power has contributed to the formation of a genuine regional state in Europe. Whether this development will be replicated in other areas remains to be seen.

The materials I have used are standard materials. The various abortion decisions make a nice basis for comparison, and they have become an important part of the literature that any beginning student ought to know. Some of the translations of cases are my own, but I have also relied on translations from journal articles and from some of the classic texts, especially Cappelletti and Cohen's Comparative Constitutional Law (1979), and deVries' Civil Law and the Anglo-American Lawyer (1975).

Different parts of the book may be relevant for different courses. American teachers may not want to spend much time on *stare decisis*, and may want to skip Chapter Two entirely. Teachers elsewhere may want to stress those very parts and go easy on some others. But a teacher anywhere might be justified in treating all four chapters equally. It is one thing to be aware of our own tradition and another to see it in a comparative setting.

I am grateful to the Law School and the Institute for the Arts and Humanities at the University of North Carolina at Chapel Hill, and to the Suffolk University Law School, for support during the writing of the book. I am indebted to my colleagues Jack Boger, John Orth and Mark Weisburd for their comments, and to the assistants who have helped with the project: Lisa Brown, Katie Miltich, Brian Oten, Brenda Thissen, James Langston.

As always I am indebted to Dr. Gail Corrado for her steadfast support.

Acknowledgments

The author is grateful for permission to use material from the following sources:

Louis M. Aucoin, "Judicial Review in France," volume 15, number 2, Boston College International and Comparative Law Review (1992), pages 443 - 469. Reprinted with permission. (c) by Boston College School of Law.

Mauro Cappelletti, "Repudiating Montesquieu?" volume 35, Catholic University Law Review (1985), pages 1 - 32. Reprinted with permission. (c) by Catholic University of America Law School.

Richard J. Cummins, "The General Principles of Law, Separation of Powers and Theories of Judicial Decision in France," volume 35, International and Comparative Law Quarterly (1986), pages 594 - 628. Reprinted with permission. (c) by The British Institute for International and Comparative Law.

Gerald Kock, "The Machinery of Law Administration in France," volume 108, University of Pennsylvania Law Review (1960), pages 366 - 386. Reprinted with permission. (c) by University of Pennsylvania Law Review.

James Beardsley, "Constitutional Review in France," 1975 Supreme Court Review, pages 189 - 259. Reprinted with permission. (c) by The University of Chicago Press.

Antonin Scalia, *A Matter of Interpretation* (1997). Reprinted with permission. (c) by Princeton University Press, Princeton, N. J.

Mitchel de S.-O.-L'E. Lasser, "Judicial (Self-) Portraits," volume 104, Yale Law Journal (1995), pages 1325 - 1410. Reprinted with permission. (c) by Yale Law Journal Co., Inc.

Dominic Massaro, "Foreordained Failure: New York's Experiment with Political Review of Constitutionality," volume 70, New York State Bar Journal (Oct. 1998), pages 12 - 19. Reprinted with permission. (c) by New York State Bar Association Journal.

L. A. Powe, "The Politics of American Judicial Review," volume 38, Wake Forest Law Review (2003), pages 697 - 732. Reprinted with permission. (c) by Wake Forest Law Review Association

Sanford Levinson, "Why I Do Not Teach *Marbury* (Except to Eastern Europeans) and Why You Shouldn't Either," volume 38, Wake Forest Law Review (2003), pages 553 - 578. Reprinted with permission. (c) by Wake Forest Law Review Association.

Gary Lawson, "The Constitutional Case against Precedent," volume 17, Harvard Journal of Law and Public Policy (1994), pages 23 - 33. Reprinted with permission. (c) by the President and Fellows of Harvard College.

Cynthia Vroom, "Equal Protection versus the Principle of Equality," volume 21, Capital University Law Review (1992), pages 199 - 223. Reprinted with permission. (c) by Capital University Law Review.

John Bell, *French Constitutional Law* (1992). Reprinted with permission. (c) by Oxford University Press, Oxford and New York.

Herbert Hausmaninger, "Judicial Referral of Constitutional Questions in Austria, Germany, and Russia," volume12, Tulane European and Civil Law Forum (1997), pages 25 - 37. Reprinted with permission. (c) by Tulane European and Civil Law Forum.

Mauro Cappelletti and John Clarke Adams, "Judicial Review of Legislation," volume 79, Harvard Law Review (1966), pages 1207 - 1224. Reprinted with permission. (c) by Harvard Law Review Association.

Stanley Paulson, "Constitutional Review in the United States and Austria," volume 16, Ratio Juris (2003), pages 223 - 237. Reprinted with permission. (c) by Blackwell Publishing, Oxford.

Guido Calabresi, "Two Functions of Formalism," volume 67, University of Chicago Law Review (2000), pages 479 - 488. Reprinted with permission. (c) by University of Chicago Law School.

Antonio Baldassare, "Structure and Organization of the Constitutional Court of Italy," volume 40, St. Louis University Law Journal (1996), pages 649 - 658. Reprinted with permission. (c) by St. Louis University School of Law.

William J. Nardini, "Passive Activism and the Limits of Judicial Self-Restraint," volume 30, Seton Hall Law Review (1999), pages 1 - 63. Reprinted with permission. (c) by Seton Hall University School of Law.

Mario Comba, "Constitutional Law," in *Introduction to Italian Law* (eds. Jeffrey S. Lena and Ugo Mattei, 2002), pages 31-40. Reprinted with permission. (c) by Kluwer Law International, London and the Hague.

Mauro Cappelletti and William Cohen, *Comparative Constitutional Law: Cases and Materials* (1979). Reprinted with permission of the publisher, Palgrave Macmillan.

Andrea Bianchi, "Venezia v. Ministero di Grazia e Giustizia, Italian Constitutional Court, June 27, 1996" (ed. Bernard H. Oxman), volume 91, number 4, American Journal of International Law (1997), pages 727 - 733. Reprinted with permission. (c) by American Society of International Law.

David S. Clark, "Selection and Accountability of Judges in West Germany," volume 61, Southern California Law Review (1988), pages 1795 - 1847. Reprinted with permission. (c) by The University of Southern California Law School.

Donald P. Kommers, "German Constitutionalism," volume 40, Emory Law Journal (1991), pages 837 - 873. Reprinted with permission. (c) by Emory University School of Law.

Wolfgang Zeidler, "The Federal Constitutional Court of the Federal Republic of Germany," volume 62, number 4, Notre Dame Law Review (1987), pages 501-525. Reprinted with permission. (c) by Notre Dame Law Review, University of Notre Dame.

Peter E. Quint, "Free Speech and Private Law in German Constitutional Theory," volume 48, Maryland Law Review (1989), pages 247 - 347. Reprinted with permission. (c) by Peter E. Quint.

Robert E. Jonas and John D. Gorby, "West German Abortion Decision: A Contrast to Roe v. Wade," volume 9, John Marshall Journal of Practice and Procedure (1976), pages 605 - 684. Reprinted with permission. (c) by John Marshall Law Review.

Deborah Goldberg, "Recent Developments in German Abortion Law," volume 5, UCLA Women's Law Journal (1995), pages 531 - 558. Reprinted with permission. (c) by UCLA Women's Law Journal.

Martin A. Rogoff, "The French (R)evolution of 1959-1998," volume 3, Columbia Journal of European Law (1997/98), pages 453 - 463. Reprinted with permission. (c) by Columbia Journal of European Law.

Henry DeVries, *The Civil Law and the Anglo-American Lawyer* (1975). Reprinted with permission. (c) Parker School of Foreign and Comparative Law, Columbia University in the City of New York.

Barry Nicholas, "Fundamental Rights and Judicial Review in France," [1978] Public Law Journal, pages 82 - 101. Reprinted with permission. (c) by Sweet & Maxwell, Ltd., London.

John H. Jackson, "Status of Treaties in Domestic Legal Systems," volume 86, number 2, American Journal of International Law (1992), pages 310 - 340. Reprinted with permission. (c) by American Society of International Law.

Gerhard Wegen and Christopher Kuner, "Federal Constitutional Court Decision Concerning the Maastricht Treaty," volume 33, International Legal Materials (1994), pages 388 - 444. Reprinted with permission. (c) by American Society of International Law.

Introduction

It is tempting for Americans to identify constitutional law with the case law of judicial review. For us, constitutional law sets limits to government power, and from the American point of view there is no limit on government power unless there is a forum in which that limit can be enforced. To steal a phrase from the American pragmatist Peirce, a limit that makes no difference *is* no difference. In the United States every ordinary court is vested with the authority to evaluate government action under the Constitution: hence the identification of constitutional law with judicial review.

But if it is tempting to make that identification it is also a little parochial. In the first place, the assumption that constitutional law requires a forum for testing government action under the constitution ignores the existence of constitutional democracies, like Great Britain, for example, and France before 1959, where no such forum exists. In the second place, and more importantly, judicial review (strictly speaking) means review by the *judiciary*, in the ordinary courts of the land. The judiciary is one of the branches of government, and in many countries with constitutional review of government action the forum is not within the judicial branch. In Germany and in post-1958 France, to take just two instances, there is constitutional review but not in the ordinary courts, which are prohibited from passing on the constitutional status of government action. There are instead special constitutional courts, with members chosen by the political branches, or by the political branches together with the judicial branch. And so in those countries we might be willing to talk about *constitutional* review, but not about judicial review in the strict sense.

This isn't just a quibble about labels. The reason for the distinction between the judiciary and the personnel of the constitutional courts is deeply rooted, as we will see. After the French revolution the power to review legislative action was taken away from the judiciary, and the parliament was left the arbiter of its own actions. The French distrust of the judiciary has left its mark on many aspects of the law of the civil law nations, and nowhere more obviously than on the question of constitutional review. Even today, with the rise of constitutional courts around the world, the ordinary judiciary has nothing to say about the constitutionality of government action. Strictly speaking, there is no judicial review.

For the sake of simplicity I will say that there is judicial review of government behavior whenever the ordinary courts of a jurisdiction have the power to con-

sider the constitutional status of that behavior. So, in the United States and in
Japan, where ordinary courts have that power, there is judicial review. In France
and Germany the ordinary courts do not have that power, and there is no judicial review. Nevertheless there is *constitutional review* in all four jurisdictions.
When I am trying to be precise, I will reserve "judicial review" for those instances of review that involve the ordinary courts, and speak more generally of
constitutional review as including both sorts of jurisdiction. Where precision is
not necessary I will follow the custom of referring to both as judicial review.

Before 1945 constitutional review was practically unknown outside the United
States. In constitutional matters, parliaments were supreme. Hans Kelsen, it is
true, had designed and helped to set up and man a constitutional court in Austria between the World Wars, and a similar court was set up in the neighboring
German (Weimar) Republic. Neither court survived the tribulations of the times
and the advance of National Socialism in the 1930s. And outside of those two
courts there was practically nothing.

There was nothing, that is, until 1945. With the end of the Second World
War the idea of constitutional control began to take hold, at least in part because of the excesses of the preceding period. It took hold first in Europe and
Japan, and then in the newly developing countries, and finally in the former socialist republics of Eastern Europe. Today varieties of constitutional review have
spread into every corner of the globe, and into every level of political association.

In fact, it is with the advance of constitutional review into the international
and supranational arenas that the distinction between judicial review and constitutional review generally comes to be most important. Countries that have
avoided judicial review—that is, constitutional review in the ordinary courts—have
seen the emergence in the ordinary courts of a new power of review under instruments of international and supranational association. If we follow the history of constitutional review in the twentieth century in France, for example,
we see first parliamentary supremacy and a complete lack of constitutional review under the Third and Fourth Republics; then constitutional review of parliamentary action in the politically appointed Constitutional Council after 1959;
and finally judicial review of parliamentary action, not under the French constitution but under the law of the European Union. This reappearance in the
ordinary courts of a power that the judiciary has been deprived of since the time
of the Revolution is one of the important parts of our story.

* * *

The material in this book is intended to provide an introduction to comparative constitutional review, an introduction that is brief enough to be included
in a general course on comparative law, or in a general course on constitutional
law. The book develops in this way: it begins with the notion of legislative su-

premacy, in which the power of the legislature is unregulated except by its own notion of constitutionality, and goes on to discuss various sorts of limits that might be placed on that supremacy-that is, various sorts of external review under some sort of fundamental law. Because of the central role that France has played in legal history, and because so many civil law countries pattern their court systems on the French system, we begin with France. France had a long history of parliamentary supremacy, and Chapter I includes materials that illustrate the reasons for that, as well as the effect that parliamentary supremacy had upon the ordinary courts of France. Since the book is intended for students both in the United States and abroad, this chapter compares French courts with American courts, and the powers of French judges with the powers of American judges. Chapters II and III discuss the development of various sorts of control that might be placed upon the legislature, from executive veto and some early and ineffective sorts of constitutional panels (for example, in New York and in France) to the American system of judicial review and the Kelsenian constitutional court, and then on to the complex French system that developed following the adoption of the 1958 constitution. In the French system there is one Council, the Constitutional Council, that examines proposed legislation for constitutionality, and another Council, the Council of State, that has taken upon itself the authority to examine administrative action for constitutionality. Chapter IV contains material relevant to the historical development of the European Court of Justice and its effect upon the power of review in the ordinary courts of the member states.

Comparative Constitutional Review

Chapter One

Parliamentary Supremacy

Constitutional review must be understood against the background of parliamentary supremacy. Constitutional review in the hands of a body external to the legislature amounts to a denial of that supremacy. We begin by exploring the reasons for thinking that parliamentary supremacy is a good thing, and constitutional review a bad thing. The Parlement in France was said to be supreme in the years prior to 1958, and we will concentrate on the development of supremacy in that body. It is true that during the formative years of the French Republic the British had already moved pretty far in that direction. French legal theorists and political philosophers were impressed by what they saw in Britain, and the British experience is at least partly responsible for the system that developed in France. But the British system is more a product of history than of theory, and it is in the development of the French system that we find the argument for legislative supremacy most clearly articulated.

1 WILLIAM BLACKSTONE, COMMENTARIES
*156–57 (1766)

The power and jurisdiction of parliament, says sir Edward Coke, is so transcendent and absolute, that it cannot be confined, either for causes or persons, within any bounds....It can change and create afresh even the constitution of the kingdom and of parliaments themselves....It can, in short, do every thing that is not naturally impossible; and therefore some have not scrupled to call its power, by a figure rather too bold, the omnipotence of parliament....So long therefore as the English constitution lasts, we may venture to affirm, that the power of parliament is absolute and without control....

Notes

1. Blackstone included the executive *within* the Parliament, and in his day the executive—the King—had the power to negate legislation. Of the Parliament narrowly conceived, consisting of the House of Lords and the House of Commons, it would be wrong to think he invested it with such absolute power as he describes; it was only Parliament broadly conceived—Parliament together

with the King—that had that power. But the Queen no longer vetoes legislation, and in Britain the narrowly conceived Parliament is now commonly described as supreme—it is not limited by constitution or court.

2. Notice that Blackstone cites Lord Coke to support his description of Parliament as supreme. As we will see, Coke is well-known for arguing something quite different, that the courts had the power to strike down legislation if it offended the common law, a power very much at odds with legislative supremacy.[1]

* * *

A. The Background of Parliamentary Supremacy in France: The Separation of Powers and the Distrust of Judges

LOUIS M. AUCOIN, JUDICIAL REVIEW IN FRANCE: ACCESS OF THE INDIVIDUAL UNDER FRENCH AND EUROPEAN LAW IN THE AFTERMATH OF FRANCE'S REJECTION OF BICENTENNIAL REFORM
15 BOSTON COLLEGE INTERNATIONAL & COMPARATIVE LAW REVIEW 443, 446–448 (1992)

Opposition to judicial review in France is a legacy of the excesses of the *ancien regime*. These excesses stemmed in part from the local administration of laws by institutions known as *parlements*, which acted as the local monarch's right arm. As the French comparativist Rene David explains in his work on French law:

The supreme courts of pre-revolutionary France, the *parlements*, made themselves very unpopular by opposing all reforms to the traditional legal system. Assiduous in their defense of an antiquated system based on the inequality of social classes and on self-serving premises, they failed in their ambition of becoming the nation's representatives. Nor did they succeed in really controlling government action or in imposing procedural rules upon it. Of their many ill-advised interferences in politics and government, people remember their opposition

---

1. See Bonham's Case, in Chapter Two below.

to those organizational reforms that the monarchy did attempt from time to time. Abolition of the *parlements* was one of the first acts of the French Revolution, on November 3, 1789.

Consequently, since the French Revolution, French authorities have always associated a strong judiciary with the concept of *"gouvernment des juges"*— government by judges.

The excesses of judicial and executive power in pre-revolutionary France led to the evolution of a new system based upon legislative supremacy after the overthrow of the ancien regime. The French began to see representative democracy as the foundation for legitimate government, associated with the idea of national sovereignty. The idea that sovereignty resides in the legislature became one of the pillars of the French Declaration of the Rights of Man and of the Citizen of 1789 (Declaration of 1789). The distinction, however, between the legislative branch and the people appeared illegitimate to the French in principle and a threat to individual liberties in practice. To the French, only an elected Parliament could effectively guarantee these liberties. Thus, the history of the French political system has been characterized by preeminent political power residing in the legislature. Even recently, under the constitutions of the Third and Fourth Republics, the power of the other branches of government has paled in comparison to that of the legislature.

The traditional philosophy of legislative supremacy continues to influence the thinking of French jurists in the twentieth century. In 1921, for example, Edouard Lambert echoed this view when he criticized U.S. judicial review as *"gouvernement des juges"*.... For many French legal scholars, according judges the power to rule on the constitutionality of laws is a potential threat to democracy.

The French opposition to judicial review is also attributable to the fear that it could upset the functioning of a parliamentary democracy. In a pure parliamentary system, the chief executive leads the party with the majority in the parliament. This executive, usually the Prime Minister, heads the Government, exercises the state's executive power, and has significant powers of legislative initiative. At the same time, parliamentary systems are prone to constant dynamic tensions between the majority and the opposition minority parties. The minority party wields significant power, for it has the right, under certain circumstances, to require the resignation of the chief executive through the process of a motion of censure. Consequently, there are constant political machinations between the majority and the opposition. Some French legal authorities have expressed a fear that the majority or opposition could use judicial review of proposed laws as a weapon to upset the sovereign legislature's agenda, causing political instability.

*   *   *

MAURO CAPPELLETTI, REPUDIATING MONTESQUIEU? THE EXPANSION AND LEGITIMACY OF "CONSTITUTIONAL JUSTICE"

35 CATHOLIC UNIVERSITY LAW REVIEW 11–15 (1985)

In France [the history of parliamentary supremacy] must be traced back, in part, to a deeply felt popular revulsion against the abuse of the judicial office by the higher courts of justice under the *ancien regime*. These courts, whose name, ironically, was *Parlements*, asserted their power to review acts of the sovereign, refusing to apply those found to be incompatible with the "fundamental laws of the realm." The reading by those courts of such—mostly unwritten—fundamental laws, however, led the courts to affirm the "*heureuse impuissance*" of the legislator to introduce even minor liberal reforms. Those judges were so deeply rooted in the feudal regime that they found any liberal innovation unacceptable. Their office was hereditary and could be bought and sold, and their activity was to be paid by each individual litigator as though it were their privilege, not their duty, to administer justice. Their status, education, and personal, family, and class interests combined to motivate their extremely conservative attitude, an attitude which eventually contributed to the triggering of the revolutionary explosion. The popular feelings against the *Parlements* were well justified, and this justification is reflected, albeit in a veiled form, in that celebrated work, *De l'Esprit des Lois*, first published in 1748 by one who, when speaking of the judges of his time and country, knew only too well what he was saying. Charles-Louis de Secondat, the offspring of an ancient family of judges "*parlementairs*," at the age of twenty-seven, in 1716, had already become "*President a mortier*" at the *Parlement* of Bordeaux, having inherited the high judicial office, as well as the name of Montesquieu, from his deceased uncle. Quite understandably given the kind of judges of the time, an enlightened Montesquieu preached that the judges should be entrusted with no political power at all: "There is no liberty... if the power to adjudicate is not separated from the legislative and the executive powers."

Even if the law, "which," he said, "is at the same time clairvoyant and blind," should appear in certain cases to be too harsh, still it is not for the judges but only for the legislator to intervene. To the judges appertains only the duty to blindly apply the law, for "the judges of the nation are...nothing but the mouth which pronounces the words of the law; they are inanimate beings who cannot moderate either the force or the rigor of the law." Thus, although Montesquieu, unlike Locke, did list the judiciary as one of the "three powers," coming after the legislative and the executive powers, he also made it clear, however, that the third branch, in a real way, is no "power" at all: "Of the three powers of which we have spoken, the judicial is, in a sense, null." Whatever the actual influence of Montesquieu on the French Revolution, this idea was to become a central part of its ideology. The Revolution proclaimed as one of its first principles the absolute supremacy of statutory law, the law enacted by the *corps legislatif* as the representatives of the people, while demoting the judiciary to what was seen as the purely mechanical task of applying that law to concrete cases. Of course, also the Rousseauian faith in the *infallibilite* of the *loi* as the expression of the *volonte generale* found its triumph in this Revolutionary development.

To be sure, the strict separation, "French style," of the governmental powers, whether or not actually "Montesquieuian" in inspiration, was miles away from the kind of separation of powers which almost contemporaneously was adopted by the American Constitution. Separation of powers in America is better described as "checks and balances"; under this principle, an extremely important role of review of both administrative and legislative action was to be reserved to the courts. *Separation des pouvoirs* French style, on the contrary, implied that the judiciary should assume a role totally subservient to, and at any rate strictly separate from, the role and activity of the political branches; as such, it soon proved to be the source of problems and difficulties no less serious than those it was intended to solve. The legal history of France throughout most of the nineteenth century is a continuous illustration of such problems, as well as of the striving efforts to find new and more appropriate solutions for these problems. Reducing the judicial function to a blind, "inanimate," slot-machine application of the laws to individual cases is oblivious of the reality, that is, of the fact that no norm, law, or code can be so clear and complete as to allow for only one "correct" interpretation. More importantly still, the Montesquieuian (and Rousseauian) approach, as implemented by French Revolutionary legislation, while intended to protect against tyranny, left the doors wide open to both legislative and executive tyranny. The famous Revolutionary *loi* of 16–24 August 1790 on "*organisation judiciaire*," whose principles were to become the pillars of the French judicial system and other Continental systems influenced by the French, established that no control whatsoever by the judiciary was allowed either of legislative or of administrative action:

> *Title II, Art. 10*: The judicial tribunals shall not take part, either directly or indirectly, in the exercise of the legislative power, nor impede or suspend the execution of the enactments of the legislative body....
>
> *Title II, Art. 12*: [The judicial tribunals] shall refer to the legislative body whenever they find it necessary either to have a statute interpreted or to have a new statute.
>
> *Title II, Art. 13*: Judicial functions are distinct and shall always remain separate from administrative functions. Under penalty of forfeiture of their offices, the judges shall not interfere in any way whatsoever with the operation of the public administration, nor shall they call administrators to account before them in respect of the exercise of their administrative functions....

This meant that both legislators and public administrators were exempt from any check by a third, independent, nonpolitical or, at least, less political branch.

* * *

CUMMINS, GENERAL PRINCIPLES OF LAW, SEPARATION OF POWERS AND THEORIES OF JUDICIAL DECISION IN FRANCE
35 INTERNATIONAL AND COMPARATIVE LAW QUARTERLY 594, 597–599 (1986)

It is important in any attempt to understand the role of the French courts and their relation to other parts of the government to place them within the constitutional tradition. Since the Revolution of 1789, France has had a variety of forms of government. Ten constitutions have been in force for a longer or shorter period. The impression of instability this gives is, however, very misleading, at least as far as the courts are concerned. For both the judicial and administrative courts have had a largely tranquil history of growth in authority, prestige and independence within a legal framework laid down by revolutionary and Napoleonic legislation. The fundamental distinguishing feature of this legal structure is a special application of the principle of separation of powers.

This famous principle, so easy to state and often so hard to apply, has in its broadest form, a chequered history in France. The most famous statement of the general doctrine is found in the chapter on the constitution of England in Montesquieu's *Spirit of the Laws* where he speaks of there existing in all states "the legislative power, the executive power concerning matters related to the law of nations and the executive power concerning matters related to civil law." In a key passage he makes clear the importance of separating the functions:

> There is no liberty if the power to judge is not separated from the legislative power and the executive power. If it is joined to the legislative power, power over the life and liberty of citizens would be arbitrary as the judge would be the legislator. If it is joined to the executive power, the judge would be able to have the force of an oppressor. . . .

A separate intellectual tradition stemming from Rousseau has from the beginning had a powerful attraction for French theorists and legislators. Rousseau's line of thought is complex and cannot be done much justice in a few lines but, as is the case with many thinkers, a few notions retained by the educated public have had more practical importance than all the rest. This oratorical tradition retains Rousseau's theory of the origin of society as based on an original compact which all men enter by surrendering the whole of their rights. Since all surrender their rights totally, all are equal and none can oppress the others without making himself subject to oppression. Sovereignty can be exercised only by the whole people. Laws adopted by the people express the general will (*volonté générale*) and cannot be subjected to any higher control. Rousseau's theory of the general will is applied in practice to a parliamentary system by regarding the members as limited to the role of expressing the will of their constituents (i.e., not having an independent voice) and regarding the laws adopted by the Parliament as the expression of the general will. It is this aspect of the tradition which excludes review of constitutionality by the courts; the law (statute), as the expression of the general will, is virtually equal to the constitution, and the courts can have no authority to strike it down.

While Rousseau's line of thought does not necessarily exclude a separation of functions between the legislature, the executive and the judiciary, it obviously places the last two in a subordinate position in a hierarchy of powers. They are powerless to interfere with either the lawmaking process or the laws (statutes) it produces and have only such independence as the legislature chooses to give them.

To these two distinct intellectual influences, the revolutionaries and the constitutional tradition after them added a view of history. The *Parlements*, the courts of the *ancien régime*, were viewed as having interfered with attempts by the monarchy to introduce reforms in the years immediately prior to 1789. The ideology of the revolution was in consequence distinctly anti-judicial and there was a determination to give the courts no more than a subsidiary role that would not interfere with the exercise of the will of the people. . . .

[L]aws of the period limited the courts to applying the laws; requiring them to refer questions of interpretation to the legislature, and created a *Tribunal de Cassation* attached to the legislature with authority to quash (*casser*) decisions of the ordinary courts which it deemed contrary to the statutes. . . .

[T]he special separation of powers established by the law of 16–24 August 1790 remains a fundamental principle of the constitutional tradition. The courts may grow in importance but they remain subordinate, with little dissent either from the populace or those learned in the law. They are confined to the role of deciding specific cases strictly on the basis of the written legislative texts. Judges are forbidden to lay down and announce general rules to guide them in their future decisions.

Despite foreign examples and the urging of some doctrinal writers, the judicial courts maintain a strict refusal to consider arguments that a statute is in conflict with the constitution. This refusal, sometimes misunderstood by foreign observers as a kind of inappropriate timidity, is in fact a recognition by the courts of their subordinate status in the hierarchy of powers and their consequent lack of right to review the actions of the legislature. The administrative courts maintain and reinforce their separate tradition. They create an independent legal system and defend and expand their right to review administrative action but maintain the same refusal as the judicial courts to consider constitutional arguments.

* * *

B. The Role of Judges in Post-Revolutionary France and in Civil Law Systems Generally

The French revolution marked a new starting point for French law. The Roman materials upon which the pre-revolutionary law had been based were put on a back shelf, new codes were created, and judges were stripped of the power to interfere with either the legislative or the executive branches — the French version of separation of powers.

> The modern French judicial system (which would fully emerge by 1804) was constructed on the principle—itself a virtual corollary of popular sovereignty—that judges must not directly, or indirectly through interpretation, make law. Democrats and generals, parliamentarians and imperialists, did not differ in their assessments of the intrinsic virtue of this principle. The law was, following Rousseau, to be codified in "simple, non-technical, and straightforward" language. As a consequence, politics would be made transparent, the legitimacy of the new social compact assured, and the multitude of intermediate institutions and social practices separating the people and State, and obscuring the fundamental relationship, could be cleared away or fatally undermined. *Le droit* was thought to be one of the more mystifying of these institutions, and it was hoped and expected that lawyers, and their penchant for doctrinal commentaries and formalist discourse, would gradually obsolesce. Judges could then proceed in a straightforward manner, as civil servants applying the codes.[2]

Only legislators were to have the power to make law: "In 1799, one such reformer put it this way:

> Only the law-maker has the authority to interpret the law....Without this principle, judges would embark on a vast unobstructed course of interpreting statutes according to their imaginations,...and even their

---

2. Alec Stone, The Birth of Judicial Politics in France: The Constitutional Council in Comparative Perspective 25 (1992).

passions. Judicial institutions would thus be entirely deformed. Judges would be able to substitute their will for *la loi*,...and establish themselves as legislators."[3]

The attitude toward judges, supported by Rousseau's argument for the supremacy of the legislature, has colored much of the development of modern French law and consequently, because of the influence of French law, much of the development of legal systems outside the common law countries. Three prominent characteristics of these systems sum up the implications of parliamentary supremacy and the distrust of judges: the distinction between private law and public law and the corresponding dual court system; the absence of judicial review of legislation; and the absence of a doctrine of precedent.

1. Private Law and Public Law

The "judicial" courts—the ordinary or civil courts—were deprived of the authority to review the behavior of the executive branch and the administrative agencies within that branch. If a citizen had a claim against a government agency in tort or in contract, or if a government agency acted outside its authority, there was nothing the ordinary courts could do about it; they were forbidden to interfere with or obstruct the actions of the executive branch.[4]

But although the ordinary courts were denied, by the law of 16–24 August 1790, the authority to review the behavior of the administration, some forum had to be provided for complaints against the administrative agencies and the executive. Since the ordinary courts could not do it that job fell to the Council of State (*Conseil d'Etat*), an advisory body within the executive branch. Later subordinate administrative courts, both first-instance tribunals and intermediate appellate courts, were created to lessen the Council's caseload. These courts are staffed by judges trained in the administrative branch; they are not members of the judiciary. Even the sources of law for the two courts systems are different: the ordinary courts are limited to applying the law set down in legislative enactments, but the administrative courts have developed a kind of case law.

Thus there are two completely independent court systems, the private law or civil "judicial" courts, a hierarchy at the top of which sits the Court of Cassation (*Cour de cassation*), and the public law administrative courts, in a hierarchy at the top of which sits the Council of State.

---

3. Id. Stone is quoting from Jean Bourdon, La reforme judiciare de l'An VIII 432–433 (1942).

4. See Article 3 of the Law of August 16–24, 1790, quoted above in Cappelletti, Repudiating Montesquieu.

Civil Courts	Administrative Courts
Court of Cassation	Council of State
Courts of Appeal	Administrative Courts of Appeal
Courts of Assizes	
Tribunals	Tribunals

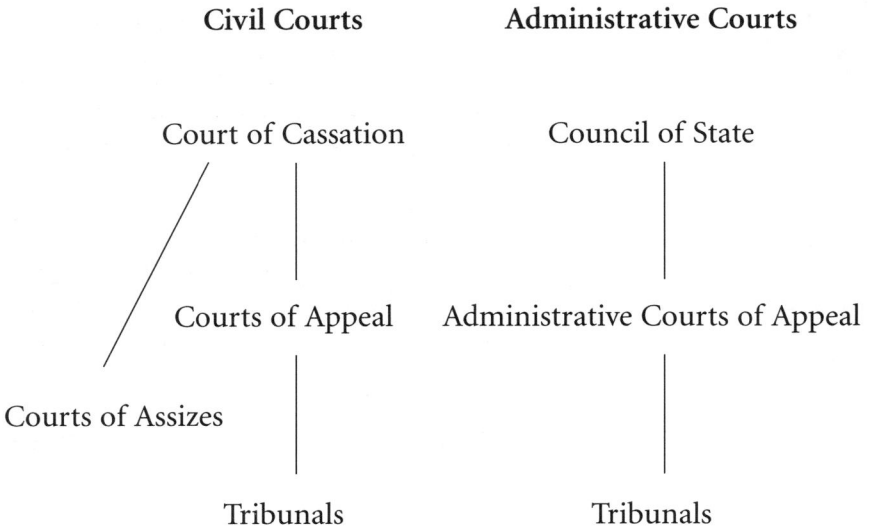

GERALD KOCK, THE MACHINERY OF LAW ADMINISTRATION IN FRANCE

108 UNIVERSITY OF PENNSYLVANIA LAW REVIEW
366, 367–380 (1960)

The judicial structure of France is perhaps most different from that to which we in the common-law system are accustomed in the existence of what amounts to two judicial systems working side by side. The picture is not that of a few specialized courts set outside the regular court structure but of a separate system of courts for trial, appeal, and review of cases which, because of the interests involved, are not within the jurisdiction of the ordinary courts. The French courts are, then, of two kinds: the ordinary, or judicial, courts and the administrative tribunals. Each system is complete in itself and capable of deciding all stages of litigation cases falling within its subject-matter competence. . . .

There are three courts of general jurisdiction within the regular judicial system—the courts of primary jurisdiction (*tribunaux de grande instance*), courts of appeal (*cours d'appel*), and a court of review (the *Cour de cassation*)....

The court of primary jurisdiction (tribunal de grande instance) has both civil and criminal jurisdiction. The court consists of at least three judges and sits in separate chambers, or divisions. When a chamber is sitting to hear a civil case it is referred to as the *tribunal civil*; the criminal chamber is usually called the *tribunal correctionnel*. The civil chambers have original jurisdiction over all civil litigation that is not limited to a special court or restricted to the administrative tribunals. Their decisions (*jugements*) are final, subject to review by the Court of Cassation, in cases involving [rights or property valued at less than a set amount]. All other decisions are subject to an appeal of right to a court of appeal. The criminal chamber has trial jurisdiction over misdemeanors (*delits*). Appeals from its decisions in criminal cases are taken to the local court of appeal....

The third regular court in the ordinary judicial system [in addition to the *tribunal de grande instance* and a court for minor cases, the *tribunal d'instance*] is the assizes court (*cour d'assises*). This court, constituted periodically for the trial of felonies, is the only court in the French system that sits with a jury....

The courts of appeal (*cours d'appel*) hear appeals from the lower courts within their jurisdiction and decide on remand cases in which the Court of Cassation has reversed the decision of another court of appeal. The court consists of a president of the court, a president for each chamber and other judges as required to complete the court. Judges who do not preside over a chamber are called councillors....

At the head of the French judicial system is found the Court of Cassation (*Cour de cassation*). This Court is a court of review,.... Its purpose is twofold: to keep the law pure by assuring that the courts below do not diverge in their decisions from the law as it is found in the codes and other legislative acts, and—as a part of the same task—to secure the uniformity of the law throughout the area in which it is applicable....

Cases come to the Court of Cassation by way of petition for review.... If after a hearing the Court finds that the lower court correctly applied the law, it dismisses the petition (*rejet de pourvoi*) and the judgment or decree rendered below becomes final. Should the Court decide that the lower court erred, it sets aside the decision (*casse le jugement*) and remands (*renvoi*) the case to another court of the same rank as that from which it came. The Court of Cassation is free to send a case to any court of the appropriate rank except that from which it came or one that has had the same case before, in the event it is the second time the case has been remanded.

It has been said that the Court of Cassation judges decisions, not suits. In a very real sense this is true, for cases may be brought before it only on the ground that a law has been violated or incorrectly applied or that a court has exceeded its authority. Nothing may be considered that has not been alleged in the original petition for review, and the decision of the Court can only be to send the case back to another court to be considered. No evidence may be looked to, and the findings of fact below may not be disturbed by the Court of Cassation even if there is no evidence in the record to support them.

The court to which the Court of Cassation remands a case (*cour de renvoi*) is not bound to follow the higher Court. If, however, the court of remand does not follow the Court of Cassation and on review that Court, all chambers sitting together, again sets the decision aside and remands the case for the same reasons, the second court to which it is remanded is bound to enter a decision in conformity with the decision of the Court of Cassation....

It is in the administrative courts that the difference between the French and our own legal system is generally thought to be greatest. . . .

Thirty-one administrative tribunals (*tribunaux administratifs*) have been established for the adjudication of administrative disputes.... The competence of the administrative tribunals extends to any subject matter that may be brought before them, since they are courts of general jurisdiction. Their jurisdiction is limited, however, with regard to the parties whose disputes they may consider. Litigation before the administrative tribunals must involve the rights or obligations of one of the administrative persons (*personnes administratives*)—the state, communes, departments, public establishments or professional orders.

Decisions of the administrative tribunals are open to appeal to the Council of State. That body's place at the summit of the administrative system invites comparison with the Court of Cassation, which we find at the top of the ordinary judicial system. In fact, the Council of State has much broader powers than has the Court of Cassation, even in its judicial duties. The Council's broader jurisdiction is evident from its power to hear appeals from the administrative tribunals and their equivalents in the overseas territories. It reviews final decisions of administrative commissions and courts just as the Court of Cassation reviews decisions of the judicial tribunals. And in addition to its judicial functions the Council of State has the position indicated by its name—it is an advisory council to the government.... The largest part of the Council's judicial business is made up of appeals from the administrative tribunals, though, as noted above, it also serves as a court of review. In addition, it has original jurisdiction in some cases: reserved to it are challenges to decisions of the President of France or of the Council of Ministers and the invalidation of decrees as unconstitutional or contrary to law.

Notes

1. In order to reduce the load on the Council of State the legislature established five intermediate courts of appeal in 1987. Since 2001, decisions of an assizes court may be appealed on issues of fact to the assizes court of another *departement*.

2. "[T]he *Conseil d'Etat... [has] been greatly aided by the* rôle of the '*commissaire du gouvernement*.' Despite the name, the *commissaire du gouvernement* is not a representative of the government or administrative authorities. The *commissaire du gouvernement* is a member of the administrative court, usually

of some seniority, who is appointed by the court to perform the functions for a specific period....The *rôle* is that of presenting arguments (*conclusions*) to the court which is deciding a case, in order to propose to the court a solution to that case which the *commissaire du gouvernement* considers appropriate, and he or she does not take part in the court's deliberations or judgment. The *rôle* of the *commissaire du gouvernement* cannot be underestimated in the development of administrative law...." David Pollard, Sourcebook On French Law xvii (2nd ed., 1998).

3. In addition to hearing complaints in tort and contract against the administration, the administrative courts also decide on the validity or invalidity of administrative actions under the legal authorization for those actions, including the statutory authorization granted by the legislature. An administrative action may be declared invalid for violating the principle of legality by exercising an *excès de pouvoir* — an "excess of power." "[P]roceedings are based on one of four grounds, namely, *incompétence, vice de forme, violation de la loi*, and *détournement de pouvoir*....[I]f an official acts completely without authority, his decision will be declared void for *incompétence*....[Vice de forme] may be rendered into English either as 'procedural *ultra vires*'...or as 'procedural impropriety'....Only failure to observe an essential formality will lead to avoidance of the subsequent proceedings....[U]nder the head of *violation de la loi* the administrative judge moves on to examine the actual contents of the administrative act itself, in order to decide whether it conforms with the legal conditions set upon administrative action in the particular case....[T]here has been a *détournement de pouvoir*, or abuse of power, if an administrative power or discretion has been exercised for some object other than that for which power or discretion was conferred by the statute...." L. Neville Brown and John S. Brown, French Administrative Law 223–230 (4th ed., 1993).

4. Referring to Montesquieu's argument for separation of powers above, and given that the argument seems to be that the legislature and the executive should not be given the power of judges (rather than the other way around), this placement of the administrative courts *within* the administration seems questionable; more so when, as in the next section, we are talking about constitutional control.

* * *

2. Judicial Review

FRENCH CONSTITUTION OF 1791, TITLE III, CHAPTER V

in FRANK MALOY ANDERSON, CONSTITUTIONS AND OTHER SELECT DOCUMENTS ILLUSTRATIVE OF THE HISTORY OF FRANCE 86 (1904)

Article 3. The tribunals cannot interfere in the exercise of the legislative power, nor suspend the execution of the laws, nor encroach upon the administrative functions, nor cite before them the administrators on account of their functions.[5]

* * *

In addition to being stripped of the power to interfere with the work of the executive branch, judges were deprived of the power to interfere with legislation. The early effort to ensure that judges would not even be able to interpret the law to fit new situations came to nothing: Interpretation is unavoidable for a judge. But there was never any question of allowing the judges of the judicial branch to examine legislation for constitutional validity. Administrative judges, of course, were there to review administrative behavior, not legislation. As a result there was no forum to which the legislature was answerable, no forum in which legislation could be struck down. All of this changed in 1958, as we will see; but until 1958, the legislature was supreme.

The French courts have stood firm on this question of constitutional review since the beginning. In the following famous French case the lower court had suspended the operation of a statute, basing its authority to do so on Article 377 of the Constitutional Act of 1795.[6] In this decision the reviewing court (called, at the time, the Tribunal of Cassation) puts the lower court in its place.

---

5. See also Article 10 of the Law of 16–24 August, 1790, quoted in Cappelletti, Repudiating Montesquieu.

6. Constitution of 1795, *in* Frank Maloy Anderson, Constitutions and other Select Documents Illustrative of the History of France 254 (1904): "*Article 377.* The French People entrust the safekeeping of the present Constitution to the fidelity of the Legislative Body, the Executive Directory, the administrators and the *judges;....*" (Emphasis added.)

TRIBUNAL OF CASSATION, DECISION OF 3 SEPTEMBER, 1797

30 DALLOZ REPERTOIRE DE LEGISLATION, DE DOCTRINE, ET DE JURISPRUDENCE 196, n.1 (1853)[7]

In light of articles 128, 131, 189, 205, and 158 of the Constitution;

Considering that it is to the Executive Directory that the Constitution delegates the power to promulgate the laws, and that it is on that body alone that any responsibility rests in these matters;

-That it is also only on the Executive Directory and its agents that punishment can be imposed in the case of an act published as law without being invested with the internal and external forms required by the Constitution;

-That even in the case of [such a] crime, the indictment and the proceedings are in the hands of certain superior authorities, namely, of the legislature and the high court of justice;[8]

-That it follows from that that subordinate authorities do not have the right to decide that the act that is sent to them as law by the Directory does not have the character of law, except to denounce it to the legislature;

Considering that the absolute terms in which the prohibition against the administration and the judiciary stopping or suspending the execution of the laws is conceived, no exception or pretext can be admitted;

-That, moreover, the central administration of Dyle published the law of 7 Vendemiaire in conformity to the decision of the Executive Directory;

-And that the criminal tribunal of the same territorial division doubly usurped the legislative power: 1st, in judging the merits of a law published by the superior authority of the Directory; 2nd, in stopping the execution of that law;

Considering that it can only be by the result of a too palpable error that the criminal tribunal of Dyle relied on the authority of article 377 of the constitution, where the people of France entrust the constitution to the legislature, to the fidelity of the Executive Directory, to administrators and judges, to the vigilance of the fathers of families, to wives and mothers, to the affection of young citizens, and to the courage of all the French;

---

7. Translated by the editor.

8. "*Article 265.* There is a high court of justice to try the accusations accepted by the Legislative Body against either its own members of those of the Executive Directory." Constitution of 1795, *in* Frank Maloy Anderson, Constitutions and other Select Documents Illustrative of the History of France 254 (1904).

-That one can only see in that touching sentence an invitation to public servants to fulfill their duties, to parents to teach the Constitution to their children, to children to love it, and to all the French to defend it;

-And that the criminal tribunal of Dyle should not have looked to that provision for the right to suspend execution of one of the laws sent or promulgated by the authority to which the Constitution delegated the right;

-That the immediate effect of such a false result would be to give the same power to all citizens, to confuse all the powers, to turn that same Constitution that it pretends to support upside down;

-The judgment of the criminal tribunal of the *departement* of Dyle of fifteen Prarial last, is quashed and annulled for *exces de pouvoir* and contravention of the articles above mentioned.

Notes

1. This interpretation of a constitutional provision entrusting the constitution to the care of judges, among others, should be compared to that found in the American *Marbury* case, found in Chapter Two below.

2. Is it ironic that the Tribunal of Cassation, in denying that courts have the right to question constitutionality, must refer to the Constitution to support its argument? The Tribunal of Cassation was originally conceived of as an arm of the legislature, and not a judicial body at all; that may account for its free reference to the Constitution. It soon became the *Court* of Cassation, a judicial body.

3. The administrative courts also refused to review legislation for constitutionality. In the Arrigi case (Council of State, November 6, 1936),[9] the Council of State denied that it had the power to review the constitutionality of a legislative delegation of power to the executive. The government commissioner, in his argument before the court, reminded the judges of the Council of State of the earlier 1797 case in the Tribunal of Cassation, reprinted above. The commissioner argued that the Council of State had no more authority in that regard than the ordinary courts. "The judgment below in that case [the lower court in the decision of September 3, 1797] believed that such control [judicial review] could be based upon article 377 of the Constitutional Act where it is said that 'the French people have entrusted the Constitution to the fidelity of the legislative body, the executive, the administrators, and the *judges*;...' But the Tribunal of Cassation found only the effect of a culpable error here." (emphasis added) (from the Commissaire's statement in the Arrighi case (1936), *translated in* Arthur von Mehren and James Gordley, The Civil Law System 251–253 (1977)).

---

9. English translation in von Mehren and Gordley, The Civil Law System 256–257.

* * *

JAMES BEARDSLEY, CONSTITUTIONAL REVIEW IN FRANCE
[1975] SUPREME COURT REVIEW 189–198 (1975)

1. *Substantive review by the judicial tribunals.*... In a number of nineteenth-century cases, the Court's refusal to judge the constitutionality of legislation was founded not on the revolutionary prohibitions on judicial intervention in the legislative process, but on those provisions of the Constitution of 1799 which had for the first time instituted nonjudicial constitutional review through the attribution of powers of review to the *Sénat conservateur*.[10] Reasoning *a contrario* from the existence of a specialized organ of review, the Court held that review by ordinary tribunals was constitutionally precluded.

With the demise of the Constitution of the 1799, and with it the *Senat conservateur*,...the Court returned to the theory of separation of powers underlying the revolutionary legislation in what has become the leading decision on the incompetence of the judicial tribunals to examine the constitutionality of legislation. In the *affaire Paulin*, decided in 1833 under the regime established by the Charte of 1830, the Court of Cassation declared: "[A] statute...adopted and promulgated in the manner constitutionally prescribed by the Charte, establishes the law for the courts, and cannot be attacked before them on the ground of unconstitutionality." There is no reference to the revolutionary legislation and no hint of a theory of incompetence in the Court's decision, but the arguments of the *avocat général* suggest adherence by the Court to the theory that any judicial refusal to give effect to an authentic act of the legislature would constitute an impermissible intervention by the judges in the legislative power.

---

10. "The *Senat conservateur* never exercised its powers of constitutional review and disappeared from the Constitution in 1815." Beardsley, Constitutional Review in France, [1975] Supreme Court Review 189, 193 (1975). According to Title II of the Constitution of 1799, there were to be eighty members of the *Senat conservateur*. Once appointed to the *Senat conservateur*, senators would remain there for life. They were appointed by the Senate from candidates proposed by the legislature, the courts, and the First Consul (Executive). They were to hold secret deliberations about the constitutionality of laws that were referred to them by either the courts or by the government. As members were nominated by the legislature and executive, their review was presumably political in nature. "These two persistent themes—hostility to judicial review and a certain receptiveness to the notion of 'political' review—marked French constitutional thought for nearly two centuries." Beardsley, at 192. The institution reappeared in the Constitution of 1852, and was no more important in its second life than in its first. Compare this institution with the Council of Revision proposed at the American Constitutional convention, see below Chapter Two, Section A.1.

But *Paulin* did not immediately settle matters. Several later decisions undercut the Court's pronouncement in *Paulin* and were to provide some support to the proponents of judicial review in the doctrinal debates of the later nineteenth and early twentieth centuries. Most important were two judgments rendered in 1851 in which the Court of Cassation explicitly examined the substantive constitutionality of a statute purporting to subject civilians to courts-martial during a state of siege. The Constitution of 4 November 1848 prohibited the creation of extraordinary tribunals, but it also authorized the National Assembly to determine by statute the conditions and effects of the declaration of a state of siege. The latter authority, declared the Court, was sufficient to sustain the statute as a constitutional exercise of legislative power. Although the 1851 decisions certainly amounted to exercises in constitutional review (albeit less intrusive than a decision striking down a statute), the Court returned to the *Paulin* position in subsequent cases.

2. *The position of the administrative courts.* The administrative courts did not squarely confront the issue until 1901. In a decision of that year, the *Conseil d'Etat* adhered to the rule adopted by the Court of Cassation in *Paulin*. The position of the *Conseil d'Etat* was more ambiguous, however, due to its development and application of nonstatutory principles which, in some applications, look remarkably like constitutional concepts.

Perhaps the best early example of this kind of decision is that which was handed down in the *Winkell* affair of 1909. Winkell was a civil servant who had participated in a strike and was, for that reason, dismissed by his employer, the postal administration. In dismissing Winkell, the administration failed to comply with the provisions of a 1905 statute requiring the government to inform a civil servant of the contents of his file before taking disciplinary action. The *Conseil d'Etat* upheld the dismissal on the ground that a strike by civil servants was illicit even if not prohibited by statute because "in accepting the employment conferred upon him, the civil servant subjects himself to all of the obligations deriving from the needs of the public service and waives all rights incompatible with the essential continuity of the national life...." The strike violated this principle of "the continuity of the public service" and the strikers were held to have suffered in consequence a kind of outlawry, "placing themselves by a collective act beyond the application of laws and regulations adopted for the purpose of guaranteeing the exercise of the rights which they derive individually from the contract of public services."

Maurice Hauriou argued that the decision could only be explained satisfactorily as a refusal to apply the 1905 statute for constitutional reasons—the "continuity of the public service" being a constitutional principle, not because it was to be found in the written document, but because it embodied a "condition necessary to the existence of the state." Hauriou's arguments—advanced in notes to *Winkell* and other decisions as well as in his other writings—provoked considerable doctrinal resistance and failed to persuade the *Conseil d'Etat* that it had embarked upon, and should continue, the exercise of judicial review of the constitutionality of acts of Parliament. Despite the remarkable effects which the application of such principles might have in cases like *Winkell*, the powers of the administrative judge in relation to parliamentary legislation were no different from those of his colleagues in the judicial tribunals. As the *Conseil d'Etat* put it in the *Arrighi* decision of 1936: "...in the present state of French public law, this ground of appeal [unconstitutionality of the statute underlying an administrative act] may not be raised before the *Conseil d'Etat*."

3. *The "general principles of law."* The principle of continuity of the public service invoked in *Winkell* is an important example of the then emerging phenomenon of "general principles of law" which was to form an important basis of the administrative case law and an aspect of that law which has been of enormous importance for the development of constitutional review in France. Although typically reticent about their nature and origin, the *Conseil d'Etat* progressively developed a catalog of principles applicable in the review of administrative action and rule-making and in the interpretation of legislation which included such notions as equality before the law, freedom of conscience, principles embodying what might be called procedural due process, the non-retroactivity of administrative acts, and the right to bring the *recours pour exces d'pouvoir* in respect of administrative decisions.

Under the regime of the Third Republic (1875–1940), it was extremely difficult to identify any legal source for these general principles other than praetorian powers of the judges. The constitutional laws of 1875 contained no declaration of rights or any other statement of similar principles. No statute explicitly consecrated such principles as rules of law to be applied by the administrative courts. Serious attempts at theoretical explanation of the general principles were not forthcoming until after World War II. Writing in 1951, M. Letourneur, a member of the *Conseil d'Etat*, argued that the general principles were nothing more than interpretations of the will of the legislator, presumed to guide legislative activity even in the absence of an explicit manifestation of that will in statutory form. Other writers pointed out that, even if, as M. Letourneur insisted, the principles are only applied in the "absence of an express manifestation of legislative will to the contrary," the influence of the general principles in the administrative courts' interpretation of statutes raised considerable doubt about whether those principles could properly be regarded as anything other than judge-made law *tout simple*.

The advent of the Fourth Republic and with it a constitution which incorporated the 1789 Declaration of Rights in its Preamble brought a new element into the theory of the general principles. The *Conseil d'Etat* came to refer in its decisions to the "general principles of law...deriving, notably, from the Preamble to the Constitution." It was never quite clear whether the Conseil regarded the Preamble as declarative of the general principles (deriving their force from some other source as the logic of continuity from the Third to Fourth Republics might seem to require) or whether the Preamble simply created a new foundation for at least some of these previously difficult to explain concepts. To the extent that the *Conseil* was applying a general principle, such as that of the continuity of the public service, which could not, by any stretch of the imagination, be derived from the Preamble, some other source was still to be supposed.

None of this was of great practical importance so long as the supremacy of Parliament remained unchallenged and the judges adhered to the rule that an act of Parliament was immune from attack either as a violation of the general principles or as an unconstitutional act.

* * *

A turning point in the development of this doctrine of "general principles" came with the open acknowledgment that the Council of State was not relying on textual justification for this move. This happened in the case of the widow Trompier-Gravier. (There is nothing in the decision itself about the absence of a text; but in argument before the Council the Government Commissioner made clear the path the Council had been taking.)

THE TROMPIER-GRAVIER CASE

COUNCIL OF STATE, MAY 5, 1944 (italics added)[11]

M. Chenot, Government Commissioner (commissaire du gouvernement), addressing the Council:

Gentlemen.—

On March 30, 1925, the Widow Trompier-Gravier, *née* Tichy, by a decree of the prefect of the Seine, was granted a license for Stand No. 69 on the Boulevard Saint-Denis, in Paris. Herself employed in the Ministry of Agriculture, she entrusted the management of her stand to one Mme. Lange. In 1939, upon complaint of M. Lange, husband of the latter and president of the federation of newspaper dealers, the administration came to the opinion that the Widow Trompier-Gravier had tried to extort the sum of 40,000 francs from Mme. Lange by threatening to withdraw the management of the stand from her. On December 26, 1939, the prefect informed the Widow Trompier-Gravier that her permit to sell from the stand would expire on December 31, 1939, and would not be renewed. This is the decision that is challenged.

---

11. Based in part on the translation of the case in Bernard Schwartz, French Administrative Law and the Common Law World 342–345 (1954).

The petition, contesting the facts on which that decision is based and contending that it is invalid because of abuse of power, raises the claim that the Widow Trompier-Gravier had not been permitted to state her defenses against the accusations brought against her....It has been established that the challenged decision was rendered without Mme. Trompier-Gravier's having been *given an opportunity to defend herself against the accusation.* The procedure that led to the revocation of Mme. Trompier-Gravier's permit therefore did not have an *adversary* character.

Is it irregular because of this fact? This is the question that we must inquire into. *Your jurisprudence, even in the absence of a legal text, has several times asserted the need for adversary procedure. This rule, based on the principles of our law, is, however, neither general nor absolute, as certain decisions show. What, then, is its scope? ...*

When an administrative decision assumes a penal quality and has a sufficiently serious adverse effect on the situation of an individual, your jurisprudence requires that the individual be given an opportunity to present his point of view on the measure affecting him. . . .

If we analyze the measure taken by the prefect with regard to Mme. Trompier-Gravier, we can see clearly that the challenged decision has a penal quality. We are certainly not dealing with a case of public employment. Mme. Trompier-Gravier is in no sense an employee of the administration. She is in the position of the holder of a permit. Such permits are revocable, and the administration could have summarily ordered the closing down of the stand. This is not what it did. It sought to punish a fault. It acted to accomplish a penal end. In these circumstances, it could not, in our opinion, disregard a principle that governs all penal procedure, even outside the field of public employment and in the absence of an express legal text. The victim of a penalty must be given notice and enabled to present his defense.

We therefore conclude that the challenged decision should be annulled.

The Council of State:

-In light of the decrees of the prefect of the Seine of March 13, 1924, December 11, 1924, and January 22, 1934; and of the law of December 18, 1940;

-Considering that it is established that the challenged decision, by which the prefect of the Seine revoked the permit that had been granted to the Widow Trompier-Gravier to sell newspapers from a stand on the Boulevard Saint-Denis, in Paris, was based on a fault of which the petitioner was said to be culpable;

-Considering that, taking into account the significance that the aforementioned revocation of the permit carried in these circumstances, and of the gravity of that penalty, such a measure could not be taken legally without the Widow Trompier-Gravier's having been given an opportunity to contest the charges against her; the petitioner, not having been afforded the opportunity of presenting evidence in her defense, can validly contend that the challenged decision was rendered by the prefect of the Seine without proper procedures and was, therefore, *ultra vires*:

The decision of the prefect of the Seine of December 26, 1939, is hereby annulled.

* * *

CUMMINS, GENERAL PRINCIPLES OF LAW, SEPARATION OF POWERS, AND THEORIES OF JUDICIAL DECISION IN FRANCE
35 INT'L & COMP. L. Q. 594, 603–605 (1986)

Since the constitutional tradition limits the role of the courts to applying texts, they have considered reference to a law or regulation as support for a decision to be an essential element of its legitimacy. The *Cour de Cassation* always cites a legal text as the basis of its decisions, however remote its relevance may be. While less strict on this point, the *Conseil d'Etat* almost always follows the same practice. Neither the specific right recognized in… *Trompier-Gravier* nor those which came to be recognized in later cases as protected general principles of law were new to the case law of the *Conseil d'Etat*. What was new and important was the *Conseil*'s assertion that it had the right to state broad principles without relying on a "text."

The phrase "general principles" in the sense of principles or rules created or found by the *Conseil d'Etat* has been used numerous times since 1944. It constitutes a well-recognised source of the power of the *Conseil* to control the action of the administration and, as such, has been largely unchallenged by other parts of the government.

There are almost as many ways of dividing the principles into categories as there are authors. Those used by Guy Braibant, head of the newly-created Section on the Report and Studies of the *Conseil d'Etat*, in his recent *Droit Administratif* (1984), are perhaps as useful as any. One category of principles relates to the organisation and functioning of public services. These include the principles of continuity, hierarchy and autonomy. The first conveys the notion that the services of the State must be maintained. In earlier days the right to strike was consequently totally prohibited. As this right is explicitly referred to in the Preamble to the 1946 Constitution, the absolute rule could no longer be maintained but the case law still limits the right to strike as much as possible. Companies providing public services may not refuse them even if existing price legislation forces them to do so at a loss. On the other hand, they are entitled to be compensated for their loss by the State. The principle of hierarchy establishes a ranking of functions and a higher level always has the right to reverse the decision of inferior ranks. More than this, the person having the higher position in the administrative hierarchy (right up to and including the minister) is obliged to consider appeals against the position of his subordinate. The principle of autonomy provides that each organ of the State (i.e., including all public entities, ministries, departments, agencies, municipalities and other subdivisions) is autonomous in the absence of a text subjecting it to the control of some other organ.

These principles may be contrasted with those which deal with the rights of citizens directly. Braibant divides these into substantive rights and procedural rights (*règles de procédure*). The first category includes the great rights of freedom of conscience, the right to come and go freely, liberty of opinion, freedom of expression and many others. The concept of equality is applied in a number of principles, e.g., the equality of users of public services (seen in the absence of discriminatory tariffs); the burden of taxation and other public charges must be distributed equally according to neutral principles; all must have equal access to public employment. Although it has not been uniformly or consistently applied in every area, the non-retroactivity of regulations remains a "general principle." This principle, which has been the source of much controversy in many contexts, finds its most general statement in Article 2 of the Civil Code: "The law only disposes for the future; it cannot have a retroactive effect."

Among the rules of procedure, Braibant classifies the rights of defence. These rights have an extensive development in criminal law. In the administrative context they include the right of a person against whom action is taken or contemplated (whether a civil servant or anyone else subject to action by the administration) to know the nature of the charges against him and have the right and opportunity reply to them. In the same category is the right to appeal. This right guarantees at least one opportunity to have any administrative action reviewed by a higher authority.

* * *

3. The Binding Effect of Judicial Decisions

What effect does the judgment of a court have? The very least effect it can reasonably have is to bind the parties that are actually before it, in the case at hand. But the courts we are acquainted with in our common law system have much broader powers than that. We expect a higher court to control a lower court in the case at hand, for example, so that if a higher court reverses a ruling and remands the case, the lower court is bound to follow the higher court's ruling in that case. Beyond that, what courts decide can have a legal effect not only in the case and on the parties before it, and on lower courts in connection with the same case and parties, but higher courts can also bind lower courts in future cases, and can even bind themselves in future cases, by setting out a principle of decision in the present case.[12]

The fact that court decisions bind courts in the future is called *stare decisis,* and it is part of what we take for granted in the American legal system. In a hierarchy of courts, an intermediate appellate court is supposed to be bound by what the supreme court has said in the past, and trial courts are supposed to be bound by what the appellate courts and the supreme court have said in the past. In addition, the appellate and supreme courts are, to some extent, expected to follow their own past rulings. The body of law composed of these court precedents is called the common law. It is trumped by legislation, but in areas in which the legislature has not acted—large tracts of tort and property law, for example— and in the interpretation of statutes, what the courts say has the effect of law.

An important difference between legal systems in the common law tradition and those in the civil law tradition, it is sometimes said, is that in the civil law tradition judicial decisions do not have the force of law. In fact that is in some ways a defining difference. Judges in the English tradition are called common law judges precisely because their decisions have this lawlike force, while judges in the French tradition (that is, the civil law tradition) have deliberately been deprived of that power.[13]

How does this feature of legal systems come to be of interest in a book on constitutional review? For one thing, the ability to modify statutes through judicial interpretations that have the force of law gives the courts the power to review legislation against the courts' own sense of what the legislation ought to say, and to incorporate the court's sense of it into the law. So *stare decisis* all by itself permits a kind of basic judicial review. That power is limited, of course, by the power of the legislature to rewrite the statute to reverse the courts' interpretation.

The more important point has to do with the effect of judicial determinations of constitutionality. As a practical matter, the study of constitutional law is the study of limits imposed on legislation by courts or other bodies interpreting a constitution. If these limits are to be imposed by the ordinary judiciary—as they are in the United States—then a question arises about the effect these court rulings will have. If they are not binding in future cases (as they are not in France), is it possible for a piece of legislation to be struck down by one court and for the same legislation to be upheld in a future case

---

12. *But see* In re Osborne, 76 F.3d 306, 309 (9th Cir., 1996); R.E.O. Industries, Inc. v. Natural Gas Pipeline Co. of America, 932 F2d 447, 454 (5th Cir., 1991).

13. Countries in the common law tradition include the countries of the United Kingdom, exclusive of Scotland, as well as the United States, Canada, Australia and others. Countries in the civil law tradition include France and Germany, most of the other countries of western Europe and Latin America, as well as many of the countries of Africa and Asia.

by the same court or by a lower level court? If there is no doctrine of precedent, then though the courts might try for consistency in such matters there is no legal requirement that they do so. And if courts are not bound by their own rulings in this matter, what about other government actors? Would the administrative agencies be bound by court rulings of constitutionality or unconstitutionality? In most of the countries of the world the judiciary—the judges who staff the ordinary courts, even those of the highest level—do not, as we will see, have the power to consider the constitutionality of legislation. And one of the arguments against allowing them to have that power is the possibility of this sort of inconsistency. As we will see, there are more powerful arguments as well.

HENRY CAMPBELL BLACK, HANDBOOK ON THE LAW OF JUDICIAL PRECEDENTS, OR THE SCIENCE OF CASE LAW
2–3, 182, 38–40, 10–11 (1912)[14]

.... [I]n the science of case-law, the primary idea of a precedent is that of a rule judicially established and presumptively binding. It is not to be considered in the light of a model which may safely be followed, nor as an example which will justify subsequent judicial action in the same direction. It declares or enunciates the rule or principle of law which must (not may) be followed in the decision of similar causes in the future, by the same court and by those courts which are under its revisory jurisdiction, or which can be disregarded only in exceptional cases and for the very strongest reasons....

Meaning of the Rule. [*Stare decisis*] embodies a rule or principle of action for the courts to follow. More fully expressed, it means that when a point or principle of law has been once officially decided or settled, by the ruling of a competent court in a case in which it was directly and necessarily involved, and more especially when it has been repeatedly decided in the same way, it will no longer be considered as open to examination, or to a new ruling, by the same tribunal or by those which are bound to follow its adjudications, unless it be for urgent reasons and in exceptional cases; ordinarily the rule so established will be adopted in all subsequent cases to which it is applicable, without any reconsideration of its correctness in point of law....

Opinion and Decision Distinguished. It is important to be noticed, as a fundamental principle in the study of precedents, that it is the decision, that is, the judgment rendered in the case, and not the opinion of the court, which settles the point of law involved and makes the precedent. The decision is the

---

14. Henry Campbell Black was the original author of Black's Law Dictionary.

conclusion of the court on the premises; the opinion sets forth the reasons of the determination, and usually states and explains them at greater or less length; and sometimes justifies and supports them by a copious citation of authorities and a wealth of argument, illustration, or analogy. The opinion, disclosing the actual determination of the court and the reasons of the judge for his decision, is of course of great importance in the information it imparts as to the principles of law which influenced the court and were supposed to govern the case, and which should guide litigants. But the opinion may far outrun the decision, not only in the way of including inferences and illustrations, but also in the way of noticing points not essential to the final conclusion or laying down principles of law far broader than is necessary for the particular case in judgment. In that case, it has no authority as a precedent beyond the point or points actually and necessarily decided. So, also, it is only the precise decision made that is authoritative in subsequent cases, and not a proposition of law which, at most, could only be inferred or implied from the point actually decided. Again, different judges may agree as to a conclusion of law, though they do not agree as to the propositions of law on which it should be based....

* * *

Still, the claim that judicial precedent is law in American courts is a little misleading. For one thing, the effect of precedent is not what it once was. Nowadays the common law judge need only overrule his earlier decisions to render them ineffective. And if they cannot be overruled, as for example decisions from a higher court cannot be, or if it would be inconvenient to overrule them, they can always be *distinguished*.

ANTONIN SCALIA, A MATTER OF INTERPRETATION
7–9, 12 (1997)

Within such a precedent-bound common-law system, it is critical for the lawyer, or the judge, to establish whether the case at hand falls within a principle that has already been decided. Hence the technique—or the art, or the game—of "distinguishing" earlier cases. It is an art or a game, rather than a science, because what constitutes the "holding" of an earlier case is not well defined and can be adjusted to suit the occasion. At its broadest, the holding of a case can be said to be the analytical principle that produced the judgment—in *Hadley v. Baxendale*, for example, the principle that damages for breach of contract must be foreseeable. In the narrowest sense, however (and courts will squint narrowly when they wish to avoid an earlier decision), the holding of a case cannot go beyond the facts that were before the court. Assume, for example, that a painter contracts with me to paint my house green and paints it instead a god-awful puce. And assume that not I, but my neighbor, sues the painter for this breach of contract. The court would dismiss the suit on the ground that (in legal terminology) there was no "privity of contract": the contract was between the painter and me, not between the painter and my neighbor. Assume, however, a later case in which a company contracts with me to repair my home computer; it does a bad job, and as a consequence my wife loses valuable files she has stored in the computer. She sues the computer company. Now the broad rationale of the earlier case (no suit will lie where there is no privity of contract) would dictate dismissal of this complaint as well. But a good common-law lawyer would argue, and some good common-law judges have held, that that rationale does not extend to this new fact situation, in which the breach of a contract relating to something used in the home harms a family member, though not the one who made the contract. The earlier case, in other words, is "distinguishable". ...

As I have described, this system of making law by judicial opinion, and making law by distinguishing earlier cases, is what every American law student, every newborn American lawyer, first sees when he opens his eyes. And the impression remains for life. His image of the great judge—the Holmes, the Cardozo—is the man (or woman) who has the intelligence to discern the best rule of law for the case at hand, and then the skill to perform the broken-field running through earlier cases that leaves him free to impose that rule....

Today, generally speaking, the old private-law fields—contracts, torts, property, trusts and estates, family law—remain firmly within the control of state common-law courts. Indeed, it is probably true that in these fields judicial lawmaking can be more freewheeling than ever, since the doctrine of *stare decisis* has appreciably eroded. Prior decisions that even the cleverest mind cannot distinguish can nowadays simply be overruled.

* * *

In the United States the theory is that judges make law. In France the theory is that judges do not make law. In France, as in the United States, the practice is a little different from the theory.

THE FRENCH CIVIL CODE
(1804)

Article 5. Judges are forbidden to issue rulings of a general statutory nature in the cases before them.[15]

---

15. See also Article 12 of the Law of 16–24 August, 1790, quoted in Cappelletti, Repudiating Montesquieu.

Note

1. "The fathers of the French revolution, such as Le Chaplier and Robespierre, were convinced that written law alone must dominate and that 'the judge-made law was the most detestable of institutions, and should be destroyed.'... Consistent with this view, legislative codes eventually were enacted which promulgated the substantive law.... [T]oday the structure of the French [judicial] courts, and their source of law, at its root retains this aversion to judge-made doctrine. Thus, in France every judicial decision must be based upon the written law. General pronouncements of legal rules, or "*arrets de reglement*"— a central characteristic of the common law court—are expressly prohibited by the French Civil Code. Likewise, French judges 'are forbidden, when giving judgment in the cases which are brought before them,...to decide a case by holding it was governed by a previous decision.' Consequently, as Planiol put it, in France

> '[t]he regulation-making power is today reserved exclusively to representatives of the executive power. The judicial authorities do not enjoy it. The effect of their decisions is purely relative. Their rulings, in other words, bind only the parties before the court. Courts have thus lost the right which they had under the old regime of rendering obligatory decisions having a binding effect upon the future and applying to all persons within their jurisdiction.'"

Sol Wachtler, Judicial Lawmaking, 65 New York University Law Review 1, 1–5 (1990).

* * *

In civil law theory it is the legislator who makes law, not the judge, and it is not up to the judge to create legal rules either from the ground up (as American judges create tort law) or in the process of interpreting statutes. Judges in ordinary courts are limited to applying statutes, and they are not to use interpretation as an excuse for inventing new rules. Moreover, their interpretations do not have the power to bind in future cases. Not only do judges lack the power to bind their own courts and lower courts in future cases, but the higher courts may not even be able to bind lower courts in the same case. Thus in France the presumption is that the lower courts are not bound by the rulings of the highest court. That means that when a case is remanded the lower court can ignore the ruling of the higher court and decide the case exactly as it did the first time. In theory, and in line with the limits the French wanted to place upon the power of judges, that could go on forever. As a practical matter, the lower court is now bound the second time the case is remanded, simply to allow litigation to come to an end.

Beyond that the rulings of the courts are to have no legal effect on future cases. No court is bound by past rulings, even of higher courts. This is true in France, and is true to a lesser extent in other civil law countries. As a practical matter, of course, courts will try for consistency, and over time trends are recognized and even relied upon by lawyers. In theory, though, court decisions make up no part of the law. Thus you will find commentators saying something like the following, in cases in which appellate courts have been resisting a certain principle that the highest court has maintained for a period of time: Appellate courts would be wise now to stop resisting this principle—though of course they have every legal right to go on doing so.

So, for example, in the famous French case *Jand'heur v. Les Galeries Belfortaises* (Cassation, Civil Chamber, February 21, 1927), the highest civil court reversed the interpretation of the court below, declared that the proper interpretation of the civil code was such as would dictate the defendant's liability, and remanded. The lower court had said that it was necessary for the plaintiff to prove fault in a traffic accident case under the code; the Court of Cassation declared that fault need not be proved. Lower appellate courts had been resisting that interpretation of the code, and a commentator said: "It was necessary to settle the case law. The new decision of the civil chamber ends all the doubts, which should never have arisen, and will, we must hope, prevent a renewal of the argument....If, hereafter, a court of appeal persists in not wanting to find liability in such cases, the court would be resisting, *as would in fact be its right*, the doctrine of the Court of Cassation." Ripert, Note to Jand'heur v. Les Galeries Belfortaises, D. 1927. I. 97 (*translated in* Arthur von Mehren and James Gordley, The Civil Law System 623 (1977)(italics added)). On remand the lower appellate court *did* persist in not wanting to find liability, and rejected the higher court's interpretation. The case thereupon was certified to the Court of Cassation a second time; the Court reiterated its interpretation of the statute and remanded once more. This time, in accord with the rule for repeated petitions to the Court of Cassation, the lower appellate court was bound by the higher court's interpretation. Even so, this binding effect did not extend to *future* cases—except insofar as it was clear that future disagreements from the lower courts would meet with the same fate.

Notes

1. Article 5 of the French Civil Code has not changed since 1804. Article 4, which was likewise intended to prevent judges from obstructing the implementation of legislation, also has not changed:

> *Article 4.* The judge who refuses to decide a case under the pretext of the silence, the obscurity, or the insufficiency of the law may be prosecuted as being guilty of a denial of justice.

2. "The rule is taken to its logical conclusion that if one court states that it has based its decision on the decision of another court relating to other litigation (even if the two situations are identical), then the decision will be

quashed." David Pollard, Sourcebook on French Law xiv, 2nd ed. (Cavendish, 1998).

3. Other civil law countries are not so single-minded about this as France has been. In Germany, for example, lower courts are bound by the rulings of the higher courts in many more kinds of cases, and some rulings have legal effect on future cases as well.

* * *

But as with American law, the theory is one thing and the practice is another. It would be wrong to conclude that French judges were utterly restrained by statutory law and utterly without power to influence the law. In the first place, in interpreting the law French judges have sometimes strayed pretty far from the words of the legislation they were applying. And in the second place, though strictly speaking there is no doctrine of *stare decisis*, the decisions of the higher courts do tend to take on a kind of inertial force, so that lawyers can rely, to a great extent, on prior cases in determining what the law is.

MITCHEL DE S.-O.-L'E. LASSER, JUDICIAL (SELF-)PORTRAITS: JUDICIAL DISCOURSE IN THE FRENCH LEGAL SYSTEM
104 YALE L.J. 1325, 1334–1346 (1995)(italics added)

The *official* French portrait of the civil judge represents an image of the judge in the performance of his or her proper role. Officially, the civil judge mechanically applies legislative provisions to given fact situations. It is the statutory law—especially the Civil Code—that determines cases. Its matrix generates outcomes in a grammatical fashion. This grammatical interpretive ideology is the product of several constitutive elements. Legislative provisions define the place of the judiciary in the French system of separation of powers and delineate basic rules concerning the proper execution of the judicial role. Judicial application and interpretation of these legislative provisions establish and enforce a specific reading of these provisions. Finally, the formal structure of the French civil judicial decision conveys a specifically grammatical conception of the judicial role implicit in the very production of such decisions....

The leading French judicial case on the proper (or improper) role of the civil judge is a damage award case, decided by the *Cour de cassation* in 1955. The trial court held Mr. Fouchereau partially liable for the injuries caused to Mr. Cornet in an accident, and ordered monetary reparations. The appellate court, without questioning the extent of Cornet's injuries or the responsibility of Fouchereau, nonetheless lowered the amount of reparations owed to Cornet. The appellate court stated as follows:

[T]hat without contesting the fall in Cornet's income after the accident nor underestimating the personal extent of his productive activity and the effect of his permanent partial disability on this activity, the court believes itself unable to go beyond its usual maximum assessment in such matters, and that there is good reason to evaluate at 2,500,000 francs the compensation related to this disability."

The *Cour de cassation* quashed the appellate court's decision, reasoning that the

appellate court modified the lower court's decision on the sole ground that "the court believes itself unable to go beyond its usual maximum assessment in such matters," although, judges being unable to pronounce by way of general and regulatory disposition on the claims that are submitted to them and the defining characteristic of damages being to repair entirely the prejudice, the court…could not limit compensation for a prejudice, the extent of which it recognized, by claiming itself bound by "its usual maximum assessment in such matters," and thus, at the least, by so ruling, by reference to "its usual maximum assessment in such matters," the challenged decision…did not give a legal basis for its decision…; but whereas it is forbidden for judges to pronounce by way of general and regulatory disposition on the claims submitted to them; whereas if, in matters of damages resulting from a crime or misdemeanor, [solely the lower court judges are empowered to determine]…the due reparations, they may not refer, in particular cases, to rules established in advance to justify their decision; whereas, there was, consequently, a violation of the texts alluded to in the claim;

On these grounds, quash[]….[16]

In this opinion, the *Cour de cassation* quashes an appellate court decision that had justified lowering a trial court's damage award on the sole basis that it exceeded the amount usually awarded in such cases. The *Cour*'s fundamental problem is that the appellate court " 'believes itself unable to go beyond its usual maximum assessment in such matters.' " Deference by a court to its own "usual maximum assessment in such matters" posits the existence and application, in violation of Article 5 of the Civil Code, of a predetermined judicial rule on how to calculate damages. According to the *Cour de cassation*, however, the statement is problematic for other reasons as well. The problem is not only that the judiciary has exercised legislative power by establishing a rule, but also that it has not properly exercised its judicial power: Civil courts cannot bind themselves with preestablished rules of their own making.…

---

16. Judgment of November 3, 1955, Cass. Crim., 1956 Recueil Dalloz [D.Jur.] I 557.

The *Cour de cassation* has therefore determined that a judge can refer to jurisprudence as long as such a reference does not constitute "the determinative argument of his decision." For this reason, appellate judges cannot even refer to jurisprudence of the *Cour* as the legal basis for overturning a decision, nor will the *Cour* sustain appeals on the basis of a lower court's violation of the *Cour*'s own jurisprudence. The *Cour* will not even entertain such an appeal. The substantive rules produced by the French judiciary turn on the distinction between what is (and what is not) considered determinative or authoritative in judicial decisions—i.e., the distinction between legislation and jurisprudence....

[On the other hand, mainstream] French academic doctrine, which both reflects and informs French legal consciousness, represents an important element of the *unofficial* portrait of the judicial role. French legal scholars identify 1899, the year of Francois Geny's first publication of *Methode d'interpretation*, as the birth of "modern" French legal consciousness. Geny's book presented a scathing, Realist-style critique of the mechanical and formalist judicial practice of his day. Since Geny, every major twentieth-century French analysis of the civil legal system has worked from the following three assumptions: (1) the Codes inevitably contain gaps, conflicts, and ambiguities inherent in the text itself and produced by the evolution of modern society; (2) the perfectly formalist conception of unproblematic, passive, and grammatical adjudication is therefore no longer tenable; and (3) the judiciary has in fact played—if only by necessity—a fundamental role in the establishment and development of legal norms....

For the nearly one hundred years since Geny first attacked "that fetishism of the written and codified statutory law," which constituted "the most distinctive and...most salient trait" of nineteenth-century academic and judicial practice, "modern" French doctrine has critiqued the rigid theory of adjudication implicit in what I have been calling the official portrait of the civil judge. The first target has been the notion of complete legislative coverage, "that pretentious notion that, under the reign of modern codification, wishes to find, simply in the dispositions of written law [legislation], all legal solutions."

According to French doctrine, two insurmountable hurdles render complete legislative coverage impossible: human imperfection and the incessant evolution of society over time. As Geny states, "even if one could imagine...a legislator sufficiently perspicacious to penetrate, with a far-ranging and profound gaze, the whole of the legal order of his time,...he still would be unable to foresee...all future relations." Modern French doctrine therefore works under the assumption that legislation must inevitably contain gaps.

The debunking of the myth of complete legislative coverage leads to a critique of the mechanical and syllogistic means by which the "traditional" French method of interpretation seeks to fill legislative gaps. As Geny states: "a) there are points requiring legal resolution that are not foreseen and settled by the statutory law; b) logic remains powerless to fill all the gaps resulting from the insufficiency of the texts." Despite this problem, notes the French academic, the French judicial decision maintains its perfectly syllogistic form, as if the Code were grammatically generating all legal solutions.

French doctrine almost universally concludes, therefore, that the traditional form of the civil judicial decision masks important facets of judicial practice. As Jean Carbonnier states:

> "Quite often, contrary to the classic syllogism where they should de-scend from the legal rule to the concrete decision, [judges] start by positing the concrete decision that strikes them as humanly desirable, and then endeavor to work back to a legal rule. Things must always have happened this way since…there have always been judges, and judges who think."

Given that legislative gaps exist, that logic cannot fill them, and that they are nonetheless filled when cases are decided, it is the judge who must be filling the gaps.

Modern French doctrine therefore takes it for granted that the judiciary plays a significant role in the creation and development of legal norms. Car-bonnier, for example, states:

> "[Modern doctrine] accepts that the judge be a creator, and not just an interpreter…That judgments, insofar as they imply judicially con-structed rules, must be seen as being part of the totality of the law, is hardly contested today when it is commonly declared that law can be judicial as well as legislative…."

French doctrine accepts the judiciary's creative normative role to such a degree that mainstream academics such as Professor Tunc can state, without explana-tion, that "as often happens today,…[the *Cour de cassation*] truly creates a rule of law."

Notes

1. "[This] suggests another question, whether credence can be accorded to the popular view that the Civil Law is differentiated from the Common Law by its refusal to accept the principle of *stare decisis*….Personally I doubt whether any general answer can be given to it….There is a possible halfway house which is popularly supposed to be that occupied by the French practice, that of regard-ing a [series] of decisions as binding. That seems to have been the French prac-tice, and probably still is the practice as far as the decisions of the lower courts are concerned, but the view of authoritative jurists now [1955] is that a single decision of the highest court, the *Cour de Cassation*, is regarded by the court it-

self as almost completely binding, at any rate until it becomes obsolete......I have heard advocates say that they rarely cite the views of jurists before any court lower than the *Cour de Cassation,* but content themselves with citing cases. I doubt whether the position is very different from that in America." F.H. Lawson, A Common Lawyer Looks at the Civil Law 83–84 (1955). Nevertheless when it comes to constitutional matters the mere possibility of inconsistency might be troubling to someone considering extending the power of constitutional review to the French courts.

2. "An interesting difference exists between the effects of a [remand] by the *Conseil d'Etat* and the *Cour de cassation*. At the beginning of the 20th century the *Cour de comptes* [a lower administrative court] took the position, that, like a lower civil court upon [remand] from the *Cour de cassation*, it was not bound by the points of law decided when the *Conseil* quashed a decision and returned it for further proceedings. In connection with the *Conseil*'s consideration of the issue, the *commissaire du gouvernement* [argued] that all decisions of the Council, contrary to the rule applicable to decisions of the *Cour*, should bind the court of [remand] on questions of law. In the *commissaire*'s view, the refusal to accord such an effect to decisions of the *Cour de cassation* 'had its origins solely in an abusive application of the principle of separation of powers and in the traditional fear of the judicial power.'" Arthur von Mehren and James Gorley, The Civil Law System 493 (1977).

3. How does it work in Germany? "Technically, statutory law is the only true source of law in Germany....By 'separation of powers' the Continental European means that the democratic legislature and its appointed executive must be protected from the undemocratic judiciary. Thus the insistence by civilian jurists that judge-made law is not real law does not mean that judge-made norms do not exist. Rather it means that judge-made norms *should* not exist. The European doctrine of separation of powers demands that the state be governed by enacted law (*Rectsstaat*), not by judicial decree (*Justizstaat*)....'A doctrine of *stare decisis* does not, in general, exist in German law but, of course, decisions of the Federal Supreme Court have a very high persuasive authority for the lower courts. The Federal Supreme Court, too, is not bound by its own previous decisions, but it tends to overrule them very rarely.'" Thomas Lundmark, Introduction to German Law, 47 American Journal of Comparative Law 677, 680–681 (1999) (*reviewing and quoting from* Werner F. Ebke and Matthew W. Finkin, Introduction to German Law (1996)).

4. Although the question does not often arise, we may ask whether the doctrine of *stare decisis* applies to the decisions of the executive and legislative branches in any legal system. In the UK, the saying is that no Parliament can bind any future Parliament; that is, that anything that has been done by one Parliament can be undone by a future Parliament. This contrasts with the rigid doctrine that applied to judicial decisions until recently: that not even the House of

Lords, the highest judicial body, could reverse an earlier decision of the House of Lords. In the United States the issue as to whether a President is bound by the acts of prior Presidents arose when President Jackson vetoed a bill establishing the Bank of the United States. The Bank had been created under earlier legislation, and approved by President Madison. The issue here was legislation *renewing* the Bank's authorization. According to Daniel Webster, Jackson's refusal to sign it was inappropriate: "[W]hen a law has been passed by Congress, and approved by the President, it is now no longer in the power, either of the same President, or his successors, to say whether the law is constitutional or not." Congressional debates, 22nd Cong., 1st Sess. 1231–1244 (1832). See below, Chapter Two.

5. "It has been seen that the ordinary courts' decisions are not considered to be a source of law, even those of the highest such court. With regard to the *Conseil d'Etat*, that body was not subject to the constitutional principles referred to above [proscribing judge-made law]....The *Conseil d'Etat* did not feel constrained or restricted to making a decision on the instant case only, but commenced to develop substantive rules of law relating to the liability of the administration in tort, the operation of contracts in which the administration had an interest, the grounds for exercising a judicial review jurisdiction and the general principles of law to which acts of the administration must conform (such as equality before the law and the right to a proper procedure)." David Pollard, Sourcebook On French Law xvii (2nd ed.1998).

Chapter Two

Inroads into Parliamentary Supremacy I: The United States

A. Political Review

1. A Council of Revision?

In the American system the states sometimes serve as laboratories in which experiments in government are carried out. One such experiment was the Council of Revision, a body specifically designed to review legislation for constitutionality. New York adopted a provision creating such a Council in its 1777 Constitution.

DOMINIC R. MASSARO, FOREORDAINED FAILURE: NEW YORK'S EXPERIMENT WITH POLITICAL REVIEW OF CONSTITUTIONALITY
70 NEW YORK STATE BAR JOURNAL 12, 17–19 (OCTOBER 1998)

It was [John] Jay who convinced the [New York] Convention that a collective body would be more suited for the exercise of constitutional review before an enactment became law. Its basic structure was straightforward and comprised of five members: the Governor, whose presence was required, the Chancellor (the chief judicial officer in equity), and the Justices (three at the time) of the Supreme Court, or any two of them acting together with the Governor. The legislature presented all bills to the Council. The Council reviewed the bills and could veto any of them by a majority vote of its members. But the legislature would have the final voice; it could override a veto by a two-thirds vote in both of its houses.

The primary purpose of the Council was to revise legislation, that is, to intervene before a law came into effect. Thus, if "it should appear improper to the said council...that said bill should become law of this state," it would be returned within ten days "together with their objections thereto in writing, to the senate or house of assembly, in whatsoever the same shall have originated." If the legislature chose not to override the objections, it could reconsider the bill to conform to those objections, or simply let the bill die....

During its existence, 6,560 bills were submitted to the Council; of these, 169 bills were returned to the legislature with objections. The legislature overrode 51 of these vetoes; the remaining 118 failed to become law. Reenacted were at least 26 bills with various degrees of modification. This activity reveals the substantial role that the Council played in the early lawmaking process of New York.

That the revisory power of the Council was plenary can readily be garnered from an analysis of its objections....Its decisions range from high judicial opinions of constitutional import to bald policy pronouncements characterized by overt moral sermonizing to blatantly political statements.

Surely the Council did not shrink from tough stands on controversial issues. In this respect it performed uncommonly well. Following the Revolution, for example, a widespread mood of radical vengefulness against those that had remained loyal to the Crown placed a severe strain on constitutional regularity; notwithstanding, the Council vetoed an ex post facto bill that deprived Tories of the vote by declaring that "to punish men for acts by laws made subsequent to the commission of such acts, hath, by all civilized nations, been deemed arbitrary and unjust." It vetoed a bill of attainder seeking forfeiture and confiscation of Tory property as "repugnant to the plain and immutable laws of justice," and rejected one that stripped them of their citizenship as "contradictory to the fundamental laws of every civilized nation."...

A bill stipulating that "no negro...shall have a legal vote" was declared "shocking [to] those principles of equal liberty which every page in [the] Constitution labors to enforce." During the second war with Great Britain in 1812, the Council vetoed an act aimed at the apprehension of suspected deserters without warrant on the ground that "it is in direct violation of all the rights of personal liberty."...

That the Council of Revision would gradually become mired in a power struggle with the legislature was inevitable given its constitutional charge to review bills on political as well as legal grounds. Indeed, the role of judges in the rough world of partisan politics and an alleged decline of public confidence in an impartial judiciary made for a major constitutional crisis. It would lead to the Council's abolition.

In 1820, the Council thwarted a call for a constitutional convention on the grounds that the Legislature did not submit the question to the voters. The

Legislature had wanted to revise the constitution in order to overhaul the system of appointments to government positions, which had deteriorated into corruption. The idea of a basic law amendable only by special convention as a shield to protect the people against their own representatives had not yet taken hold in New York. A resolution calling for a convention with general authority to change the constitution had been passed. The Council, in a message written by Chancellor Kent, held that it "doubted whether it belongs to the ordinary legislature…to call a convention…before they have received a legitimate and full expression of the people."

A Select Committee of the Assembly issued a lengthy partisan report highly critical of the Council for usurping the legislature's role as representative of the people's will. It flayed it as "so dangerous an authority" inconsistent with "the principles of republican government." Unable to garner sufficient votes to override the veto, however, the legislature was forced in 1821 to enact a bill providing for a referendum. It was overwhelmingly approved by the people.…

At the convention, the Council thus became the victim of retribution. Its inherent political and structural weaknesses were exposed. Opponents argued that it had "usurped the power of judging the expediency as well as the constitutionality of bills passed by the legislature" and that it should therefore be abolished. It was argued that "the council had…in fact become a third branch of the legislature…." Delegates contended that New York should follow the example of the national government and replace it with a purely executive veto.…

New York's Second Constitution abolished the Council of Revision. In its place the convention followed the Federal design of constitutional order, redistributing the Council's functions by allowing for the executive veto and full acceptance of judicial review. The convention thus affirmed that democratic representation should pervade all of public policy making. Its decision, ratified by the electorate the following year, would prove more palatable down to the present day.

And thus the Council of Revision passed into history on the last day of December, 1822.

Notes

1. Review of a bill before passage is called *a priori* review. We will see this sort of review again in the constitutional courts discussed in subsequent chapters.

2. The actions of the Council in blocking reform legislation and the resulting attacks upon the Council are reminiscent of the French experience with judges. See above, Chapter One, Section A.

3. In France, the Constitution of 1799 gave powers of (political) review to a body similar to the Council of Revision, the *Senat conservateur*. See above, Chapter One, Section B.2.

4. The drafters of the American Constitution initially considered creating a Council of Revision with the power to review and veto legislation:

> Resolved that the Executive and a convenient number of the National Judiciary, ought to compose a Council of Revision with authority to examine every act of the National Legislature before it shall operate, & every act of a particular Legislature before a Negative thereon shall be final; and that the dissent of the said Council shall amount to a rejection, unless the Act of the National Legislature be again passed....

"Resolutions proposed by Mr. Randolph...," in Notes of Debates in the Federal Convention of 1787 32 (1966).

5. The proposed Council was to consist of the President and several members of the federal judiciary. "Supporters of the proposed Council...argued that the Council of Revision provided a needed check on the legislature in the separation of powers system. James Madison and James Wilson argued that the President would need the judiciary's help to check the power of the legislature because an executive veto alone would not suffice. Wilson asserted that the executive and the judiciary could only 'preserve their full importance against the legislature' by jointly exercising the veto power. Madison added that a Council, unlike a single, weak executive, would 'render [the] Check or negative more respectable....' Since the legislature would have 'a powerful tendency... to absorb all power into its vortex' the Constitution had to give 'every defensive authority to the other departments' as long as such authority was 'consistent with republican principles.' At the time of the Federal Convention, the widespread phenomenon of overbearing state legislatures supported Madison and Wilson's warning that the President alone would be an ineffective check against the Congress. The delegates to the Federal Convention, like those at the New York Convention of 1777, were justifiably concerned about the potential for either executive or legislative tyranny. As in New York, the proposed Council of Revision offered a compromise between these two extremes by placing a weighty check upon the legislature while diluting the President's power by forcing him to act in concert with the judicial branch in exercising the veto." James T. Barry, The Council of Revision and the Limits of Judicial Power, 56 University of Chicago Law Review 235, 235, 249–250 (1989).

* * *

This provision obviously was not adopted; there never was a federal Council of Revision. It was argued at the Convention that the power of review ought to be granted to the executive only, since judges (it was asserted) already had the power to expand the law, "which involved a power of deciding on their Constitutionality. In some states the judges had actually set aside laws as being against the Constitution." *See* Notes of Debates in the Federal Convention of 1787 (1966) at 61. The argument seems to have prevailed, *see id.* at 66.

2. Executive Review

In the United States, the president can veto legislation on any ground, including unconstitutionality. Constitutional issues are, in fact, rarely involved; vetoes are generally based on policy and political considerations. From time to time, however, the question of constitutionality does enter into the veto question.

In 1791 Thomas Jefferson, then Secretary of State, wrote, at the request of President George Washington, an opinion on legislation creating a national bank. Jefferson argued that the bank would be unconstitutional and that the legislation ought to be vetoed for that reason. "The negative [*i.e.*, the veto] of the President is the shield provided by the Constitution to protect against the invasions of the legislature: 1. the right of the executive. 2. of the judiciary. 3. of the states and state legislatures. The present [*i.e.*, the creation of the bank] is the case of a right remaining exclusively within the states, and consequently one of those intended by the Constitution to be placed under its protection." Against the Constitutionality of the Bank of the United States, *in* VII H.A. Washington, ed., Writings of Thomas Jefferson 561 (1853–1855).

Nevertheless Washington signed the bill and the first Bank of the United States, modeled on the Bank of England, was established. Its charter was not renewed by Congress and it died in 1811. In 1816 the second Bank of the United States was chartered. Its constitutionality was upheld by the Supreme Court in McCulloch v. Maryland, 17 U.S. 316 (1819), as necessary to the accomplishment of ends permitted to Congress by the Constitution. When Congress passed a bill renewing its charter in 1832, President Andrew Jackson, relying on arguments like those Jefferson had used some thirty years before, vetoed it.

ANDREW JACKSON, VETO MESSAGE
OF JULY 10, 1832

If our power over means is so absolute that the Supreme Court will not call in question the constitutionality of an act of Congress the subject of which "is not prohibited, and is really calculated to effect any of the objects intrusted [sic] to the government," although, as in the case before me, it takes away powers expressly granted to Congress and rights scrupulously reserved to the States, it becomes us to proceed in our legislation with the utmost caution. Though not directly, our own powers and the rights of the States may be indirectly legislated away in the use of means to execute substantive powers. We may not enact that Congress shall have the power of exclusive legislation over the District of Columbia, but we may pledge the faith of the United States that as a means of executing other powers it shall not be exercised for twenty years or forever. We may not pass an act prohibiting the States to tax the banking business carried on within their limits, but we may, as a means of executing our powers over other objects, place that business in the hands of our agents and then declare it exempt from State taxation in their hands. Thus may our own powers and the rights of the States, which we can not directly curtail or invade, be frittered away and extinguished in the use of means employed by us to execute other powers. That a bank of the United States, competent in all the duties which may be required by the Government, might be so organized as to not infringe on our own delegated powers or the reserved rights of the States I do not entertain a doubt. Had the Executive been called upon to furnish the project of such an institution, the duty would have been cheerfully performed. In the absence of such a call it was obviously proper that he should confine himself to pointing out those prominent features in the act presented which in his opinion make it incompatible with the Constitution and sound policy....

The bank is professedly established as an agent of the executive branch of the Government, and its constitutionality is maintained on that ground. Neither upon the propriety of present action nor upon the provisions of this act was the Executive consulted. It has had no opportunity to say that it neither needs nor wants an agent clothed with such powers and favored by such exemptions. There is nothing in its legitimate functions which makes it necessary or proper. Whatever interest or influence, whether public or private, has given birth to this act, it can not be found either in the wishes or necessities of the executive department, by which present action is deemed premature, and the powers conferred upon its agent not only unnecessary, but dangerous to the Government and country....

Nor is our government to be maintained or our Union preserved by invasions of the rights and powers of the several States. In thus attempting to make our General Government strong we make it weak. Its true strength consists in leaving individuals and States as much as possible to themselves — in making itself felt, not in its power, but in its beneficence; not in control, but in its protection; not in binding the States more closely to the center, but leaving each to move unobstructed in its proper orbit.

Experience should teach us wisdom. Most of the difficulties our Government now encounters and most of the dangers which impend over our Union have sprung from an abandonment of the legitimate objects of Government by our national legislation, and the adoption of such principles as are embodied in this act. Many of our rich men have not been content with equal protection and equal benefits, but have besought us to make them richer by act of Congress. By attempting to gratify their desires we have in the results of our legislation arrayed section against section, interest against interest, and man against man, in a fearful commotion which threatens to shake the foundations of our Union. It is time to pause in our career to review our principles, and if possible revive that devoted patriotism and spirit of compromise which distinguished the sages of the Revolution and the fathers of our Union. If we can not at once, in justice to interests vested under improvident legislation, make our Government what it ought to be, we can at least take a stand against all new grants of monopolies and exclusive privileges, against any prostitution of our Government to the advancement of the few at the expense of the many, and in favor of compromise and gradual reform in our code of laws and system of political economy.

* * *

B. Judicial Review

The question whether the ordinary courts may decide on the validity of legislation has a long history. In England there was a brief period during which some argued that legislation was subject to the common law, and that judges might strike down statutes that conflict with the common law. In Bonham's Case, the issue was the validity of a statute authorizing the President and Censors of the College of Physicians to fine someone for practicing medicine in violation of the statute. The decision of the court is set down in Lord Coke's words:

DR. BONHAM'S CASE
8 COKE'S REPORTS 113B, 118A (1610)

The censors cannot be judges, ministers, and parties; judges to give sentence or judgment; ministers to make summons; and parties to have the moiety of the forfeiture [for no one should be a judge in his own cause...]; and one cannot be [both] Judge and attorney for any of the parties.... And it appears in our books, that in many cases, the common law will controul Acts of Parliament, and sometimes adjudge them to be utterly void: for when an Act of Parliament is against common right and reason, or repugnant, or impossible to be performed, the common law will controul it, and adjudge such Act to be void.

Notes

1. "Elsewhere Coke further asserted: 'Fortescue and Littleton and all others agree that the law consists of three parts: first, common law; secondly, statute law; third, custom, which takes away the common law. But the common law

corrects, allows and disallows both statute law and custom, for if there be repugnancy in statute or unreasonableness in custom, the common law disallows
and rejects it.' But who ought to control and ascertain such 'repugnancy or unreasonableness,' and who ought to guarantee the supremacy of the common
law against arbitrary decisions of the sovereign on the one hand and of Parliament on the other? This was the essential question, and Coke's answer, at this
point in his life, was clear and precise: that control and that guarantee were the
task of the judges....While the influence of Coke's doctrine in Bonham's Case
is debatable, Coke unquestionably reflected the attitude of many common law
judges." Mauro Cappelletti, Judicial Review in the Contemporary World 37–38
(1971).

2. The dalliance with judicial review was brief, and had no lasting effect in
British law. (Indeed, some commentators wonder whether the whole episode
was not exaggerated by Coke.) By the time of the American revolution parliament was undoubtedly supreme in Britain. "But if the parliament will positively enact a thing to be done which is unreasonable, I know of no power that
can control it: and the examples usually alleged in support of this sense of the
rule do none of them prove, that where the main object of a statute is unreasonable the judges are at liberty to reject it; for that were to set the judicial
power above that of the legislature, which would be subversive of all government." 1William Blackstone, Commentaries *91 (1766).

3. But Lord Coke's daring assertion of judicial power was well-known in the
American colonies, and is part of the background of the American doctrine of
judicial review. In 1766, for example, a Virginia court held the Stamp Act unconstitutional, a judgment announced in the following brief order:

> On the motion of the Clerk, and other Officers of this Court, praying
> their opinion whether the act entitled "an act for granting and applying
> certain Stamp Duties, and other Duties, in America & c." was binding
> on the inhabitants in this colony, and whether they the said officers
> should incur any penalties by not using stamped paper, agreeable to the
> directions of the said act, the Court unanimously declared it to be their
> opinion that the said act did not bind, affect, or concern the inhabi-
> tants of this colony, inasmuch as they conceive the same to be uncon-
> stitutional, and that the said several officers may proceed to the execu-
> tion of their respective offices without incurring any penalties by means
> thereof; which opinion [the] court doth order to be recorded.

The Richmond Gazette (March 21, 1766); *reprinted in* Thomas Grey, Origins
of the Unwritten Constitution: Fundamental Law in American Revolutionary
Thought, 30 Stanford Law Review 843, 881 n. 180 (1978).

4. In the Virginia case of Robin v. Hardaway, 2 Va. (1 Jefferson) 109 (1772),
the plaintiffs made an appeal to natural law in urging the court to find a statute

invalid. The 1682 statute made slaves of Indian servants brought into Virginia, and the plaintiffs were the descendants of Indian servants brought into Virginia, and themselves were held in slavery on those grounds.

> "*Mason, for the plaintiffs:*.... Now all acts of legislature apparently contrary to natural right and justice are, in our laws, and must be in the nature of things, considered as void. The laws of nature are the laws of God; whose authority can be superseded by no power on earth. A legislature must not obstruct our obedience to him from whose punishments they cannot protect us. All human constitutions which contradict his laws, we are in conscience bound to disobey. Such have been the adjudications of our courts of justice....8 Co. 118. a. Bonham's case."[1]

Some Americans, at least, had come to think of judicial control as a good thing, and a bulwark against the forces of evil and corruption.

1. An Impetuous Vortex?

One of the evils to be avoided was the voracious legislature which, if the powers were not both separate and mutually limiting, might swallow up the other two branches.

JAMES MADISON, THE FEDERALIST NO. 48
(1788)

To the People of the State of New York:

It was shown in the last paper that the political apothegm there examined does not require that the legislative, executive, and judiciary departments should be wholly unconnected with each other. I shall undertake, in the next place, to show that unless these departments be so far connected and blended as to give to each a constitutional control over the others, the degree of separation which the maxim requires, as essential to a free government, can never in practice be duly maintained.

It is agreed on all sides, that the powers properly belonging to one of the departments ought not to be directly and completely administered by either of the other departments. It is equally evident, that none of them ought to possess, directly or indirectly, an overruling influence over the others, in the administration of their respective powers. It will not be denied, that power is of an encroaching

---

1. 1 (Jefferson) 109, 114 (Va 1772) (The court, in its published decision, took no note of the argument.)

nature, and that it ought to be effectually restrained from passing the limits assigned to it. After discriminating, therefore, in theory, the several classes of power, as they may in their nature be legislative, executive, or judiciary, the next and most difficult task is to provide some practical security for each, against the invasion of the others. What this security ought to be, is the great problem to be solved.

Will it be sufficient to mark, with precision, the boundaries of these departments, in the constitution of the government, and to trust to these parchment barriers against the encroaching spirit of power? This is the security which appears to have been principally relied on by the compilers of most of the American constitutions. But experience assures us, that the efficacy of the provision has been greatly overrated; and that some more adequate defense is indispensably necessary for the more feeble, against the more powerful, members of the government. The legislative department is everywhere extending the sphere of its activity, and drawing all power into its impetuous vortex....

2. A Rampant Judiciary?

"Aware that the Ratifiers distrusted a rampant judiciary, Hamilton assured them that of the three branches 'the judiciary is next to nothing,' that judges would be impeached for 'deliberate usurpations of the authority of the legislature.'" Raoul Berger, An Argument Against Government by Judiciary, 2 National Law Journal 18, 18 (February 18, 1980).

ALEXANDER HAMILTON, THE FEDERALIST NO. 78
(1788)

To the People of the State of New York:...

Whoever attentively considers the different departments of power must perceive, that, in a government in which they are separated from each other, the judiciary, from the nature of its functions, will always be the least dangerous to the political rights of the Constitution; because it will be least in a capacity to annoy or injure them. The Executive not only dispenses the honors, but holds the sword of the community. The legislature not only commands the purse, but prescribes the rules by which the duties and rights of every citizen are to be regulated. The judiciary, on the contrary, has no influence over either the sword or the purse; no direction either of the strength or of the wealth of the society; and can take no active resolution whatever. It may truly be said to have neither FORCE nor WILL, but merely judgment; and must ultimately depend upon the aid of the executive arm even for the efficacy of its judgments.

This simple view of the matter suggests several important consequences. It proves incontestably, that the judiciary is beyond comparison the weakest of the three departments of power; that it can never attack with success either of the other two; and that all possible care is requisite to enable it to defend itself against their attacks. It equally proves, that though individual oppression may now and then proceed from the courts of justice, the general liberty of the people can never be endangered from that quarter; I mean so long as the judiciary remains truly distinct from both the legislature and the Executive. For I agree, that "there is no liberty, if the power of judging be not separated from the legislative and executive powers"....

The complete independence of the courts of justice is peculiarly essential in a limited Constitution. By a limited Constitution, I understand one which contains certain specified exceptions to the legislative authority; such, for instance, as that it shall pass no bills of attainder, no ex-post-facto laws, and the like. Limitations of this kind can be preserved in practice no other way than through the medium of courts of justice, whose duty it must be to declare all acts contrary to the manifest tenor of the Constitution void. Without this, all the reservations of particular rights or privileges would amount to nothing.

Some perplexity respecting the rights of the courts to pronounce legislative acts void, because contrary to the Constitution, has arisen from an imagination that the doctrine would imply a superiority of the judiciary to the legislative power. It is urged that the authority which can declare the acts of another void, must necessarily be superior to the one whose acts may be declared void. As this doctrine is of great importance in all the American constitutions, a brief discussion of the ground on which it rests cannot be unacceptable.

There is no position which depends on clearer principles, than that every act of a delegated authority, contrary to the tenor of the commission under which it is exercised, is void. No legislative act, therefore, contrary to the Constitution, can be valid. To deny this, would be to affirm, that the deputy is greater than his principal; that the servant is above his master; that the representatives of the people are superior to the people themselves; that men acting by virtue of powers, may do not only what their powers do not authorize, but what they forbid.

If it be said that the legislative body are themselves the constitutional judges of their own powers, and that the construction they put upon them is conclusive upon the other departments, it may be answered, that this cannot be the natural presumption, where it is not to be collected from any particular provisions in the Constitution. It is not otherwise to be supposed, that the Constitution could intend to enable the representatives of the people to substitute their WILL to that of their constituents. It is far more rational to suppose, that the courts were designed to be an intermediate body between the people and the legislature, in order, among other things, to keep the latter within the limits assigned to their authority. The interpretation of the laws is the proper and peculiar province of the courts. A constitution is, in fact, and must be regarded by the judges, as a fundamental law. It therefore belongs to them to ascertain its meaning, as well as the meaning of any particular act proceeding from the legislative body. If there should happen to be an irreconcilable variance between the two, that which has the superior obligation and validity ought, of course, to be preferred; or, in other words, the Constitution ought to be preferred to the statute, the intention of the people to the intention of their agents.

Nor does this conclusion by any means suppose a superiority of the judicial to the legislative power. It only supposes that the power of the people is superior to both; and that where the will of the legislature, declared in its statutes, stands in opposition to that of the people, declared in the Constitution, the judges ought to be governed by the latter rather than the former. They ought to regulate their decisions by the fundamental laws, rather than by those which are not fundamental....

It can be of no weight to say that the courts, on the pretense of a repugnancy, may substitute their own pleasure to the constitutional intentions of the legislature. This might as well happen in the case of two contradictory statutes; or it might as well happen in every adjudication upon any single statute. The courts must declare the sense of the law; and if they should be disposed to exercise WILL instead of JUDGMENT, the consequence would equally be the substitution of their pleasure to that of the legislative body. The observation, if it prove any thing, would prove that there ought to be no judges distinct from that body.

* * *

ALEXANDER HAMILTON, THE FEDERALIST NO. 81
(1788)

....That there ought to be one court of supreme and final jurisdiction, is a proposition which is not likely to be contested. The reasons for it have been assigned in another place, and are too obvious to need repetition. The only question that seems to have been raised concerning it, is, whether it ought to be a distinct body or a branch of the legislature. The same contradiction is observable in regard to this matter which has been remarked in several other cases. The very men who object to the Senate as a court of impeachments, on the ground of an improper intermixture of powers, advocate, by implication at least, the propriety of vesting the ultimate decision of all causes, in the whole or in a part of the legislative body.

The arguments, or rather suggestions, upon which this charge is founded, are to this effect: "The authority of the proposed Supreme Court of the United States, which is to be a separate and independent body, will be superior to that of the legislature. The power of construing the laws according to the SPIRIT of the Constitution, will enable that court to mould them into whatever shape it may think proper; especially as its decisions will not be in any manner subject to the revision or correction of the legislative body. This is as unprecedented as it is dangerous. In Britain, the judicial power, in the last resort, resides in the House of Lords, which is a branch of the legislature; and this part of the British government has been imitated in the State constitutions in general. The Parliament of Great Britain, and the legislatures of the several States, can at any time rectify, by law, the exceptionable decisions of their respective courts. But the errors and usurpations of the Supreme Court of the United States will be uncontrollable and remediless." This, upon examination, will be found to be made up altogether of false reasoning upon misconceived fact.

In the first place, there is not a syllable in the plan under consideration which DIRECTLY empowers the national courts to construe the laws according to the spirit of the Constitution, or which gives them any greater latitude in this respect than may be claimed by the courts of every State. I admit, however, that the Constitution ought to be the standard of construction for the laws, and that wherever there is an evident opposition, the laws ought to give place to the Constitution. But this doctrine is not deducible from any circumstance peculiar to the plan of the convention, but from the general theory of a limited Constitution; and as far as it is true, is equally applicable to most, if not to all the State governments. There can be no objection, therefore, on this account, to the federal judicature which will not lie against the local judicatures in general, and which will not serve to condemn every constitution that attempts to set bounds to legislative discretion....

It is not true, in the second place, that the Parliament of Great Britain, or the legislatures of the particular States, can rectify the exceptionable decisions of their respective courts, in any other sense than might be done by a future legislature of the United States. The theory, neither of the British, nor the State constitutions, authorizes the revisal of a judicial sentence by a legislative act. Nor is there any thing in the proposed Constitution, more than in either of them, by which it is forbidden. In the former, as well as in the latter, the impropriety of the thing, on the general principles of law and reason, is the sole obstacle. A legislature, without exceeding its province, cannot reverse a determination once made in a particular case; though it may prescribe a new rule for future cases. This is the principle, and it applies in all its consequences, exactly in the same manner and extent, to the State governments, as to the national government now under consideration. Not the least difference can be pointed out in any view of the subject.

Note

1. "A legislature, without exceeding its province, cannot reverse a determination once made in a particular case; though it may prescribe a new rule for future cases." Does Hamilton mean that although the legislature cannot change the outcome of a case already decided, by correcting the court's interpretation of the Constitution, it might nevertheless change the interpretation for future cases by simply overruling the court's interpretation legislatively?

* * *

3. The Text

CONSTITUTION OF THE
UNITED STATES OF AMERICA
(1789)

Article I. Section 8. The Congress shall have the Power...To make all Laws which shall be necessary and proper for carrying into Execution the foregoing Powers, and all other Powers vested by this Constitution in the Government of the United States, or in any Department or Officer thereof.

Article II. Section 1. Before he enter on the Execution of his Office, he shall take the following Oath or Affirmation:—"I do solemnly swear (or affirm) that I will faithfully execute the Office of President of the United States, and will to the best of my Ability, preserve, protect and defend the Constitution of the United States."

Article III. Section 2. (1) The judicial Power shall extend to all Cases, in Law and Equity, arising under this Constitution, the Laws of the United States, and Treaties made, or which shall be made, under their Authority; —to all cases affecting ambassadors, other public ministers and consuls—to all cases of admiralty and maritime jurisdiction—to controversies to which the United States shall be a party—to controversies between two or more states, between a state and citizens of another state—between citizens of different states—between citizens of the same state claiming land under grants of two different states, and between a state, or the citizens thereof, and foreign states, citizens, or subjects.

(2) In all cases affecting ambassadors, other public ministers and consuls, and those in which a state shall be a party, the Supreme Court shall have origi-

nal jurisdiction. In all the other cases before mentioned, the Supreme Court shall have appellate jurisdiction, both as to law and fact, with such exceptions, and under such regulations as the Congress shall make.

Article VI. .... This Constitution, and the Laws of the United States which shall be made in Pursuance thereof; and all Treaties made, or which shall be made, under the Authority of the United States, shall be the supreme Law of the Land; and the Judges in every State shall be bound thereby, any Thing in the Constitution or Laws of any State to the Contrary notwithstanding.

The Senators and Representatives before mentioned, and the Members of the several State Legislatures, and all executive and judicial Officers, both of the United States and of the several States, shall be bound by Oath or Affirmation, to support this Constitution; but no religious Test shall ever be required as a Qualification to any Office or public Trust under the United States.

Notes

1. The "arising under this Constitution" language of Article III was not in the original drafts of the Constitution, in which the judicial power extended only to cases arising under "the Laws of the United States," etc. The fact that "this Constitution" was later inserted suggests that, in the final considered opinion of the drafters, the judicial power included the power to settle controversies involving the interpretation of the Constitution. On the other hand, there seems to have been a consensus at the Convention that the power was limited to cases "of a Judiciary nature." 2 Max Farrand, Records of the Federal Convention of 1787 430 (1911). Madison had contrasted extending the judicial power to include the Constitution with limiting it to "cases of a Judiciary Nature." *Id.* The implication would seem to be that constitutional review was not intended by the delegates to the Convention to be included within the judicial power. There is nothing in the text to help us to decide between these two possible implications.

2. In 1795 a lower federal court, sitting in Philadelphia, instructed a jury to find for the plaintiff, partly on the ground that one of the statutes that the defendant relied upon was unconstitutional. The judge declared that the Constitution was superior to mere statutory law, something which was generally acknowledged, but he also declared what was more controversial, that where a legislative act does conflict with the Constitution, "it will be the duty of the Court to adhere to the Constitution and declare the act null and void.... It is an important principle, which...ought never to be lost sight of, that the Judiciary in this is not a subordinate, but co-ordinate, branch of the government." Vanhorne's Lessee v. Dorrace, 2 U.S. (Dall.) 304, 309 (1795).

3. In a series of Supreme Court cases prior to 1803 the justices took various positions on the possibility of judicial review. In Hylton v. United States, 3

U.S. (Dall.) 171, 175 (1796), Justice Chase said that the statute before them did not contradict the Constitution, making it unnecessary to decide whether the Court had the power to declare an act of Congress void on the ground that it was in violation of the Constitution. "[B]ut if the court have such power, I am free to declare, that I will never exercise it, but in a very clear case." In Calder v. Bull, 3 U.S. (Dall.) 386 (1798), Justice Chase asserted that the legislature was limited not only by the Constitution but by certain fundamental principles of law, such as that a man may not be a judge in his own case. But he remained tentative as to whether it was the place of the Court to declare such laws, whether violative of the constitution or of some fundamental unwritten law, void. Justice Iredell, in the same case, seemed more certain of that power; but he disagreed about the authority of unwritten principles. In Cooper v. Telfair, 4 U.S. (Dall.) 14, 19 (1800), Justice Chase once more took his cautious stand:

> [A]lthough it is alleged that all acts of the legislature, in direct opposition to the prohibitions of the constitution, would be void; yet, it still remains a question, where the power resides to declare it void?

4. The supremacy of the constitution is thus one thing, and the power of the courts to declare acts of the legislature unconstitutional is another thing entirely. Given the experience of constitutional democracies like France where, until 1958 at least, constitutionality went hand in hand with parliamentary supremacy, that observation would not be worth making, were it not for the fact that in Marbury v. Madison John Marshall declares it to be self-evidently false. Marbury is the first case in which the Supreme Court of the United States struck down a statute as unconstitutional, and it is recognized as the great landmark in the history of judicial review.

4. Marbury v. Madison

Marbury had been named a justice of the peace during the last moments of John Adams' administration. The incoming Jefferson administration refused to deliver Marbury's commission. Marbury, relying on the Judiciary Act of 1789, which gave original jurisdiction over such matters to the Supreme Court, sued in that Court for a writ of mandamus, which would require the Secretary of State, Madison, to deliver the commission.

MARBURY V. MADISON
5 U.S. (1 Cr.) 137 (1803)

[The attorney representing Marbury had argued among other things that the Court had the power to issue the writ:

"Congress, by a law passed at the very first session after the adoption of the constitution, vol. 1, p. 68, s. 13, have expressly given the Supreme Court the power of issuing writs of mandamus. The words are, 'the Supreme Court shall also have appellate jurisdiction from the circuit courts, and courts of the several states, in the cases hereinafter specially provided for; and shall have power to issue writs of prohibition to the district courts, when proceeding as courts of admiralty and maritime jurisdiction, and writs of *mandamus*, in cases warranted by the principles and usages of law, to any courts appointed, or *persons holding office*, under the authority of the United States.'

"Congress is not restrained from conferring original jurisdiction in other cases than those mentioned in the constitution. 2 Dal. Rep. 298.

"This court has entertained jurisdiction on a mandamus in one case, and on a prohibition in another....In none of these cases nor in any other, was the power of the court to issue a mandamus ever denied. Hence it appears there has been a legislative construction of the constitution upon this point and a judicial practice under it, for the whole time since the formation of the government."]

Mr. Chief Justice Marshall delivered the opinion of the court.

In the order in which the court has viewed this subject, the following questions have been considered and decided.

1st. Has the applicant a right to the commission he demands?

2d. If he has a right, and that right has been violated, do the laws of his country afford him a remedy?

3d. If they do afford him a remedy, is it a mandamus issuing from this court?

[The Court reaches an affirmative answer to the first two questions, and goes on to the third:]

This, then, is a plain case of a mandamus, either to deliver the commission, or a copy of it from the record; and it only remains to be inquired,

Whether it can issue from this court.

The act to establish the judicial courts of the United States authorizes the supreme court to "issue writs of mandamus in cases warranted by the principles and usages of law, to any courts appointed, or persons holding office, under the authority of the United States."

The secretary of state, being a person, holding an office under the authority of the United States, is precisely within the letter of the description; and if this court is not authorized to issue a writ of mandamus to such an officer, it must be because the law is unconstitutional, and therefore absolutely incapable of conferring the authority, and assigning the duties which its words purport to confer and assign.

The constitution vests the whole judicial power of the United States in one supreme court, and such inferior courts as congress shall, from time to time, ordain and establish. This power is expressly extended to all cases arising under the laws of the United States; and consequently, in some form, may be exercised over the present case; because the right claimed is given by a law of the United States.

In the distribution of this power it is declared that "the supreme court shall have original jurisdiction in all cases affecting ambassadors, other public ministers and consuls, and those in which a state shall be a party. In all other cases, the supreme court shall have appellate jurisdiction."

It has been insisted, at the bar, that as the original grant of jurisdiction, to the supreme and inferior courts, is general, and the clause, assigning original jurisdiction to the Supreme Court, contains no negative or restrictive words, the power remains to the legislature, to assign original jurisdiction to that court, in other cases than those specified in the article which has been re-cited, provided those cases belong to the judicial power of the United States....

It cannot be presumed that any clause in the Constitution is intended to be without effect; and, therefore, such a construction is inadmissible, unless the words require it.

If the solicitude of the conventions, respecting our peace with foreign powers, induced a provision that the Supreme Court should take original jurisdiction in cases which might be supposed to affect them; yet the cause would have proceeded no further than to provide for such cases, if no further restriction on the powers of Congress had been intended. That they should have appellate jurisdiction in all other cases, with such exceptions as Congress might make, is no restriction, unless the words be deemed exclusive of original jurisdiction....

To enable the Court, then, to issue a mandamus, it must be shown to be an exercise of appellate jurisdiction or to be necessary to enable them to exercise appellate jurisdiction....

It is the essential criterion of appellate jurisdiction, that it revises and corrects the proceedings in a cause already instituted and does not create that cause. Although, therefore, a mandamus may be directed to courts, yet to issue such a writ to an officer for the delivery of a paper is, in effect, the same as to sustain an original action for that paper and, therefore, seems not to belong to appellate but to original jurisdiction. Neither is it necessary in such a case as this to enable the Court to exercise its appellate jurisdiction. The authority, therefore, given to the supreme court, by the act establishing the judicial courts of the United States, to issue writs of mandamus to public officers, appears not to be warranted by the constitution; and it becomes necessary to inquire whether a jurisdiction, so conferred, can be exercised.

Judiciary Act is unconstitutional. Congress may not vest the Supreme Court with original jurisdiction over cases in which the Constitution vests

The question, whether an act, repugnant to the constitution, can become the law of the land, is a question deeply interesting to the United States; but, happily, not of an intricacy proportioned to its interest. It seems only necessary to recognize certain principles, supposed to have been long and well established, to decide it.

That the people have an original right to establish for their future government, such principles as, in their opinion, shall most conduce to their own happiness, is the basis on which the whole American fabric has been erected. The exercise of this original right is a very great exertion; nor can it nor ought it to be frequently repeated. The principles, therefore, so established are deemed fundamental. And as the authority, from which they proceed, is supreme, and can seldom act, they are designed to be permanent.

This original and supreme will organizes the government, and assigns to different departments their respective powers. It may either stop here, or establish certain limits not to be transcended by those departments.

The government of the United States is of the latter description. The powers of the legislature are defined and limited; and that those limits may not be mistaken or forgotten, the constitution is written. To what purpose are powers limited, and to what purpose is that limitation committed to writing, if these limits may, at any time, be passed by those intended to be restrained? The distinction between a government with limited and unlimited powers is abolished, if those limits do not confine the persons on whom they are imposed, and if acts prohibited and acts allowed are of equal obligation. It is a proposition too plain to be contested, that the constitution controls any legislative act repugnant to it; or, that the legislature may alter the constitution by an ordinary act.

Between these alternatives there is no middle ground. The constitution is either a superior paramount law, unchangeable by ordinary means, or it is on a level with ordinary legislative acts, and like other acts, is alterable when the legislature shall please to alter it.

If the former part of the alternative be true, then a legislative act contrary to the constitution is not law: if the latter part be true, then written constitutions are absurd attempts, on the part of the people, to limit a power in its own nature illimitable.

Certainly all those who have framed written constitutions contemplate them as forming the fundamental and paramount law of the nation, and consequently the theory of every such government must be, that an act of the legislature repugnant to the constitution is void.

This theory is essentially attached to a written constitution, and is consequently to be considered by this court as one of the fundamental principles of our society. It is not therefore to be lost sight of in the further consideration of this subject.

the judge with appellate jurisdiction.

If an act of the legislature, repugnant to the constitution, is void, does it, notwithstanding its invalidity, bind the courts and oblige them to give it effect? Or, in other words, though it be not law, does it constitute a rule as operative as if it was a law? This would be to overthrow in fact what was established in theory; and would seem, at first view, an absurdity too gross to be insisted on. It shall, however, receive a more attentive consideration.

It is emphatically the province and duty of the judicial department to say what the law is. Those who apply the rule to particular cases, must of necessity expound and interpret that rule. If two laws conflict with each other, the courts must decide on the operation of each.

So if a law be in opposition to the constitution: if both the law and the constitution apply to a particular case, so that the court must either decide that case conformably to the law, disregarding the constitution; or conformably to the constitution, disregarding the law: the court must determine which of these conflicting rules governs the case. This is of the very essence of judicial duty.

If then the courts are to regard the constitution; and the constitution is superior to any ordinary act of the legislature, the constitution, and not such ordinary act, must govern the case to which they both apply.

Those then who controvert the principle that the constitution is to be considered, in court, as a paramount law, are reduced to the necessity of maintaining that courts must close their eyes on the constitution, and see only the law.

This doctrine would subvert the very foundation of all written constitutions. It would declare that an act, which, according to the principles and theory of our government, is entirely void, is yet, in practice, completely obligatory. It would declare, that if the legislature shall do what is expressly forbidden, such act, notwithstanding the express prohibition, is in reality effectual. It would be given to the legislature a practical and real omnipotence with the same breath which professes to restrict their powers within narrow limits. It is prescribing limits, and declaring that those limits may be passed at pleasure.

That it thus reduces to nothing what we have deemed the greatest improvement on political institutions, a written constitution, would of itself be sufficient, in America where written constitutions have been viewed with so much reverence, for rejecting the construction. But the peculiar expressions of the constitution of the United States furnish additional arguments in favor of its rejection.

The judicial power of the United States is extended to all cases arising under the constitution.

Could it be the intention of those who gave this power, to say that, in using it, the constitution should not be looked into? That a case arising under the constitution should be decided without examining the instrument under which it arises?

This is too extravagant to be maintained.

In some cases then, the constitution must be looked into by the judges. And if they can open it at all, what part of it are they forbidden to read, or to obey?

There are many other parts of the constitution which serve to illustrate this subject.

It is declared that "no tax or duty shall be laid on articles exported from any state." Suppose a duty on the export of cotton, of tobacco, or of flour; and a suit instituted to recover it. Ought judgment to be rendered in such a case? ought the judges to close their eyes on the constitution, and only see the law.

The constitution declares "that no bill of attainder or ex post facto law shall be passed."

If, however, such a bill should be passed and a person should be prosecuted under it; must the court condemn to death those victims whom the constitution endeavors to preserve?

"No person," says the constitution, "shall be convicted of treason unless on the testimony of two witnesses to the same overt act, or on confession in open court."

Here the language of the constitution is addressed especially to the courts. It prescribes directly for them, a rule of evidence not to be departed from. If the legislature should change that rule, and declare *one* witness, or a confession *out* of court, sufficient for conviction, must the constitutional principle yield to the legislative act?

From these, and many other selections which might be made, it is apparent, that the framers of the constitution contemplated that instrument as a rule for the government of *courts*, as well as of the legislature. Why otherwise does it direct the judges to take an oath to support it? This oath certainly applies, in an especial manner, to their conduct in their official character. How immoral to impose it on them, if they were to be used as the instruments, and the knowing instruments, for violating what they swear to support!

The oath of office, too, imposed by the legislature, is completely demonstrative of the legislative opinion on this subject. It is in these words: "I do solemnly swear that I will administer justice without respect to persons, and do equal right to the poor and to the rich; and that I will faithfully and impartially discharge all the duties incumbent on me as according to the best of my abilities and understanding agreeably to the constitution and laws of the United States."

Why does a judge swear to discharge his duties agreeably to the constitution of the United States, if that constitution forms no rule for his government? if it is closed upon him, and cannot be inspected by him.

If such be the real state of things, this is worse than solemn mockery. To prescribe, or to take this oath, becomes equally a crime.

It is also not entirely unworthy of observation, that in declaring what shall be the supreme law of the land, the constitution itself is first mentioned; and not the laws of the United States generally, but those only which shall be made in pursuance of the constitution, have that rank.

Thus, the particular phraseology of the constitution of the United States confirms and strengthens the principle, supposed to be essential to all written constitutions, that a law repugnant to the constitution is void, and that courts, as well as other departments, are bound by that instrument.

The rule must be discharged.

Notes

1. The power of review taken by the Court did not include abstract review, mentioned above in connection with the Councils of Revision. "As far back as Marbury v. Madison...this Court held that the judicial power may be exercised only in a 'case or controversy' not suffering any of the limitations of the political question doctrine, not then moot or calling for an advisory opinion." U.S. v. Richardson, 94 S.Ct. 2940, 2943 (1974)(Burger, C.J.)

2. Justice Marshall derives part of his argument from the fact that judges are sworn to uphold the Constitution. Compare his interpretation of this fact with that of the French Tribunal of Cassation in the Decision of September 3, 1797, *supra*, in Chapter One, Section B.2.

* * *

L.A. POWE, THE POLITICS OF AMERICAN JUDICIAL REVIEW: REFLECTIONS ON THE MARSHALL, WARREN, AND REHNQUIST COURTS
WAKE FOREST LAW REVIEW 697, 697–704 (2003)

Marbury v. Madison was a result of the Federalist defeats in the elections of 1800. With the House of Representatives deciding between Thomas Jefferson and Aaron Burr, the lame-duck Federalist Congress was busy creating judicial offices to be filled quickly by the outgoing John Adams. William Marbury was to be a justice of the peace in the District of Columbia, but his signed and sealed commission was not delivered before the end of the Adams Administration. After Jefferson instructed his Acting Secretary of State, the Attorney General Levi Lincoln, to withhold it, Marbury sued in the original jurisdiction of the Supreme Court. The Administration refused even to defend its decision.

Marshall's opinion begins by finding Marbury has a legal right to his commission and that if we are indeed a government of laws and not men there must be a remedy. He then absolutely butchers the construction of section 13 of the Judiciary Act of 1789 to find that it authorizes mandamus under the circumstances and follows with a silly construction of article III, section 2 which puts the two, as misconstrued, into conflict. Because there is no point to a written constitution unless it is superior to ordinary legislation Marshall asks the rhetorical question: "[D]oes [such a law] notwithstanding its invalidity, bind the courts, and oblige them to give it effect?" No. "It is emphatically the province and duty of the judicial department to say what the law is," with "law" in this case referring to the constitution itself.

The conclusion that the Court had the right to strike down a federal statute that was in conflict with the Constitution was not controversial. *The Federalist* had stated that judges could declare a federal statute unconstitutional, and a young John Marshall, when a delegate to the Virginia convention on ratification, had said so too. Since ratification of the Constitution, courts had increasingly struck down state statutes as inconsistent with both state and federal constitutions, and several Justices had assumed they had the power to similarly strike down federal statutes. Indeed, the Jeffersonians had wished some judge would have done it to the Sedition Act of 1798.

What was controversial was Marshall's conclusion that Jefferson and his Secretary of State were instigating a government of men and not of law. In this, he was delivering a verbal blow in a political contest that had already swung decisively in favor of Jefferson. As everyone knows, finding a way not to order James Madison to deliver the commission to Marbury was essential because if such an order were made, "the order would surely be ignored by Madison, [and] the Court would be exposed as impotent to enforce its mandates, [thus] the shakiness of judicial prestige would be dramatically emphasized." Indeed it might have "trigger[ed] a rash of judicial impeachments, and possibly a compete reformation of the federal judiciary."

A major locus of Marshall's and Jefferson's problems was that neither the Framers nor the Constitution itself had anticipated the (almost immediate) rise of political parties. By the time Adams succeeded George Washington, the Republicans thought the Federalists wished to establish a monarchy. The Federalists reciprocated by viewing the Republicans as Jacobins. *Marbury* is one act of the transition of the new nation to a two-party democracy where the losers accept the verdict of the voters.

The two parties' dispute had escalated in the aftermath of the breaking of diplomatic relations by France and the XYZ Affair. On receiving the diplomatic dispatches from the American ministers in France, Adams informed Congress that no settlement was likely with France, and he called for increased military expenditures. It looked like preparation for war. Jefferson thought Adams's message was "insane," and Republicans demanded Adams release the dispatches. They were dynamite, especially Y's boast that France had its own party in America — the Jeffersonians: "The diplomatic skill of France and the means she possesses in your country, are sufficient to enable her, with the French party in America, to throw the blame which will attend the rupture of the negotiations on the Federalists...."

The outcome was the Sedition Act, which protected both the President and Congress, but not the Vice President (Jefferson), from libels, and which Republicans rightly feared would be turned on them....

Then came the elections of 1800. Defeated for the presidency and defeated for the Seventh Congress, the Federalists, still controlling all the elected branches, used their still existent power to retreat to their exclusive preserve—the judiciary. "The judges of the federal bench were almost to a man ardent Federalist partisans, and they had enthusiastically shouldered the task of enforcing the Sedition Act....Supreme Court justices like [William] Paterson, [James] Iredell, and above all Samuel Chase earned the hatred of Jefferson's fast growing Republican Party...." The antipathy to the judiciary could not have been helped when Chief Justice Oliver Ellsworth decided to retire early rather than let Jefferson appoint a successor. Following a rejection by John Jay, Adams selected Marshall (who continued on as Secretary of State even after he was unanimously confirmed).

The lame-duck Federalist Congress started creating new federal judgeships for Adams to fill even as the House deadlocked on the unpalatable choice between Jefferson and Burr. First came the Judiciary Act of 1801, eliminating circuit riding for Supreme Court justices, creating six new circuits and sixteen accompanying judgeships, and reducing the Court from six to five (effective on the next vacancy). All sixteen slots went to Federalist partisans. Next were the "midnight judges," created in an act passed at the end of February setting up a government for the District of Columbia. Adams quickly nominated forty-two justices of the peace (with five year terms); the Senate confirmed them all, but after Adams signed the commissions and Marshall affixed the formal seal, some, including that for William Marbury, could not be delivered before March 4 and were left in the Department of State....

Marbury's lawyer, Adams' Attorney General Charles Lee, moved for a show of cause on why mandamus should not issue against Madison. Madison had already declined to appear, and Attorney General Levi Lincoln, who was present, stated that he had no instructions. The Court, through Marshall, ruled that the next term they would hear arguments on whether the petitioners were entitled to the writ....

Marbury and the appeal of *Stuart v. Laird* gave the justices a number of options, none good. The "cases threatened to produce a constitutional crisis, which Marshall recognized the Court could not win." The justices could decide against the Republicans both times, thereby giving the more extreme republicans the fight they were looking for. The justices could try to split the difference by deciding for Marbury while okaying the Repeal Act or against Marbury while invalidating the Repeal Act. In either of these cases they could expect a strong response from the Republicans. Finally they could rule twice in favor of the Republicans and wait for the future to sort itself out.

Marshall's genius, as everyone recognizes, is that he found another option that saved the Federalists and the judiciary from total defeat. When ruling against Marbury, he verbally sided with his [Marbury's] claim while simultaneously declaring and exercising the power of judicial review. Congress and the President were not the only national actors with a right to make a constitutional determination. The federal judiciary was more than a political pawn to be expanded and shrunk as political needs demanded. Judges could—must—declare the law; they, too, could construe and apply the Constitution. Indeed it was just that (mis)application of the Constitution in Marshall's interpretation of Article III that caused Marbury to lose.

* * *

SANFORD LEVINSON, WHY I DO NOT TEACH *MARBURY* (EXCEPT TO EASTERN EUROPEANS) AND WHY YOU SHOULDN'T EITHER
38 WAKE FOREST LAW REVIEW 553, 562–563, 566–567 (2003)

I confess that one reason I stopped teaching *Marbury* is that I got angry, every single year, when reading Marshall's mangling of section 13 of the Judiciary Act 36 and then Article III of the Constitution....

Why should students' first experience with constitutional analysis be a case that can be fully understood only if one applies a fairly vulgar version of Legal Realism demonstrating that a judge will do *anything* necessary to achieve his or her policy goals?

One response, of course, is that vulgar Legal Realism is correct, a view that I am sometimes drawn to, especially in the era of *Bush v. Gore* and the zealotry of the current Supreme Court majority with regard to protecting states against the possibility of being sued by aggrieved citizens. But even the desire to make that point certainly does not justify the emphasis that Marbury gets. There are so many more important cases that could be used to demonstrate that interplay of law and politics. Of the "older" cases, my own "favorite" is...*Prigg v. Pennsylvania*, in which Justice Story, who was also Dane Professor of Constitutional Law at Harvard and the author in 1833 of the most influential constitutional law treatise of his time, admitted in effect that there is no better way of defending the egregious results of that case than by pointing to the possible threat to the Union that would follow if the Court recognized fugitive slaves as even minimal rightsholders—i.e., not to be returned to slavery without the guarantee of a judicial hearing that they were in fact the fugitives they were alleged to be. Thus, slaveowners have a constitutional right to engage in "self-help repossession" of their chattels. Or a more recent case that certainly is the focus of much contemporary discussion, *Ex parte Quirin,* in which the Supreme Court might well be thought to have submitted to pressures from the President of the United States to rubberstamp the summary trial and execution of German saboteurs. One could go on and on citing cases that demonstrate the interplay of law and politics. Why anyone would prefer *Marbury* to any of these other cases, if one is simply interested in conveying to students a Realist mode of analysis, is beyond me. Persons with more conservative views than mine might have their own candidates, including, perhaps, *Blaisdell, Baker v. Carr,* or *Casey,* but the point still stands. All of these, by any stretch of the imagination, are more significant that *Marbury.*

Even if one uses *Marbury* to "make the case" for judicial review, certainly an important issue, just have students read *Federalist Number 78* and then explain that Hamilton's arguments were substantially accepted in an otherwise obscure 1803 case. Moreover, the important arguments thereafter were about the actual occasions for, and scope of, review rather than the theoretical existence of the power in such non-existent cases as, for example, Congress declaring that one witness was enough to convict for treason.

One need not be a full-fledged Legal Realist to believe that courts are especially "political" during times of political transformation. (This is, after all, the distinction between "normal" science and what occurs during times of paradigm shifts.) So if one shares my own interest in looking at how courts respond to political "transitions" or "constitutional moments," then, of course, I would submit that the events of 1860 to 1877 are of almost infinitely more importance than those of 1800 to 1804 in terms of the continuing consequences for our present polity. Others might pick the New Deal Revolution or, indeed, the present constitutional moment itself, which calls into attention important aspects of what had heretofore been perceived as the New Deal "settlement," not to mention, in more recent days, the potential slippage toward a 1984-like version of "constitutionalism" in which the Executive Branch is able to restrict rights at will so long as it labels someone, without the need to present corroborating evidence, a "terrorist" or "enemy combatant...."

* * *

C. Binding on All?

We should distinguish three questions. The first is whether, in the course of applying legislation, the courts have the power to examine that legislation for constitutional validity; this is the fundamental question of judicial review. For the United States that question was answered in the affirmative in *Marbury*. The second question is whether court determinations (and particularly Supreme Court determinations) of constitutionality and unconstitutionality are binding in future cases; this is the question of the precedential effect of court interpretations of the Constitution. The third question is whether court determinations of constitutionality and unconstitutionality are binding on other organs of government; this is the question of the universal effect of court interpretations—or of the supremacy of judicial interpretations of the Constitution.

The first proposition, that courts have the authority to review legislation for constitutionality, was not without its critics. Some twenty-two years after *Marbury* a justice of the Pennsylvania high court wrote an eloquent refutation:

> The constitution and the right of the legislature to pass the act, may be in collision. But is that a legitimate subject for judicial determination? If it be, the judiciary must be a peculiar organ, to revise the proceedings of the legislature, and to correct its mistakes; and in what part of the constitution are we to look for this proud pre-eminence? Viewing the matter in the opposite direction, what would be thought of an act of assembly in which it should be declared that the Supreme Court had, in a particular case, put a wrong construction on the constitution of the United States, and that the judgment should therefore be reversed? It would doubtless be thought a usurpation of judicial power. But it is by no means clear, that to declare a law void which has been enacted according to the forms prescribed in the constitution, is not a usurpation of legislative power. It is an act of sovereignty; and sovereignty and legislative power are said by Sir William Blackstone to be convertible terms. It is the business of the judiciary to interpret the laws, not scan the authority of the lawgiver; and without the latter, it cannot take cognizance of a collision between a law and the constitution. So that to affirm that the judiciary has a right to judge of the existence of such collision, is to take for granted the very thing to be proved. And, that a very cogent argument may be made in this way, I am not disposed to deny; for no conclusions are so strong as those that are drawn from the petitio principii.

Eakin v. Raub, 12 S&R 330, 348 (Pa. 1825)(Gibson, dissenting).

Gibson made one exception: State courts were bound to invalidate state laws that conflicted with the federal constitution or federal statutes. "By becoming parties to the federal constitution, the states have agreed to several limitations of their individual sovereignty, to enforce which, it was thought to be absolutely necessary to prevent them from giving effect to laws in violation of those limitations, through the instrumentality of their own judges." *Id.* at 356. Compare the situation today in Europe (see Chapter Four below) where ordinary courts, generally deprived of the right to review legislation, are required to do just that when it conflicts with the laws of the European Union.

As to the precedential value of a judicial finding of unconstitutionality, consider Andrew Jackson's point, in his explanation of his veto of the bill creating a Bank of the United States: "Mere precedent is a dangerous source of authority, and should not be regarded as deciding questions of constitutional power except where the acquiescence of the people and the States can be considered as well settled." Veto Message, July 10, 1832, Andrew Jackson, Veto Message of July 10, 1832, *reprinted in* 2 Compilation of the Messages and Papers of the Presidents, 1789–1897, James D. Richardson, ed., at 581–82 (1896–1899). Jackson also denied that the Court's ruling would bind other branches of government. The Supreme Court had upheld the constitutionality of the Bank some years earlier; Jackson asserted that the Court's opinion as to constitutionality does not remove the executive's (and the legislature's) obligation and authority to decide for themselves whether the law is constitutional.

ABRAHAM LINCOLN, SPEECH AT SPRINGFIELD
JUNE 26, 1857

And now as to the Dred Scott decision. That decision declares two propositions—first, that a negro cannot sue in the U.S. Courts; and secondly, that Congress cannot prohibit slavery in the Territories. It was made by a divided court—dividing differently on the different points. Judge Douglas does not discuss the merits of the decision; and in that respect, I shall follow his example, believing I could no more improve on McLean and Curtis, than he could on Taney.

He denounces all who question the correctness of that decision, as offering violent resistance to it. But who resists it? Who has, in spite of the decision, declared Dred Scott free, and resisted the authority of his master over him?

Judicial decisions have two uses—first, to absolutely determine the case decided; and secondly, to indicate to the public how other similar cases will be decided when they arise. For the latter use, they are called "precedents" and "authorities."

We believe, as much as Judge Douglas, (perhaps more) in obedience to, and respect for, the judicial department of government. We think its decisions on Constitutional questions, when fully settled, should control, not only the particular cases decided, but the general policy of the country, subject to be disturbed only by amendments of the Constitution as provided in that instrument itself. More than this would be revolution. But we think the Dred Scott decision is erroneous. We know the court that made it, has often overruled its own decisions, and we shall do what we can to have it to overrule this. We offer no *resistance* to it.

Judicial decisions are of greater or less authority as precedents, according to circumstances. That this should be so, accords both with common sense, and the customary understanding of the legal profession.

If this important decision had been made by the unanimous concurrence of the judges, and without any apparent partisan bias, and in accordance with legal public expectation, and with the steady practice of the departments throughout our history, and had been in no part, based on assumed historical facts which are not really true; or, if wanting in some of these, it had been before the court more than once, and had there been affirmed and re-affirmed through a course of years, it then might be, perhaps would be, factious, nay, even revolutionary, not to acquiesce in it as a precedent.

But when, as it is true we find it wanting in all these claims to the public confidence, it is not resistance, it is not factious, it is not even disrespectful, to treat it as not having yet quite established a settled doctrine for the country. But Judge Douglas considers this view awful. Hear him:

> The courts are the tribunals prescribed by the Constitution and created by the authority of the people to determine, expound and enforce the law. Hence, whoever resists the final decision of the highest judicial tribunal, aims a deadly blow to our whole Republican system of government—a blow, which if successful would place all our rights and liberties at the mercy of passion, anarchy and violence. I repeat, therefore, that if resistance to the decisions of the Supreme Court of the United States, in a matter like the points decided in the Dred Scott case, clearly within their jurisdiction as defined by the Constitution, shall be forced upon the country as a political issue, it will become a distinct and naked issue between the friends and enemies of the Constitution—the friends and enemies of the supremacy of the laws.

Why this same Supreme Court once decided a national bank to be constitutional; but Gen. Jackson, as President of the United States, disregarded the decision, and vetoed a bill for a re-charter, partly on constitutional grounds, declaring that each public functionary must support the Constitution, "*as he understands it.*" But hear the General's own words. Here they are, taken from his veto message:

> It is maintained by the advocates of the bank, that its constitutionality, in all its features, ought to be considered as settled by precedent, and by the decision of the Supreme Court. To this conclusion I cannot assent. Mere precedent is a dangerous source of authority, and should not be regarded as deciding questions of constitutional power, except where the acquiescence of the people and the States can be

considered as well settled. So far from this being the case on this subject, an argument against the bank might be based on precedent. One Congress in 1791, decided in favor of a bank; another in 1811, decided against it. One Congress in 1815 decided against a bank; another in 1816 decided in its favor. Prior to the present Congress, therefore, the precedents drawn from that source were equal. If we resort to the States, the expressions of legislative, judicial and executive opinions against the bank have been probably to those in its favor as four to one. There is nothing in precedent, therefore, which if its authority were admitted, ought to weigh in favor of the act before me.

I drop the quotations merely to remark that all there ever was, in the way of precedent up to the Dred Scott decision, on the points therein decided, had been against that decision. But hear Gen. Jackson further —

> If the opinion of the Supreme Court covered the whole ground of this act, it ought not to control the co-ordinate authorities of this Government. The Congress, the executive and the court, must each for itself be guided by its own opinion of the Constitution. Each public officer, who takes an oath to support the Constitution, swears that he will support it as he understands it, and not as it is understood by others.

Again and again have I heard Judge Douglas denounce that bank decision, and applaud Gen. Jackson for disregarding it. It would be interesting for him to look over his recent speech, and see how exactly his fierce philippics against us for resisting Supreme Court decisions, fall upon his own head. It will call to his mind a long and fierce political war in this country, upon an issue which, in his own language, and, of course, in his own changeless estimation, was "a distinct and naked issue between the friends and the enemies of the Constitution," and in which war he fought in the ranks of the enemies of the Constitution.

* * *

COOPER V. AARON
358 U.S. 1, 18 (1958)

Per curiam.

....Article VI of the Constitution makes the Constitution the 'supreme Law of the Land.' In 1803, Chief Justice Marshall, speaking for a unanimous Court, referring to the Constitution as 'the fundamental and paramount law of the nation,' declared in the notable case of Marbury v. Madison, 1 Cranch 137, 177, 2 L.Ed. 60, that 'It is emphatically the province and duty of the judicial department to say what the law is.' This decision declared the basic principle that the federal judiciary is supreme in the exposition of the law of the Constitution, and that principle has ever since been respected by this Court and the Country as a permanent and indispensable feature of our constitutional system. It follows that the interpretation of the Fourteenth Amendment enunciated by this Court in the Brown case is the supreme law of the land, and Art. VI of the Constitution makes it of binding effect on the States 'any Thing in the Constitution or Laws of any State to the Contrary notwithstanding.' Every state legislator and executive and judicial officer is solemnly committed by oath taken pursuant to Art. VI, ¶3 'to support this Constitution' ....

* * *

GARY LAWSON, THE CONSTITUTIONAL CASE AGAINST PRECEDENT
17 HARVARD JOURNAL OF LAW AND PUBLIC POLICY 23, 26–28 (1994)

Suppose that the enacting Congress (and perhaps also the signing President) objects that it has already determined that the statute is constitutional. The court's proper answer is, "thanks, but we'll check anyway." On Marshallian premises, legislative or executive interpretations of the Constitution are no substitute for the Constitution itself. The court's job is to figure out the true meaning of the Constitution, not the meaning ascribed to the Constitution by the legislative or executive departments.

Precisely the same analysis holds if the court is called upon to judge an exercise of the executive power. Executive action that violates the Constitution can have no valid legal status in an adjudication. It would be affirmatively wrong for a court to give such action the force and effect of law when the hierarchically supreme Constitution says otherwise. Again, the court's task is to ascertain the Constitution's true meaning, not the meaning ascribed to it by the President.

Suppose now that a court is faced with a conflict between the Constitution on the one hand and a prior judicial decision on the other. Is there any doubt that, under the reasoning of Marbury, the court must choose the Constitution over the prior decision? If a statute, enacted with all of the majestic formalities for lawmaking prescribed by the Constitution, and stamped with the imprimatur of representative democracy, cannot legitimately be given effect in an adjudication when it conflicts with the Constitution, how can a mere judicial decision possibly have a greater legal status? If the Constitution says X and a prior judicial decision says Y, a court has not merely the power, but the obligation, to prefer the Constitution. Furthermore, if courts must search for the true meaning of the Constitution, rather than the meaning ascribed to it by the Congress or the President, there is no apparent reason why they must not also prefer the document's true meaning to the meaning ascribed to it by a precedent court.

Thus, the case for judicial review of legislative or executive action is precisely coterminous with the case for judicial review of prior judicial action. What's sauce for the legislative or executive goose is also sauce for the judicial gander. At least as a prima facie matter, the reasoning of Marbury thoroughly delegitimizes precedent.

Note

1. Harrison summarizes Lawson's argument as follows: "An examination of the Supremacy Clause, which does not confer supremacy on [Supreme Court precedents], shows that they are subordinate to the Constitution, statutes and treaties, just as is state law. Invoking *Marbury* for the principle that superior law trumps inferior law in case of a conflict, Lawson concludes that precedent cannot overcome any of the kinds of law listed in Article VI"—in particular, it cannot overcome a statutory determination of constitutionality. Harrison, "Coordination, the Constitution, and the Binding Effect of Judicial Opinions," University of Virginia Working Papers (August 7, 2000), at 11.

* * *

JOHN HARRISON, COORDINATION, THE CONSTITUTION, AND THE BINDING EFFECT OF JUDICIAL OPINIONS
UNIVERSITY OF VIRGINIA WORKING PAPERS 3(August 7, 2000)

To say that courts are final is not to say final as to what. The root-level judicial function is the resolution of concrete disputes, usually concerning the application of law to specific facts. Who owns Blackacre, must A pay for the goods B has delivered, must C go to jail, are the kinds of questions courts answer when they decide cases. In American law their judgments conclusively resolve certain issues between the parties. For future purposes the court's answer to the question is taken as correct whether it is or not. Judicial finality is thus as familiar as preclusion.

American courts, when they decide cases, often write opinions. Those opinions generally derive their concrete conclusions concerning A and B from abstract propositions of law. Sometimes an authoritative text explicitly provides the answer to the abstract question the court is interested in. More often the answer cannot be read off the text, so the text must be construed. The court must deduce a conclusion that is at the level of specificity it needs. The court might need to know, for example, not whether levying war against the United

States constitutes treason, but whether firing a few bullets at an empty Army recruiting office constitutes levying war.

Courts gloss the text. The Supreme Court in *Brown* deduced from the Fourteenth Amendment the abstract principle that racial segregation in public schools is forbidden. It then entered judgments that as such bound only the parties to the cases before it. A few years later in *Cooper* the Court announced that it was not just the final case decider but the final annotator. Everyone else who was bound to the Constitution was thereby bound to follow it as the Court expounded it, whether the Court was right or not. The gloss on its opinions was to the whole world what the decrees in its judgments were to the parties.

Notes

1. According to Harrison, the "judicial finality" thesis is equivalent to the claim that the Supreme Court's interpretations have an authority as great as the Constitution's own authority. Harrison gives a number of reasons for thinking that such a rule of judicial finality in constitutional interpretation is not warranted. First of all, the Constitution lists and ranks the sources of law. Precedent is not listed as an authoritative source of law. How then can it trump other recognized sources of law? Perhaps as a gloss on an authoritative text (the Constitution), authoritative court interpretations of the Constitution derive their authority as law from the Constitution itself. To this Harrison replies that if the original contemplation had been to make the courts, or the Supreme Court, authoritative and final interpreters, it would have been natural to provide for reporters and require written opinions, which was not done; the question whether lower courts also have the power would have been addressed; and the question whether federal courts can review implementation of federal precedents by state courts would also have been addressed. Precedent was not really a universal feature of judicial decisions, so the precedential effect of judicial rulings, let alone their universal binding effect, was not something that would have been taken for granted. *Id.*

2. A question that is not considered much of an issue by American jurists, but which is of necessity taken very seriously in France and other civil law countries, is this: If judicial review in the ordinary courts is authorized, are those courts competent to review legislation only, or administrative action only, or both, for constitutional nonconformity? In the United States courts assume the jurisdiction to do both. By way of comparison, ordinary courts (to be distinguished from administrative and constitutional "courts") in France and other civil law countries are presently empowered to do neither. (This statement deserves some qualification, which it will get in Chapter Four.)

*   *   *

D. The Scope of Judicial Review

Almost no one, I think, even those who oppose judicial review, would object to a court striking down—or at least refusing to apply—a statute that had not been passed and promulgated according to the procedures laid out in the Constitution. The real issue arises when the courts inquire "into anything beside the form of enactment." Eakin v. Raub,12 S&R 330, 353 (Pa. 1825) (Gibson, J., dissenting). If there was to be substantive judicial review in American courts, would it address only separation of powers issues? Or individual rights as well? There is no indication that the issue was completely thought out, but one of the arguments in favor of review was that it would enable the courts to protect *themselves* from legislative encroachment—i.e., to safeguard at least this aspect of the separation of powers (1 Max Farrand, Records of the Federal Convention of 1787 21 (1911)—and it seems to have been taken for granted by many that the federal courts would be able to review state legislation for encroachment upon federal powers. On the other hand, Madison denied at one point that the courts would have the power to police the lines of demarcation. 1 Annals of Congress 500 (June 17, 1789).

As to individual rights, there was of course debate as to the inclusion of a Bill of Rights. Madison, in support of the Bill of Rights that he introduced in the House of Representatives, argued that the courts would enforce the rights included therein against arbitrary assumptions of power by the legislature and the executive. 1 Annals of Congress 439. Hamilton, who argued against the inclusion of a Bill of Rights, nevertheless argued in favor of granting the independent judiciary the power to enforce rights that appeared in the text of the Constitution itself.

1. Separation of Powers

UNITED STATES V. NIXON
418 U.S. 683, 686–687, 703–713 (1974)

Chief Justice Burger delivered the opinion of the Court.

This litigation presents for review the denial of a motion, filed in the District Court on behalf of the President of the United States, in the case of United States v. Mitchell (D. C. Crim. No. 74–110), to quash a third-party subpoena duces tecum issued by the United States District Court for the District of Columbia, pursuant to Fed. Rule Crim. Proc. 17 (c). The subpoena directed the President to produce certain tape recordings and documents relating to his conversations with aides and advisers. The court rejected the President's claims of absolute executive privilege, of lack of jurisdiction, and of failure to satisfy the requirements of Rule 17 (c). The President appealed to the Court of Appeals. We granted both the United States' petition for certiorari before judgment (No. 73–1766), and also the President's cross-petition for certiorari before judgment (No. 73–1834), because of the public importance of the issues presented and the need for their prompt resolution....

[W]e turn to the claim that the subpoena should be quashed because it demands "confidential conversations between a President and his close advisors that it would be inconsistent with the public interest to produce." The first contention is a broad claim that the separation of powers doctrine precludes judicial review of a President's claim of privilege. The second contention is that if he does not prevail on the claim of absolute privilege, the court should hold as a matter of constitutional law that the privilege prevails over the subpoena duces tecum .

In the performance of assigned constitutional duties each branch of the Government must initially interpret the Constitution, and the interpretation of its powers by any branch is due great respect from the others. The President's counsel, as we have noted, reads the Constitution as providing an absolute privilege of confidentiality for all Presidential communications. Many decisions of this Court, however, have unequivocally reaffirmed the holding of Marbury v. Madison, 1 Cranch 137 (1803), that "[i]t is emphatically the province and duty of the judicial department to say what the law is."

No holding of the Court has defined the scope of judicial power specifically relating to the enforcement of a subpoena for confidential Presidential communications for use in a criminal prosecution, but other exercises of power by the Executive Branch and the Legislative Branch have been found invalid as in conflict with the Constitution. Powell v. McCormack, 395 U.S. 486 (1969); Youngstown Sheet & Tube Co. v. Sawyer, 343 U.S. 579 (1952). In a series of cases, the Court interpreted the explicit immunity conferred by express provisions of the Constitution on Members of the House and Senate by the Speech or Debate Clause, U.S. Const. Art. I, §6. Doe v. McMillan, 412 U.S. 306 (1973); Gravel v. United States, 408 U.S. 606 (1972); United States v. Brewster, 408 U.S. 501 (1972); United States v. Johnson, 383 U.S. 169 (1966). Since this Court has consistently exercised the power to construe and delineate claims arising under express powers, it must follow that the Court has authority to interpret claims with respect to powers alleged to derive from enumerated powers.

Our system of government "requires that federal courts on occasion interpret the Constitution in a manner at variance with the construction given the document by another branch." Powell v. McCormack, supra, at 549. And in Baker v. Carr, 369 U.S., at 211, the Court stated:

> Deciding whether a matter has in any measure been committed by the Constitution to another branch of government, or whether the action

of that branch exceeds whatever authority has been committed, is itself a delicate exercise in constitutional interpretation, and is a responsibility of this Court as ultimate interpreter of the Constitution. Notwithstanding the deference each branch must accord the others, the "judicial Power of the United States" vested in the federal courts by Art. III, § 1, of the Constitution can no more be shared with the Executive Branch than the Chief Executive, for example, can share with the Judiciary the veto power, or the Congress share with the Judiciary the power to override a Presidential veto. Any other conclusion would be contrary to the basic concept of separation of powers and the checks and balances that flow from the scheme of a tripartite government. The Federalist, No. 47, p. 313 (S. Mittell ed., 1938). We therefore reaffirm that it is the province and duty of this Court "to say what the law is" with respect to the claim of privilege presented in this case. Marbury v. Madison, supra, at 177.

In support of his claim of absolute privilege, the President's counsel urges two grounds, one of which is common to all governments and one of which is peculiar to our system of separation of powers. The first ground is the valid need for protection of communications between high Government officials and those who advise and assist them in the performance of their manifold duties; the importance of this confidentiality is too plain to require further discussion....

The second ground asserted by the President's counsel in support of the claim of absolute privilege rests on the doctrine of separation of powers. Here it is argued that the independence of the Executive Branch within its own sphere, Humphrey's Executor v. United States, 295 U.S. 602, 629–630 (1935); Kilbourn v. Thompson, 103 U.S. 168, 190–191 (1881), insulates a President from a judicial subpoena in an ongoing criminal prosecution, and thereby protects confidential Presidential communications.

However, neither the doctrine of separation of powers, nor the need for confidentiality of high-level communications, without more, can sustain an absolute, unqualified Presidential privilege of immunity from judicial process under all circumstances. The President's need for complete candor and objectivity from advisers calls for great deference from the courts. However, when the privilege depends solely on the broad, undifferentiated claim of public interest in the confidentiality of such conversations, a confrontation with other values arises. Absent a claim of need to protect military, diplomatic, or sensitive national security secrets, we find it difficult to accept the argument that even the very important interest in confidentiality of Presidential communications is significantly diminished by production of such material for in camera inspection with all the protection that a district court will be obliged to provide.

The impediment that an absolute, unqualified privilege would place in the way of the primary constitutional duty of the Judicial Branch to do justice in criminal prosecutions would plainly conflict with the function of the courts under Art. III. In designing the structure of our Government and dividing and allocating the sovereign power among three co-equal branches, the Framers of the Constitution sought to provide a comprehensive system, but the separate powers were not intended to operate with absolute independence.

> "While the Constitution diffuses power the better to secure liberty, it also contemplates that practice will integrate the dispersed powers into a workable government. It enjoins upon its branches separateness but interdependence, autonomy but reciprocity." Youngstown Sheet & Tube Co. v. Sawyer, 343 U.S. 579, 635 (1952) (Jackson, J., concurring).

To read the Art. II powers of the President as providing an absolute privilege as against a subpoena essential to enforcement of criminal statutes on no more than a generalized claim of the public interest in confidentiality of nonmilitary and nondiplomatic discussions would upset the constitutional balance of "a workable government" and gravely impair the role of the courts under Art. III.

Since we conclude that the legitimate needs of the judicial process may outweigh Presidential privilege, it is necessary to resolve those competing interests in a manner that preserves the essential functions of each branch. The right and indeed the duty to resolve that question does not free the Judiciary from according high respect to the representations made on behalf of the President. United States v. Burr, 25 F. Cas. 187, 190, 191–192 (No. 14,694) (CC Va. 1807)....

In this case we must weigh the importance of the general privilege of confidentiality of Presidential communications in performance of the President's responsibilities against the inroads of such a privilege on the fair administration of criminal justice. The interest in preserving confidentiality is weighty indeed and entitled to great respect. However, we cannot conclude that advisers will be moved to temper the candor of their remarks by the infrequent occasions of disclosure because of the possibility that such conversations will be called for in the context of a criminal prosecution.

On the other hand, the allowance of the privilege to withhold evidence that is demonstrably relevant in a criminal trial would cut deeply into the guarantee of due process of law and gravely impair the basic function of the courts. A President's acknowledged need for confidentiality in the communications of his office is general in nature, whereas the constitutional need for production of relevant evidence in a criminal proceeding is specific and central to the fair adjudication of a particular criminal case in the administration of justice. Without access to specific facts a criminal prosecution may be totally frustrated. The President's broad interest in confidentiality of communications will not be vitiated by disclosure of a limited number of conversations preliminarily shown to have some bearing on the pending criminal cases.

We conclude that when the ground for asserting privilege as to subpoenaed materials sought for use in a criminal trial is based only on the generalized interest in confidentiality, it cannot prevail over the fundamental demands of due process of law in the fair administration of criminal justice. The generalized assertion of privilege must yield to the demonstrated, specific need for evidence in a pending criminal trial.

Notes

1. "[A]lthough judicial review is incompatible with a fundamental precept of American democracy—majority rule—the Court must exercise this power in order to protect individual rights, which are not adequately represented in the political processes. When judicial review is unnecessary for the effective preservation of our constitutional scheme, however, the Court should decline to exercise its authority.... [T]he thesis to be urged—hereafter referred to as the Separation Proposal—is as follows: The federal judiciary should not decide constitutional questions concerning the respective powers of Congress and the President vis-á-vis one another;...But such controversies do not exhaust the range of constitutional issues that fall within the...category of separation of powers at the national level. An obvious subclassification remains: fundamental conflicts between the political branches, on the one hand, and the federal judiciary on the other.... [The Judicial Proposal] is that the Supreme Court should pass final constitutional judgment on questions concerning the permissible reach and circumscription of 'the judicial power.'...The Judicial Proposal [proceeds] from the same functional analysis as its companion proposals respecting individual rights, federalism, and the separation of powers, by recognizing the distinctive ability of the Justices (in contrast to elected officials—lawyers and laymen alike) to define the proper boundaries of judicial power." Jesse Choper, Judicial Review and the National Political Process 2, 263, 382–385 (1980).

* * *

2. Rights

CYNTHIA VROOM, EQUAL PROTECTION VERSUS THE PRINCIPLE OF EQUALITY: AMERICAN AND FRENCH VIEWS ON EQUALITY IN THE LAW
21 CAPITAL UNIVERSITY LAW REVIEW
199, 199, 208–213 (1992)

At first glance, the American doctrine of equal protection of the law and the French principle of equality seem similar: they are both designed to eliminate discrimination in the law; they both operate in western democratic societies with shared values; and they are both shaped by supralegisla-tive bodies (the American Supreme Court and the French *Conseil constitu-tionnel*). The surface similarities are deceptive, however, for equal protec-tion of the law in the United States and the principle of equality in France are far from identical. They arise from different legal and cultural traditions and are rooted in different constitutional models. As a result, the jurispru-dence of equality in the two countries varies significantly in nature and con-tent....

In the United States, equal protection analysis is divided into the categories of "classifications" and "fundamental rights." Certain kinds of classifications are considered to be inherently suspect and given the most intensive degree of re-view. Classifications not considered to be inherently suspect receive a less in-tensive degree of review. Laws which limit the exercise of fundamental rights are also given intensive scrutiny, while laws limiting the exercise of rights not considered to be fundamental are given a lower level of review.

A. Classifications

Strict scrutiny. Race is the most obvious suspect classification. The Supreme Court's modern jurisprudence on race, including the school deseg-regation cases and affirmative action, is well known and will not be discussed in this paper.

Alienage is another suspect classification. The government may not treat resident aliens differently from citizens unless the distinction is necessary to promote a compelling state interest. A distinction between aliens and citizens has been upheld with respect to the right to vote or hold office, and rejected with respect to land ownership, welfare benefits, access to competitive civil rights jobs, financial aid for higher education, and the right to practice law.

Mid-level review. Certain classifications are not considered as inherently "sus-pect," and thus are given a less rigorous level of review. Among these are gender and illegitimacy.

Unlike the French Constitution, the American Constitution contains no ex-press guarantee of equality for women. The Fourteenth Amendment, which by its terms could serve this function, had no immediate impact on the use of sex-based classifications, and the courts continued to uphold laws providing differ-ent treatment for men and women. The turning point did not come until 1971 with the landmark decision *Reed v. Reed*, involving a statute which gave males preference over females in the selection of an administrator of an intestate es-tate. The Supreme Court struck down this sex-based classification, relying for the first time on the equal protection clause of the Fourteenth Amendment. Since *Reed*, sex-based classifications have been struck down in several contexts: for example, where a female member of the military had to prove her spouse was a dependent in order to obtain increased housing and medical benefits, while married male servicemen received these benefits automatically; and where a statute granted payments based on earnings of a deceased husband to his widow and children, but payments based on earnings of a deceased wife only to her children.

A sex-based classification was upheld where a statute allowed a property tax exemption for widows but not widowers, on the ground that widows face greater financial difficulty than widowers and have greater problems in the job market. The distinction between acceptable sex-based classifications and unacceptable ones is not very clear, and there is inevitably a subjective character to the judgment of the Supreme Court; a decision in a given case depends upon the Justices' view of the purpose of the classification and the extent of the burden.

With respect to legitimacy, a law may not discriminate against illegitimate children unless the distinction is reasonably related to an important governmental interest. Laws excluding illegitimate children from welfare, workers' compensation benefits, inheritance, or financial support have been struck down as violating the equal protection clause.

Rational basis. Perhaps the most common example of a classification receiving minimal review is wealth. Laws which burden the poor, if they do not involve the exercise of a fundamental right, are given the same minimal scrutiny as any economic or social legislation and will be upheld if the classification has any rational relationship to a legitimate end of government. "It is apparently the view of the majority of the justices that there is nothing in the judicial function which makes them institutionally capable of deciding economic policy as to the allocation of income and wealth through the review of legislative classifications."

Perhaps the most controversial issue in this category is government funding of abortions for poor women. The Supreme Court has held that states need not subsidize nontherapeutic abortions, on the ground that the fundamental right to privacy only prohibits governments from limiting the abortion decision and does not require them to affirmatively fund abortions.

B. Fundamental Rights

Laws which limit the exercise of these rights by certain persons are analyzed under the Equal Protection Clause. They are subject to strict scrutiny and will be upheld only if the limitation is necessary to promote a compelling governmental interest.

Voting. Equal protection jurisprudence is especially abundant in the area of voting. Impermissible limitations of this right include poll taxes, literacy tests, residency requirements, restrictions based on party affiliations, and racial restrictions. The right to vote extends to the right to be a candidate, and restrictions on this right have been struck down, including wealth restrictions, property ownership requirements, and racial restrictions. The right to vote also includes having each person's vote count equally, and this has resulted in a series of laws on reapportionment, beginning in 1962 with *Baker v. Carr.*

Restrictions on the right to vote have been upheld as justified where laws imposed residency requirements on candidates and required party affiliation for placement on the ballot.

Privacy. The most controversial fundamental right is that of privacy. The debate in the United States over the inclusion of abortion in the right to privacy has been well publicized and will not be discussed here. Other aspects of the right to privacy include contraception and marriage. Equal protection analysis focuses on limitations on the exercise of these rights for certain categories of persons.

In the seminal case on the right to privacy, a statute forbidding the use of contraceptive devices was struck down on the ground that it impermissibly limited the right of privacy of married persons. Seven years later, a statute prohibiting the distribution of contraceptives to unmarried persons was found to violate the Equal Protection Clause by limiting the right of privacy of unmarried persons.

Laws restricting the right of certain persons to marry are also invalid unless a compelling reason can be shown for the classification. In *Loving v. Virginia*, a statute prohibiting interracial marriage was found to violate the Equal Protection Clause because its classification was based solely on race.

Travel. The right to travel is also considered to be a fundamental right. The principal equal protection case is *Shapiro v. Thompson*, which struck down three statutes denying welfare benefits to persons who had resided in the jurisdiction for less than one year. The Court held that this residency requirement would deter the entry of indigent persons into the state, which effectively limited their right to interstate travel. A state does not have the right to distinguish between old and new residents in the exercise of a fundamental right absent a compelling justification, and none was found here.

The fundamental guarantees of the Bill of Rights, including freedom of speech, the press, and religion, as well as the guarantees of the criminal justice system, have generally not played a large part in the jurisprudence of equal protection, largely because of the strong substantive protection offered by the Bill of Rights in these areas.

Nonfundamental rights. Certain rights are not considered to be "fundamental"; in cases involving such rights, the Supreme Court will use the rational basis test, which allows the legislature maximum discretion. The law will be upheld if it is rationally related to a legitimate government interest.

"Nonfundamental" rights are primarily found in economic and social legislation. The Supreme Court has held, for example, that there is no fundamental right to welfare payments. As long as the legislative scheme does not discriminate against suspect classes or deny due process to those entitled to receive benefits, welfare laws will not be closely scrutinized by the courts. In *Dandridge v. Williams*, the Supreme Court upheld a law limiting the number of children for whom a family could receive welfare payments

There is also no fundamental right to governmental assistance in obtaining housing. However, housing authorities may not discriminate against minorities in allocating public housing.

Public education has never been declared a fundamental right, although the Supreme Court came close in *San Antonio Independent School District v. Rodriguez*, in which it upheld a statute allowing local property taxes to finance public education, even though the money was not spent equally throughout the school district. The Court left open the question of the right to education: "Even if it were conceded that some identifiable quantum of education is a constitutionally protected [right], we have no indication that the [allocation of taxes] fails to provide each child with an opportunity to acquire the basic minimal skills."

Government employment is not a fundamental right in the United States, and laws restricting it will receive only minimal review. In *Vance v. Bradley*, for example, the Supreme Court upheld a mandatory retirement age of sixty for the foreign service, even though the general federal retirement age was seventy.

This broad outline of American equal protection doctrine reveals a close concentration on the kinds of discrimination arising from inherent characteristics of a particular group, and from restrictions on the exercise of a limited number of fundamental rights by certain persons. Economic and social equality is not an important goal of equal protection in the United States; this goal is largely left to the discretion of legislature.

* * *

3. Abortion: The Right to Privacy

CONSTITUTION OF THE
UNITED STATES OF AMERICA

Amendment XIV. (1) All persons born or naturalized in the United States, and subject to the jurisdiction thereof, are citizens of the United States and of the State wherein they reside. No State shall make or enforce any law which shall abridge the privileges of immunities of citizens of the United States; nor shall any State deprive any person of life, liberty, or property, without due process of law; nor deny to any person within its jurisdiction the equal protection of the laws.

* * *

TEXAS PENAL CODE
(1925)

Article 1191. If any person shall designedly administer to a pregnant woman or knowingly procure to be administered with her consent any drug or medicine, or shall use towards her any violence or means whatever externally or internally applied, and thereby procure an abortion, he shall be confined in the penitentiary not less than two nor more than five years;....

Article 1192. Whoever furnishes the means for procuring an abortion knowing the purpose intended is guilty as an accomplice.

* * *

ROE V. WADE
410 U.S. 113, 117–118, 129, 152–165, 172–177 (1973)

Justice Blackmun delivered the opinion of the Court....

The principal thrust of appellant's attack on the Texas statutes is that they improperly invade a right, said to be possessed by the pregnant woman, to choose to terminate her pregnancy. Appellant would discover this right in the concept of personal "liberty" embodied in the Fourteenth Amendment's Due Process Clause; or in personal, marital, familial, and sexual privacy said to be protected by the Bill of Rights or its penumbras, see *Griswold v. Connecticut*, 381 U.S. 479 (1965);*Eisenstadt v. Baird*, 405 U.S. 438 (1972); *id.*, at 460 (White, J., concurring in result); or among those rights reserved to the people by the Ninth Amendment, *Griswold v. Connecticut*, 381 U.S., at 486 (Goldberg, J., concurring)....

The Constitution does not explicitly mention any right of privacy. In a line of decisions, however, going back perhaps as far as *Union Pacific R. Co. v. Botsford*, 141 U.S. 250, 251 (1891), the Court has recognized that a right of personal privacy, or a guarantee of certain areas or zones of privacy, does exist under the Constitution. In varying contexts, the Court or individual Justices have, indeed, found at least the roots of that right in the First Amendment, *Stanley v. Georgia*, 394 U.S. 557, 564 (1969); in the Fourth and Fifth Amendments, *Terry v. Ohio*, 392 U.S. 1, 8–9 (1968), *Katz v. United States*, 389 U.S. 347, 350 (1967), *Boyd v. United States*, 116 U.S. 616 (1886), see *Olmstead v. United States,* 277 U.S. 438, 478 (1928) (Brandeis, J., dissenting); in the penumbras of the Bill of Rights, *Griswold v. Connecticut,* 381 U.S., at 484–485; in the Ninth Amendment, *id.*, at 486 (Goldberg, J., concurring); or in the concept of liberty guaranteed by the first section of the Fourteenth Amendment, see *Meyer v. Nebraska*, 262 U.S. 390, 399 (1923). These decisions make it clear that only personal rights that can be deemed "fundamental" or "implicit in the concept of ordered liberty," *Palko v. Connecticut,* 302 U.S. 319, 325 (1937), are included in this guarantee of personal privacy. They also make it clear that the right has some extension to activities relating to marriage, *Loving v. Virginia,* 388 U.S. 1, 12 (1967); procreation, *Skinner v. Oklahoma,* 316 U.S. 535, 541–542 (1942); contraception, *Eisenstadt v. Baird,* 405 U.S., at 453–454; id., at 460, 463–465 (White, J., concurring in result); family relationships, *Prince v. Massachusetts,* 321 U.S. 158, 166 (1944); and child rearing, id. at 460, 463–465 (White, J., concurring in result); family relationships, *Prince v. Massachusetts,* 321 U.S. 158, 166 (1944); and child rearing and education, *Pierce v. Society of Sisters,* 268 U.S. 510, 535 (1925), *Meyer v. Nebraska, supra.* This right of privacy, whether it be founded in the Fourteenth Amendment's concept of personal liberty and restrictions upon state action, as we feel it is, or, as the District Court determined, in the Ninth Amendment's reservation of rights to the people, is broad enough to encompass a woman's decision whether or not to terminate her pregnancy. The detriment that the State would impose upon the pregnant woman by denying this choice altogether is apparent. Specific and direct harm medically diagnosable even in early pregnancy may be involved. Maternity, or additional offspring, may force upon the woman a distressful life and future. Psychological harm may be imminent. Mental and physical health may be taxed by child care. There is also the distress, for all concerned, associated with the unwanted child, and there is the problem of bringing a child into a family already unable, psychologically and otherwise, to care for it. In other cases, as in this one, the additional difficulties and continuing stigma of unwed motherhood may be involved. All these are factors the woman and her responsible physician necessarily will consider in consultation.

On the basis of elements such as these, appellant and some amici argue that the woman's right is absolute and that she is entitled to terminate her pregnancy at whatever time, in whatever way, and for whatever reason she alone chooses. With this we do not agree. Appellant's arguments that Texas either has no valid interest at all in regulating the abortion decision, or no interest strong enough to support any limitation upon the woman's sole determination, are unpersuasive. The Court's decisions recognizing a right of privacy also acknowledge that some state regulation in areas protected by that right is appropriate. As noted above, a State may properly assert important interests in safeguarding health, in maintaining medical standards, and in protecting potential life. At some point in pregnancy, these respective interests become sufficiently compelling to sustain regulation of the factors that govern the abortion decision. The privacy right involved, therefore, cannot be said to be absolute. In fact, it is not clear to us that the claim asserted by some amici that one has an unlimited right to do with one's body as one pleases bears a close relationship to the right of privacy previously articulated in the

Court's decisions. The Court has refused to recognize an unlimited right of this kind in the past. *Jacobson v. Massachusetts*, 197 U.S. 11 (1905) (vaccination); *Buck v. Bell*, 274 U.S. 200 (1927) (sterilization).

We, therefore, conclude that the right of personal privacy includes the abortion decision, but that this right is not unqualified and must be considered against important state interests in regulation....

Where certain "fundamental rights" are involved, the Court has held that regulation limiting these rights may be justified only by a "compelling state interest," *Kramer v. Union Free School District*, 395 U.S. 621, 627 (1969); *Shapiro v. Thompson*, 394 U.S. 618, 634 (1969), *Sherbert v. Verner*, 374 U.S. 398, 406 (1963), and that legislative enactments must be narrowly drawn to express only the legitimate state interests at stake. *Griswold v. Connecticut*, 381 U.S., at 485; *Aptheker v. Secretary of State*, 378 U.S. 500, 508 (1964); *Cantwell v. Connecticut*, 310 U.S. 296, 307–308 (1940); see *Eisenstadt v. Baird*, 405 U.S., at 460, 463–464 (White, J., concurring in result)....

The appellee and certain amici argue that the fetus is a "person" within the language and meaning of the Fourteenth Amendment. In support of this, they outline at length and in detail the well-known facts of fetal development. If this suggestion of personhood is established, the appellant's case, of course, collapses, for the fetus' right to life would then be guaranteed specifically by the Amendment. The appellant conceded as much on reargument. On the other hand, the appellee conceded on reargument that no case could be cited that holds that a fetus is a person within the meaning of the Fourteenth Amendment.

The Constitution does not define "person" in so many words. Section 1 of the Fourteenth Amendment contains three references to "person." .... "Person" is used in other places in the Constitution....But in nearly all these instances, the use of the word is such that it has application only postnatally. None indicates, with any assurance, that it has any possible pre-natal application.

All this, together with our observation, supra, that throughout the major portion of the 19th century prevailing legal abortion practices were far freer than they are today, persuades us that the word "person," as used in the Fourteenth Amendment, does not include the unborn....This conclusion, however, does not of itself fully answer the contentions raised by Texas, and we pass on to other considerations.

The pregnant woman cannot be isolated in her privacy. She carries an embryo and, later, a fetus, if one accepts the medical definitions of the developing young in the human uterus. See Dorland's Illustrated Medical Dictionary 478–479, 547 (24th ed. 1965). The situation therefore is inherently different from marital intimacy, or bedroom possession of obscene material, or marriage, or procreation, or education, with which *Eisenstadt* and *Griswold*, *Stan-*

ley, Loving, Skinner, and *Pierce* and *Meyer* were respectively concerned. As we have intimated above, it is reasonable and appropriate for a State to decide that at some point in time another interest, that of health of the mother or that of potential human life, becomes significantly involved. The woman's privacy is no longer sole and any right of privacy she possesses must be measured accordingly.

Texas urges that, apart from the Fourteenth Amendment, life begins at conception and is present throughout pregnancy, and that, therefore, the State has a compelling interest in protecting that life from and after conception. We need not resolve the difficult question of when life begins. When those trained in the respective disciplines of medicine, philosophy, and theology are unable to arrive at any consensus, the judiciary, at this point in the development of man's knowledge, is not in a position to speculate as to the answer....

In areas other than criminal abortion, the law has been reluctant to endorse any theory that life, as we recognize it, begins before live birth or to accord legal rights to the unborn except in narrowly defined situations and except when the rights are contingent upon live birth. For example, the traditional rule of tort law denied recovery for prenatal injuries even though the child was born alive. That rule has been changed in almost every jurisdiction. In most States, recovery is said to be permitted only if the fetus was viable, or at least quick, when the injuries were sustained, though few courts have squarely so held. In a recent development, generally opposed by the commentators, some States permit the parents of a stillborn child to maintain an action for wrongful death because of prenatal injuries. Such an action, however, would appear to be one to vindicate the parents' interest and is thus consistent with the view that the fetus, at most, represents only the potentiality of life. Similarly, unborn children have been recognized as acquiring rights or interests by way of inheritance or other devolution of property, and have been represented by guardians ad litem. Perfection of the interests involved, again, has generally been contingent upon live birth. In short, the unborn have never been recognized in the law as persons in the whole sense.

In view of all this, we do not agree that, by adopting one theory of life, Texas may override the rights of the pregnant woman that are at stake. We repeat, however, that the State does have an important and legitimate interest in preserving and protecting the health of the pregnant woman, whether she be a resident of the State or a nonresident who seeks medical consultation and treatment there, and that it has still another important and legitimate interest in protecting the potentiality of human life. These interests are separate and distinct. Each grows in substantiality as the woman approaches term and, at a point during pregnancy, each becomes "compelling."

With respect to the State's important and legitimate interest in the health of the mother, the "compelling" point, in the light of present medical knowledge, is at approximately the end of the first trimester. This is so because of the now-established medical fact, referred to above…, that until the end of the first trimester mortality in abortion may be less than mortality in normal childbirth. It follows that, from and after this point, a State may regulate the abortion procedure to the extent that the regulation reasonably relates to the preservation and protection of maternal health. Examples of permissible state regulation in this area are requirements as to the qualifications of the person who is to perform the abortion; as to the licensure of that person; as to the facility in which the procedure is to be performed, that is, whether it must be a hospital or may be a clinic or some other place of less-than-hospital status; as to the licensing of the facility; and the like.

This means, on the other hand, that, for the period of pregnancy prior to this "compelling" point, the attending physician, in consultation with his patient, is free to determine, without regulation by the State, that, in his medical judgment, the patient's pregnancy should be terminated. If that decision is reached, the judgment may be effectuated by an abortion free of interference by the State.

With respect to the State's important and legitimate interest in potential life, the "compelling" point is at viability. This is so because the fetus then presumably has the capability of meaningful life outside the mother's womb. State regulation protective of fetal life after viability thus has both logical and biological justifications. If the State is interested in protecting fetal life after viability, it may go so far as to proscribe abortion during that period, except when it is necessary to preserve the life or health of the mother.

Measured against these standards, Art. 1196 of the Texas Penal Code, in restricting legal abortions to those "procured or attempted by medical advice for the purpose of saving the life of the mother," sweeps too broadly. The statute makes no distinction between abortions performed early in pregnancy and those performed later, and it limits to a single reason, "saving" the mother's life, the legal justification for the procedure. The statute, therefore, cannot survive the constitutional attack made upon it here.

This conclusion makes it unnecessary for us to consider the additional challenge to the Texas statute asserted on grounds of vagueness. See *United States v. Vuitch*, 402 U.S., at 67–72.

To summarize and to repeat:

1. A state criminal abortion statute of the current Texas type, that excepts from criminality only a lifesaving procedure on behalf of the mother, without regard to pregnancy stage and without recognition of the other interests involved, is violative of the Due Process Clause of the Fourteenth Amendment.

(a) For the stage prior to approximately the end of the first trimester, the abortion decision and its effectuation must be left to the medical judgment of the pregnant woman's attending physician.

(b) For the stage subsequent to approximately the end of the first trimester, the State, in promoting its interest in the health of the mother, may, if it chooses, regulate the abortion procedure in ways that are reasonably related to maternal health.

(c) For the stage subsequent to viability, the State in promoting its interest in the potentiality of human life may, if it chooses, regulate, and even proscribe, abortion except where it is necessary, in appropriate medical judgment, for the preservation of the life or health of the mother.

* * *

Justice Rehnquist, dissenting.

I have difficulty in concluding, as the Court does, that the right of "privacy" is involved in this case. Texas, by the statute here challenged, bars the performance of a medical abortion by a licensed physician on a plaintiff such as Roe. A transaction resulting in an operation such as this is not "private" in the ordinary usage of that word. Nor is the "privacy" that the Court finds here even a distant relative of the freedom from searches and seizures protected by the Fourth Amendment to the Constitution, which the Court has referred to as embodying a right to privacy. *Katz v. United States*, 389 U.S. 347 (1967).

If the Court means by the term "privacy" no more than that the claim of a person to be free from unwanted state regulation of consensual transactions may be a form of "liberty" protected by the Fourteenth Amendment, there is no doubt that similar claims have been upheld in our earlier decisions on the basis of that liberty. I agree with the statement of Mr. Justice Stewart in his concurring opinion that the "liberty," against deprivation of which without due process the Fourteenth Amendment protects, embraces more than the rights found in the Bill of Rights. But that liberty is not guaranteed absolutely against deprivation, only against deprivation without due process of law. The test traditionally applied in the area of social and economic legislation is whether or not a law such as that challenged has a rational relation to a valid state objective. *Williamson v. Lee Optical Co.*, 348 U.S. 483, 491 (1955). The Due Process Clause of the Fourteenth Amendment undoubtedly does place a limit, albeit a broad one, on legislative power to enact laws such as this. If the Texas statute were to prohibit an abortion even where the mother's life is in jeopardy, I have little doubt that such a statute would lack a rational relation to a valid state objective under the test stated in Williamson, supra. But the Court's sweeping invalidation of any restrictions on abortion during the first trimester is impossible to justify under that standard, and the conscious weighing of competing factors that the Court's opinion apparently substitutes for the established test is far more appropriate to a legislative judgment than to a judicial one.

The Court eschews the history of the Fourteenth Amendment in its reliance on the "compelling state interest" test. See *Weber v. Aetna Casualty & Surety Co.*, 406 U.S. 164, 179 (1972) (dissenting opinion). But the Court adds a new wrinkle to this test by transposing it from the legal considerations associated with the Equal Protection Clause of the Fourteenth Amendment to this case arising under the Due Process Clause of the Fourteenth Amendment. Unless I misapprehend the consequences of this transplanting of the "compelling state interest test," the Court's opinion will accomplish the seemingly impossible feat of leaving this area of the law more confused than it found it.

While the Court's opinion quotes from the dissent of Mr. Justice Holmes in *Lochner v. New York*, 198 U.S. 45, 74 (1905), the result it reaches is more closely attuned to the majority opinion of Mr. Justice Peckham in that case. As in Lochner and similar cases applying substantive due process standards to economic and social welfare legislation, the adoption of the compelling state interest standard will inevitably require this Court to examine the legislative policies and pass on the wisdom of these policies in the very process of deciding whether a particular state interest put forward may or may not be "compelling." The decision here to break pregnancy into three distinct terms and to outline the permissible restrictions the State may impose in each one, for example, partakes more of judicial legislation than it does of a determination of the intent of the drafters of the Fourteenth Amendment.

[handwritten margin note: parallel to Lochner v. New York]

The fact that a majority of the States reflecting, after all, the majority sentiment in those States, have had restrictions on abortions for at least a century is a strong indication, it seems to me, that the asserted right to an abortion is not "so rooted in the traditions and conscience of our people as to be ranked as fundamental," *Snyder v. Massachusetts*, 291 U.S. 97, 105 (1934). Even today, when society's views on abortion are changing, the very existence of the debate is evidence that the "right" to an abortion is not so universally accepted as the appellant would have us believe.

To reach its result, the Court necessarily has had to find within the scope of the Fourteenth Amendment a right that was apparently completely unknown to the drafters of the Amendment. As early as 1821, the first state law dealing directly with abortion was enacted by the Connecticut Legislature. Conn. Stat., Tit. 20, §§ 14, 16. By the time of the adoption of the Fourteenth Amendment in 1868, there were at least 36 laws enacted by state or territorial legislatures limiting abortion. While many States have amended or updated their laws, 21 of the laws on the books in 1868 remain in effect today. Indeed, the Texas statute struck down today was, as the majority notes, first enacted in 1857 and "has remained substantially unchanged to the present time."

There apparently was no question concerning the validity of this provision or of any of the other state statutes when the Fourteenth Amendment was adopted. The only conclusion possible from this history is that the drafters did not intend to have the Fourteenth Amendment withdraw from the States the power to legislate with respect to this matter.

Notes

1. The holding in *Roe v. Wade* was revisited in 1992, in Planned Parenthood of Southeastern Pennsylvania v. Casey, 505 U.S. 833 (1992). While claiming to reaffirm the earlier case, the Court made some significant changes:

> We give this summary:
>
> (a) To protect the central right recognized by Roe v. Wade while at the same time accommodating the State's profound interest in potential life, we will employ the undue burden analysis.... An undue burden exists, and therefore a provision of law is invalid, if its purpose or effect is to place a substantial obstacle in the path of a woman seeking an abortion before the fetus attains viability.
>
> (b) We reject the rigid trimester framework of Roe v. Wade. To promote the State's profound interest in potential life, throughout pregnancy the State may take measures to ensure that the woman's choice is informed, and measures designed to advance this interest will not be invalidated as long as their purpose is to persuade the woman to choose childbirth over abortion. These measures must not be an undue burden on the right.
>
> (c) As with any medical procedure, the State may enact regulations to further the health or safety of a woman seeking an abortion. Unnecessary health regulations that have the purpose or effect of presenting a substantial obstacle to a woman seeking an abortion impose an undue burden on the right....

505 U.S. 833, at 878.

2. "Consider... cases where groups that win legal victories are nonetheless worse off.... Consider the following version of the history of abortion litigation in the United States. The Supreme Court struck down most states' abortion laws in 1973. Its decision provided some opportunities for anti-choice forces to try to enact restrictive legislation. Pro-choice activists, though, believed—correctly, for two decades—that the courts would strike down restrictive abortion laws. Sensibly enough, they devoted their political energies to other issues, relying on the low-cost courts for protection against restrictive abortion laws. Meanwhile their opponents mobilized around the abortion issue, but their political concerns were broader. Their efforts to enact and enforce restrictive *abortion* laws were unavailing, but they had real influence over other issues. That is, pro-choice forces found themselves facing stronger forces on issues

other than abortion than they had faced before their legal victory in the abortion cases.... The overall composition of the federal judiciary was among those other issues. The pro-choice legal victories contributed to the right-wing transformation of the federal courts.... Perhaps on balance the benefits for the pro-choice forces, measured by what happened on the abortion issue over the years since 1973—including the erosion but not the overruling of the initial victory —exceeded their losses on other issues. But examining the abortion decisions standing alone does not show that judicial review was a good thing even for advocates of women's rights." Mark Tushnet, Taking the Constitution Away From the Courts 138–139 (1999).

3. Norway claims the honor of being the first democratic nation outside the United States to have judicial review in the ordinary courts. "The closest comparable Norwegian decision [to *Marbury*] was a case between a naval officer and the naval authorities of 1866.... [T]his case is our first example of a publicised judgment in which the principle of judicial review was clearly applied." Chief Justice Carsten Smith, University of London Annual Coffin Memorial Lecture (2000), online at <http://www.hoyesterett.no/artikler/2694.asp>.

4. Japan is an example of a country with judicial review more or less on the American model. The legal system in Japan is in the civil law tradition, and has been for over a century. Under the pre-World War II constitution, known as the Meiji Constitution, there was no constitutional review. "[T]he laws are promulgated with the consent of the [legislature] and with Imperial sanction; therefore the judges need not question whether or not they are just." Fuji, Essentials of Japanese Constitutional Law 315 (1940). After the surrender of Japan in 1945, General Douglas MacArthur implemented Allied policy in Japan. His aims were to make sure that Japan was no longer a military menace to the United States, and to create a basis for democratic institutions in Japan. He insisted that a new constitution be drafted by the transitional government; when that failed, his own staff wrote a constitution in eight days. See Murphy and Tanenhaus, Comparative Constitutional Law 37 (1977). What would you expect of a constitution for the Japanese written by Americans? You would expect it to look very much like the American constitution; and you would not expect it to work very well at all for Japan. The truth is that it did look very much like the American constitution, and that it has worked so well over fifty years, and the Japanese have come to identify so closely with it, that nationalist agitation to replace it with a more Japanese document is almost unheard of. (Article 9, governing Japan's right to wage war, is an exception to that statement; it *has* been controversial.) Under Article 81 of the post-war constitution, the Japanese Supreme Court is the court of last resort with power to determine the constitutionality of any law, order, regulation or official act. The Supreme Court has decided that all lower courts have the same power, but only when confronted by an actual case or controversy—a system of review close to the American model.

Chapter Three

Inroads into Parliamentary Supremacy II: Kelsen and the Constitutional Court

If there is to be a forum for constitutional review of legislative and administrative action, should it be in the ordinary courts, as it is in the United States, or in a special tribunal? If it is to be in the ordinary courts, how far should those courts be involved? Should they be limited to making a preliminary appraisal and then sending the difficult cases on to a special tribunal? Or should they be able to conduct a full determination of the constitutionality of laws and regulations? In the United States, as we saw in the last chapter, every court has the power, and the responsibility, to decide on the constitutionality of government action. In this chapter we take up examples in which constitutional review is provided for, but either (1) the ordinary courts have no role at all, or (2) their role is limited to initial appraisal and referral to a special constitutional tribunal. In these cases it is correct to speak of *constitutional review*, but not, strictly speaking, of *judicial review*, since review is not carried out by the judiciary.

HERBERT HAUSMANINGER, JUDICIAL REFERRAL OF CONSTITUTIONAL QUESTIONS IN AUSTRIA, GERMANY, AND RUSSIA
12 TULANE EUROPEAN AND CIVIL LAW FORUM 25, 26–27 (1997)

The Austrian system has its roots in the constitutional law discussions of the late nineteenth century. It was further developed by Hans Kelsen, a prominent legal theorist, constitutional law scholar, and the "father" of the Austrian Constitution of 1920. After the Second World War, it was this system rather than the American that profoundly influenced the creation of constitutional courts within the new constitutions of Italy (1948) and Germany (1949). In the following years, the Austrian model of constitutional review—often as modified by contemporary German theory and experience—was adopted by most West European as well as by several Central and Latin American states. Most recently, virtually all emerging democracies in Eastern Europe have established constitutional courts based on the Austrian and/or German experience.

There are several reasons why the older American system was not adopted by European nations in the course of their constitutional reforms following World War II. European constitutional review is the product of a specific model of separation of powers and rule of law in continental Europe, a model that emphasizes the notions of supremacy of parliament and the product of its legislative activity, the statute. In European civil law countries, statutory regulation is comprehensive, and judges have no overt law-making function similar to that of their common law brethren. They are faithfully to apply the statute, not to challenge it. Their activism is also curbed by the fact that they are part of a civil service hierarchy, in which they are promoted from lower to higher courts according to professional competence and seniority. Constitutional review being a quasi-legislative function, it is considered to differ substantially from "regular" judicial work. It is, therefore, assigned to a special procedure before a separate constitutional organ with justices particularly selected for this politically sensitive activity.

One should note in particular that in times of radical political change from totalitarian to democratic systems, e.g., after the collapse of the Soviet regime in Eastern Europe, the regular judiciary is invariably tainted but cannot be quickly replaced, whereas a specialized constitutional court may be staffed with competent and reputable jurists (such as law professors). If sufficiently broad access is provided (like for instance in Hungary today), this court may swiftly impose constitutionality from above.

Note

1. Hausmaninger points out that the judiciary in Germany and elsewhere after World War II was tainted by its involvement in the Fascist regimes, and that a specially appointed court was better suited to enforcing the provisions of a democratic constitution. Why was the same strategy not adopted in Japan which, with its civil law background and court system, would have been a suitable candidate for it? The answer may have more to do with the personalities involved in the transition than with any feature of the Japanese legal system.

* * *

MAURO CAPPELLETTI AND JOHN CLARKE ADAMS, JUDICIAL REVIEW OF LEGISLATION: EUROPEAN ANTECEDENTS AND ADAPTATIONS

79 HARVARD LAW REVIEW 1207, 1215–1216 (1966)

[An additional reason for denying ordinary courts the right of judicial review is the lack of *stare decisis* in courts that are not in the common law tradition.] Under the Anglo-American doctrine of *stare decisis*, a decision by the highest court in any jurisdiction is binding on all lower courts in the same jurisdiction, and thus does not need a specific grant of the power to declare a law invalid, nor must it decide anything beyond the applicability of the law in question to the concrete case; *stare decisis* does the rest by requiring other courts to follow the precedent in all succeeding cases. Thus, although the unconstitutional statute may remain on the books, it is a "dead law." Stare decisis, however, is not normally part of the Roman law systems, and thus in these systems the courts are not generally bound even by the decisions of the highest court. Under these circumstances the American system of judicial review can lead to grave uncertainty and confusion, as one court may decide to enforce a statute that another court will find invalid.

Another difficulty of quite a different nature is also likely to arise when the American system of judicial review is superimposed on typical European systems. In such systems the magistrates form a career service, the higher echelons of which are composed of elderly men who have reached a position of eminence based in large measure on their ability to interpret laws with logic and precision. They have been trained in the execution of the law as it stands, and they tend to shy away from the type of policy-making decisions that are involved in judicial review. It is difficult and perhaps distasteful for these magistrates to change their whole mode of thinking from the traditional one of applying any law that has been duly enacted, to that of questioning and determining the validity of legislation. The norms in modern constitutions are quite different from the legal norms with which these judges have long been in the habit of dealing. Modern constitutions do not limit themselves to a statement of the law; they are concerned with ultimate values relating to the future activity of the state and the society. This incompatibility between the training and traditions of the regular judges in a career service and the requirements for the effective operation of judicial review played a major role in the unsatisfactory operation of judicial review in German under the Weimar Republic, and in Italy from 1948 until the special constitutional court went into operation in 1956. If one accepts [the] thesis that the regular French courts have the power to disallow unconstitutional law, this incompatibility must be a primary cause of the absence of judicial review in France; and some responsibility for the poor performance of judicial review in Japan may also be attributed to the same cause.

A. Kelsen's Vision: Abstract Review

STANLEY L. PAULSON, CONSTITUTIONAL REVIEW IN THE UNITED STATES AND AUSTRIA: NOTES ON THE BEGINNINGS

16 RATIO JURIS 223, 223–224, 228–229, 231–233, 234–237 (2003)

Introduction. If the "beginnings" of constitutional review are the field of inquiry, the question arises right at the outset: Why talk about these two countries, the United States and Austria, in the same breath? The answer is straightforward: The first and most prominent development of what is known as *decentralized* constitutional review can be traced to the United States of America in the early decades of the republic. The first—although not, today, the most prominent[1]—system of *centralized* constitutional review was developed in Austria, in the period immediately following World War I.

It goes without saying that the development of constitutional review in the United States and in Austria was informed by—was, indeed, one response to —the greater political situation in each country. And, equally obvious, the respective political situations could scarcely have been more different. America, near the end of the eighteenth century, had won its war of independence, its emancipation from the British crown. Its task was the formation of a new state. In sharp contrast, Austria, early in the twentieth century, did not seek emancipation. Rather, as one of the many national divisions emerging from the collapse of the Austro-Hungarian Empire at the end of the War, the rump state Austria required a new political framework, a new constitution. What resulted, thanks to the Austrian Federal Constitution of October 1920, was the First Austrian Republic.

Despite taking place at very different points in time under extraordinarily different political circumstances, in legal systems reflecting altogether different traditions, the development of constitutional review in the two countries manifests some striking similarities. Both countries introduced, at the outset, constitutional review of federalist issues (that is, competing claims of federal and state or *Land* law)—America by means of a statute, section 25 of the Judiciary Act of 1789, Austria in article 140 of its new constitution of October 1920. And both countries introduced forms of constitutional review reaching to the enactments of the federal legislature, that is, the Congress or Parliament—

---

1. Widely admired, the German Federal Constitutional Court has become the most prominent system of centralized constitutional review in the world. The Court was established by statute, 12 March 1951, pursuant to the Constitution or Basic Law of 1949. [Footnote in original text.]

America in John Marshall's decision, *Marbury v. Madison* (1803), fourteen years after the founding of the Republic, and Austria from the outset, once again on the basis of article 140....

Early Developments in Austria: 1918–1920. The Austro-Hungarian Empire collapsed in October of 1918. On 16 October 1918, the last monarch of the Empire, Emperor Karl, who had assumed the throne in 1916 upon the death of Franz Joseph, made a last attempt to save the old order. Looking to that part of the Empire controlled by Austria, he announced its reorganization in the form of a federal state whose various regions, representing the various ethnic groups in the Empire, would be reconstituted as member states of the federation. The effort came too late. The non-German peoples of the Empire had already begun the process of forming independent states, prompting those in the German-speaking regions of the Empire to do the same. Their initial step, taken on 21 October 1918, was to form a Provisional National Assembly (*die provisorische Nationalversammlung des selbständigen deutschösterreichischen Staates*). Nine days later, 30 October 1918, the Provisional National Assembly took a second major step, declaring that it would assume power in the German-speaking regions of the Empire. It was this latter step that marked the founding of the post-War Austrian state, "German-Austria" ("*Deutschösterreich*"), as it was known in the immediate post-War period.

The Constitution of German-Austria, the "provisional constitution," as it is sometimes called, consisted not of a single document but of a number of decisions taken by the Provisional National Assembly and embodied in statutes, among them the foundational decision of 30 October 1918 and a decision of 12 November in which the Provisional National Assembly declared that the state would adopt a republican form of government....

The Provisional National Assembly did not take up its central task of developing a full-fledged constitution for Austria until the spring of 1919. Hans Kelsen, who had been appointed in November 1918 as legal consultant to Chancellor Karl Renner, was now called upon by Renner to draft a new federal constitution....

In his work on the Constitution of 1920, as Kelsen remarked many years later, it was the provisions on constitutional review, articles 137–48, that had meant the most to him.... First, the powers taken over from the earlier *Reichsgericht* comprise articles 137, 138, and 144 of the Federal Constitution of 1920. [These sections concern the jurisdiction of the Constitutional Court over disputes between governmental departments, between *Länder* (states), and between *Länder* and the federal government, and over complaints from citizens concerning the unconstitutionality of certain administrative actions.] ... In addition to these powers taken over from the old *Reichsgericht*, the Federal Constitution of 1920 also conferred certain entirely new powers on the Constitutional Court. Article 139 provides that the Constitutional Court is empowered, on the application of a court of ordinary jurisdiction, to hear cases respecting the legality of ordinances issued by a federal or *Land* authority. Article 140 provides that the Constitutional Court is empowered to hear claims respecting the constitutionality of *Land* statutes, this on the application of the federal government, and to hear claims respecting the constitutionality of federal statutes, this on the application of one of the *Land* governments. The Court is also empowered to decide cases of the constitutionality of a federal or *Land* statute *ex officio*, that is, on its own initiative, insofar as this is required in order to pass on the constitutionality of a statute in a case before the Court.

It is this development, the powers conferred on the Constitutional Court in article 140, that counts, in Kelsen's words, as "the high point of [the Court's] function as the guarantor of the constitution (*Garant der Verfassung*)"....

Kelsen's Explication and Defense of Centralized Constitutional Review. Presupposed in Kelsen's inquiry into the concept of constitution is his *Stufenbaulehre* or doctrine of hierarchical structure, according to which "the law regulates its own creation." That is, one legal norm governs the process whereby another legal norm is created—and the idea applies to the full range of legal norms in the hierarchical structure. The effect of this dynamic conception, reaching all the way up and down the hierarchy, is to relativize the differences between law creation and law application, thereby relativizing the standing of the different species of law themselves. In particular, legislation, the standard-bearer of later nineteenth-century statutory legal positivism (*Gesetzespositivismus*) in Europe and Britain, loses its privileged position.

It is only from the vantage point of this "theory of hierarchy," Kelsen argues, that the immanent meaning of the concept of constitution is accessible. For it is the constitution that serves as the fundamental positive-law rule—more precisely, the set of fundamental positive-law rules—determining the organs and procedures of legislation, and these organs and procedures provide for the remaining *Stufen* or levels of hierarchy. Thus understood, we have in view the "original and narrower concept of the constitution," according to Kelsen, namely, constitution *qua* means of allocating legal powers. A wider concept of the constitution includes, in addition to the norms addressing the organs and procedures of legislation, a catalog of basic rights. Here Kelsen mentions the equality of citizens before the law, freedom of expression, freedom of belief and conscience, and the inviolability of property.[2] As Kelsen understands them, basic rights and freedoms represent certain constraints on the scope, or the manner of exercise, of legal powers....

---

2. Elsewhere in the same paper, however, Kelsen expresses great scepticism about whether "the ideals of 'justice,' 'freedom,' 'equality,' 'equity,' 'morality,' and the like" are legally explicable at all, arguing at one point that these "formulae" represent nothing "more than a typical political ideology...." [Footnote in original text.]

In his lecture of 1928, Kelsen's most expansive statement on constitutional review, he considers, first, options other than a constitutional court, including preventive as well as repressive measures, and argues in every instance that the option in question is unsuitable. In particular, the legislative body—the body enacting the putatively unconstitutional statute—is ill-equipped to monitor itself either before or after the fact, that is, either preventively or repressively. Nothing short of an independent organ with power to invalidate the unconstitutional statute is worthy of consideration, Kelsen argues. That independent organ is a constitutional court....

In a paper of 1942, Kelsen addresses the merits, as he sees them, of a centralized system of constitutional review over the decentralized system in America. As is well known, all American courts of ordinary jurisdiction, federal and state courts alike, have power to hear questions of federal constitutional law so long as the case posing the question has been brought before the court in the appropriate way. When, however, the American court holds that a legal norm is invalid for want of constitutionality, that is an inflated way of saying that the court is setting the norm aside for the case at hand. Unlike the European constitutional courts, no American court—neither the state courts of Wyoming nor the Supreme Court in Washington—has power literally to abrogate the offending legal norm. What might loosely be described as the "abrogation" of an offending legal norm comes about, if at all, only by way of the doctrine of *stare decisis*, which has the courts "standing by what has been decided...."

Concluding Remark. Kelsen's leitmotif, expressed again and again both in the materials on the formation of the Austrian Federal Constitution and in his own historico-constitutional writings, was the need for constitutional review in a federal system. By contrast, Kelsen treated "the ideals of 'justice,' 'freedom,' 'equality,' 'equity,' 'morality,' and the like" with great scepticism. In a word, constitutional protection of basic rights was not driving the effort that culminated in the Austrian Constitutional Court.

The situation in the United States was not markedly different. The jury is still out on the question of whether the rule of *Marbury v. Madison* was understood by the Constitutional Framers in Philadelphia as inevitable, or whether it was a fluke, prompted by an extraordinary political constellation. What is clear, however, is that a half-century would pass before federal law was again overturned on constitutional grounds—and then only in the utterly wrongheaded and tragic *Dred Scott* case. In fact, the power of constitutional review addressed to congressional legislation did not begin to aggregate until late in the nineteenth century, almost a hundred years after the founding of the Republic. By contrast, the power of constitutional review addressed to federalist questions had become everyday fare, with countless cases throughout the nineteenth century and beyond.

* * *

THE AUSTRIAN CONSTITUTION OF 1920[3]

Article 139. The Constitutional Court has jurisdiction over questions of illegality of state (*landes*) and federal (*bundes*) ordinances upon application by another court, or, upon its own motion, where such an ordinance serves as the basis for a judgment in a case before the Constitutional Court; over questions of illegality of state ordinances upon application by the federal government; and over questions of illegality of a federal ordinance upon application by a state government....

Article 140. The Constitutional Court has jurisdiction over questions of unconstitutionality of state legislation upon application of the federal government, over questions of illegality of federal legislation upon application of a state government, and, upon its own motion, where such a legislation serves as the basis for a judgment in a case before the Constitutional Court.

Notes

1. Whereas in the United States constitutional review of legislation is decentralized—every court has the power to review legislation—where there is a Kelsen-type court review is centralized. Some other distinctions to be aware of: Review in American courts takes place in the context of, and is incidental to the resolution of, particular cases involving disputes between parties; it is said to be *inci-denter* (to use the Latin term). In the original Austrian Constitutional Court, by contrast, the issue of the unconstitutionality of legislation was raised by government parties who were affected by the promulgation of a certain statute. Unconstitutionality was the principal issue; hence such review is said to be *principaliter.* Review in the context of a dispute between parties is said to be concrete, while review at the behest of government actors not directly affected by the legislation is said to be abstract, both for obvious reasons. (Abstract review is not advisory; it is binding on all.) Finally, American courts, when they declare legislation unconstitutional, do so "for the case at hand," as Paulson puts it. They decide the issue for the parties to the case: the decision is binding *inter partes.* It is only *stare decisis* that gives such decisions further authority. In European courts, on the other hand, *stare decisis* is not the rule; consequently for the decisions of a constitutional court to have proper universal effect the decisions must be *erga*

---

3. The German text is found at <www.rechtsgeschichte.jku.at/Lehrverstaltungen/B-VG%201.Oktober%201920.htm>. The translation is based largely upon a 1945 translation by the U.S. Foreign Economic Administration, Enemy Branch (!), entitled "The Constitutions of Austria from 1920–1934" and dated July, 1945. There is a copy in the U.C.L.A. Libraries.

omnes: binding on all. *See* Mauro Cappelletti and William Cohen, Comparative Constitutional Law, Chapter Four, Modern Systems of Judicial Review, *passim* (1979).

2. Under 1930 legislation implementing Article 140, the Constitutional Court had jurisdiction to assess the validity of a statute already enacted (*a posteriori* review), or a bill yet to be voted on by the legislature (*a priori* review). *See* J.A.C. Grant, Judicial Review under the Austrian Constitution of 1920, 28 American Political Science Review 670, 673 (1934). Most modern constitutional courts can exercise only *a posteriori* review; in contrast, the French Constitutional Council can exercise only review *a priori*. See below, section D. *A priori* review is of necessity abstract; *a posteriori* review may be either abstract or concrete.

3. Under the 1920 Austrian Constitution, there was a roundabout way of getting a determination of the unconstitutionality of a statute *incidenter*, in a concrete case. Article 139 permits review of questions of the *illegality*—presumably the *ultra vires* sort—of administrative *ordinances* arising in concrete cases. Such cases would arise in the administrative courts. If a court believed that an ordinance involved in a case was illegal, it could halt proceedings and refer the matter to the Constitutional Court under Article 139. If, in the course of deciding on the illegality of an ordinance, it appeared to the Constitutional Court that the statute on which the ordinance was based might be unconstitutional, the Court could, on its own motion, halt its own proceedings to take up the question of the statute's constitutionality, under the last clause of Article 140. *See* Hans Kelsen, Judicial Review of Legislation: A Comparative Study of the Austrian and the American Constitution, 4 Journal of Politics 183, 194–195 (1942).

4. "When the Constitution of 1920 was prepared...other methods for putting into motion the judicial review of legislation were discussed. The first was to grant to every citizen the right to make an application to the Constitutional Court which would have been obliged to pass upon the validity of the statute. It was a kind of *actio popularis* in constitutional questions. The second possibility was to institute at the Constitutional Court the office of a General Prosecutor in charge of the protection of the Constitution. His function would have been to examine all federal and state statutes and to submit those of doubtful constitutionality to the consideration of the Constitutional Court. Neither of these methods was utilized. With respect to the protection of minorities a third possibility may be mentioned, namely the proposal to grant to an outvoted minority the right of contesting the constitutionality of the statute adopted by the majority through application made to the Constitutional Court." Kelsen, *supra* note 3, at 197. The first of these, the *direct appeal*, was adopted by Germany in implementing the Basic Law of 1949. That procedure is taken up in section C, below. The third, allowing the minority in the legislature to protest a statute adopted by

the majority, was adopted by Germany in Article 93 of the Basic Law, and by France in a 1974 amendment to the 1958 constitution. More about that in section D.

5. In Kelsen's vision, the Constitutional Court was to "ensure the smooth running of the constitutional process of government. That function is to resolve any dispute with regard to the boundaries of the constitutional authority between, or repair any usurpation of power by governmental departments or bodies." Mario Patrono, The Protection of Fundamental Rights by Constitutional Courts—A Comparative Perspective, 31 Victoria University of Wellington Law Review 401, 408 (2000). Kelsen apparently was not concerned with the protection of individual rights by the Constitutional Court. In his defense of the Court against Carl Schmitt, Kelsen argued that the Court should avoid the temptation to rely on broad words like "justice" and "public welfare," even if they were found in the constitution. Indeed, the Austrian constitution avoids generalities of that sort. "What is found is an extreme terminological precision, a precision that to a foreign observer might appear to be that of administrative law rather than of Constitutional law." Id. at 404.

6. Kelsen thought the constitutional court especially important for federal systems. This issue arises again in connection with the power of the European Court of Justice to give shape to the developing entity called Europe. The issue is discussed in Chapter Four.

7. The Austrian constitution was amended in 1929. Among other things, the power was granted to the highest judicial court and to the highest administrative courts to halt proceedings and forward explicit questions of constitutionality to the Constitutional Court-review incidenter by way of judicial referral. (This idea reappears in the Italian and German Constitutional Courts after the war. See below, Section B.) There were, perhaps, more important amendments. "The reform of the Austrian Constitution in 1929 was [not least] directed against the Constitutional Court because of a conflict between the latter and the administration. The amendment did not alter the jurisdiction of the Court but provided that its members should no longer be elected by the Parliament but be appointed by the Administration.... The old Court was, in fact, dissolved and replaced by a new one almost all the members of which were party followers of the Administration. This was the beginning of a political evolution which inevitably had to lead to Fascism and was responsible for the fact that the annexation of Austria by the Nazis did not encounter any resistance." Kelsen, supra note 2, at 188. The Court was finally abolished in the Fascist constitution of 1934.

8. The Austrian Constitutional Court's determinations of unconstitutionality were effective prospectively; earlier effects of the degraded law were not affected by the Court's ruling. There was one exception to this: when, after the 1929 amendments, the issue of constitutionality arose in the context of a case

sent up by the highest judicial court or the highest administrative court, the ruling was effective as to the parties to that case. The point was to give the judges of those courts some reason for requesting review. *See* J.A.C. Grant, Judicial Review of Legislation under the Austrian Constitution of 1920, 28 American Political Science Review 670, 675 (1934).

* * *

B. The Italian Constitutional Court and Judicial Referral of Constitutional Questions

GUIDO CALABRESI, TWO FUNCTIONS OF FORMALISM
67 UNIVERSITY OF CHICAGO LAW SCHOOL 479, 481–484 (2000)[4]

The functional approach to law, law as a "doer" of things, continued to remain very important in Italy throughout the Renaissance and into the Enlightenment. Beccaria's discussion of criminal law in the eighteenth century, which talked about *why* criminal law, *what* it did, and therefore what types of criminal punishments were justified, is a perfect example. This attitude continued throughout the early nineteenth century. Thus, the law reforms brought about by the French Revolution and the great Codifications that followed it closely reflected notions of what ends the law ought to serve.

Toward the end of the nineteenth century, however, the codes and law generally became rigidified. German influences, which came to the United States too, though here there were other influences as well, came to be felt. The scholars who followed this approach propounded a notion of law as a science, with a logic of its own. Law came to be viewed as a formal legal system answering to strict rules. And legal scholarship was asked to look not to the functions law served, what it was supposed to do, but only to the internal consistency of the system.

In the United States this approach started breaking down in the first thirty or forty years of the twentieth century. People started realizing that the laws enforced served nineteenth-century social goals, and began asking what kinds of laws, or what kind of law reform, could make the law answer to the social goals of the present, of the twentieth century.

---

4. This publication in the University of Chicago Law Review is the first appearance in print of a lecture delivered in the 1960s.

Perhaps the same would have occurred in Italy, had it not been for the coming of Fascism, and that, in a way, is the essence of our story. To the scholars opposing Fascism, the nineteenth-century self-contained formalistic system became a great weapon. Why? Well, a formal, self-contained, uncriticizable system of law is conservative. It can't be changed. Now, what did it conserve in Italy in the 1920s? What it conserved was the liberal, nineteenth-century political approach, as well as nineteenth-century economic laissez-faire. But, in a time of Fascism, the important thing was that it conserved basic democratic attitudes.

The functionalists, those who wanted law to be responsive to social goals, were in the 1920s necessarily Fascists, because in the 1920s and '30s, the goal of the society, since it was totalitarian and Fascist, could only be stated in terms of Fascist ideology. So it was no accident actually that the great American functionalist, Roscoe Pound, the Dean of the Harvard Law School, who was rather a liberal in many of these things, was a close friend of the most famous of the Italian functionalists, Giorgio Del Vecchio, Dean of the Law School at Rome, and later President of Rome University, who was in fact a Fascist. He was the most responsible of these Fascists, but, more important to Pound, he was one of the few Italian legal scholars who could talk Pound's language and let law answer to social goals.

The anti-Fascist scholars, by contrast, took defense in the fact that law could not be changed. Thus, in a broader sense Italian legal formalism, in its unresponsiveness, sterility if you wish, was itself serving a much greater constitutional function—that of preserving a democratic legal system from Fascist pressures.

Well, as one would expect, the fall of Fascism changed things dramatically. And one might think that it would have totally changed this attitude toward law. For some it did; some of the people who had been traditionalists—formalists in their view of law, like Ascarelli and Calamandrei, and their students—at the very end of Fascism made clear that now the only thing that a formal system of law preserved was nineteenth-century economic ideals. Formalism was no longer necessary to preserve democratic freedoms, and therefore, one must look beyond Fascism to what law could do to order the society in terms of modern-day goals.

For others, however, the identification of functional law—of law which served purposes, of law which did things—with Fascism, remained too strong. And the fear that any law that responded to social ends, even if now the social ends were democratic, might in the future be corruptible to bad social ends, continued to have an influence. In a way, these people said, it is better to have a legal system that cannot change, than to put it in the hands of human beings who are fallible....

Well, of course, this conflict, between those like Ascarelli and Calamandrei, who said it was now time to make law respond to social ends, and the others, who continued to identify functional law with Fascism, couldn't be won totally by one side or the other. In the newer areas of law, the group that took what one might think of as an American approach to law tended to win out. This is seen most dramatically in the establishment of a constitutional court and in the growth of "constitutional law" in Italy.

This was a very real response of a functional sort to Fascism.

* * *

Like the 1920 Austrian Constitution, the postwar Italian Constitution provided for abstract review of national and regional legislation at the behest of government actors. But Italy also provided for judicial referral of constitutional issues, *incidenter*, in concrete cases. Constitutional courts take cases by judicial referral when the ordinary and administrative courts of the land encounter a constitutional issue in the course of a case, stop the proceedings in the case, and refer the constitutional issue to the constitutional court for resolution. Italy's was apparently the first of the new postwar constitutions under which provision was made for cases to be taken by judicial referral. That procedure was provided for in a 1948 statute implementing the constitutional court provisions of the constitution.

THE CONSTITUTION OF ITALY[5]

Article 123. Every Region is to have an organic law which, in harmony with the Constitution, determines its form of government and its fundamental principles of organization and operation. The organic law is to regulate the exercise of the right of initiatives and of referendums under laws and administrative provisions of the Region, and the publication of the laws and the regional regulations.

The organic law is to be approved and modified by the regional Council with a law approved by an absolute majority of its members and adopted in two separate hearings not less than two months apart. That law does not require the signature of the Government Commissioner. The Government of the Republic can raise the question of constitutionality of that law in the Constitutional Court within thirty days of its publication....

Article 127. The Government, if it believes that a regional law exceeds the authority of the Region, may raise the question of constitutionality in the Constitutional Court within sixty days of its publication.

A Region, if it believes that a statute, or an act having the force of a statute, of the [Italian] State or of another Region exceeds its authority, may raise the

---

5. Translation by the editor of provisions from the version of the 1948 Italian Constitution (updated as of May 30, 2003) published online at <http://www.senato.it/funz/cost/home.htm> .

question of constitutionality in the Constitutional Court within sixty days of the publication of the statute or the act having the force of a statute.

Article 134. The Constitutional Court has jurisdiction:

-Over controversies concerning the constitutionality of statutes and acts having the force of statutes, of the State and of the Regions;

-Over conflicts of authority between the departments of government of the State, and over those between the State and the Regions, and between the Regions;

-Over charges brought against the President of the Republic, under the provisions of the Constitution.

Article 136. When the Court declares the unconstitutionality of a statute or of an act having the force of a statute, the provision ceases to be effective the day after the publication of the decision....

* * *

CONSTITUTIONAL STATUTE NUMBER 1 OF 1948
GAZZETTA UFFICIALE NO. 43 (FEBRUARY 20, 1948)[6]

Article 1. The question of the constitutionality of a statute or of any act of the Republic having the force of a statute, observed by the judge *ex officio [sua sponte]* or raised by one of the parties in the course of a trial, and not considered manifestly unfounded by the judge, must be referred to the Constitutional Court for its consideration.

* * *

ANTONIO BALDASSARRE, STRUCTURE AND ORGANIZATION OF THE CONSTITUTIONAL COURT OF ITALY
40 ST. LOUIS UNIVERSITY LAW JOURNAL
649, 649–650, 652–653 (1996)

The Judiciary is organized as a national court system, which is historically patterned on the French legal model and consists of two judicial hierarchies: the ordinary courts and the administrative courts....

Because the judicial personnel of the ordinary court systems are chosen from a career service into which one enters by examination, in order to safe-

---

6. Translation by the editor. The statute is found online at <http://www.giurcost.org/fonti/lcost1-48.htm>.

guard the independence of the Judiciary, the framers of the 1948 Constitution decided to take the control of the judicial careers away from the Minister of Justice (as it has been established in previous regimes) and vest it in an independent organ, the "Superior Council of the Judiciary." This organ, whose chairman is the President of the Republic, is composed of the president and the general prosecutor of the Court of Cassation as *de jure* members and thirty members elected as follows: two-thirds by all the career judges from those belonging to the various categories of the Judiciary and one third by Parliament in joint session from the full professors of law and lawyers with fifteen years practice. As the organ of "self-government of the Judiciary," the Superior Council of the Judiciary has full powers over appointments, assignments, transfers and disciplinary measures in regard to judges.

The hierarchy of the administrative courts is not part of the judicial order and no judge pertaining to that hierarchy is therefore subject to the Superior Council of the Judiciary's authority. Nevertheless, the administrative courts are now staffed by judicial personnel, who, like the regular judges, are drawn from career service and recruited by competitive examination (except for some members of the Council of State, up to fifty percent, which are filled by political appointment, often of senior civil servants). The administrative courts, which are primarily concerned with the legality of the acts of the public administration, consist of the Regional Administrative Courts at the lowest level and the Council of State which has appellate jurisdiction in administrative litigation. Another check against administrative illegality and arbitrariness is given by the Court of Auditors, which is a judicial body having jurisdiction in matters of public accounting and in some other matters specified by law. The administrative courts' independence is guaranteed by the method of entry and the career structure of the judicial personnel, as well as by the constitutional principle to which they perform their functions, subject only to the law, like any other judge.

The Constitutional Court stands outside the Judiciary both ordinary and administrative. The Constitution does not place it in the section dedicated to the Judiciary (Part two, Title IV), but under the separate section regarding the "Constitutional guarantees" (Part two, Title VI), dealing with amendments to the Constitution and constitutional law-making. In other words, the Constitutional Court is a special institution acting in a judicial manner, established to safeguard the Constitution in the event of infringements of fundamental principles by the legislature....

In order to perform all the functions connected with the Constitutional Court's role in guaranteeing the Constitution, the framers of the 1948 constitution established a body composed of fifteen justices: five appointed by the President of the Republic, five elected by two-thirds majority (or a three-fifths majority after the third ballot) in a joint session of Parliament, and five elected by the highest courts, such as three by the Court of Cassation, one by the Council of State, and one by the Court of Auditors....

Since the Constitutional Court began operating in 1956, it has gradually broadened its power and strengthened its role in the Italian legal system. The Court is primarily concerned with judicial review and it therefore produces decisions on [statutory] laws declaring them void, totally or partially. At its very beginning, the major problem lay in the enforceability of the Court's decisions, so that the first President of the Constitutional Court, the former Head of State, Enrico De Nicola, resigned after one year because a Cabinet minister refused to comply with a decision of the Court. However, the battle was won in a short time. Realizing the ignorance of its decisions on the part of civil servants and politicians, the Court began to use its power in a very pervasive way during the 1960s, thanks to widespread support by public opinion. In particular, declaring a [statutory] law partially void, the Court sometimes replaces one or more words in the law with other words in order to make the same statute conform to the Constitution. Furthermore, to overcome the Government's failure to carry out decisions of the Court, when it is requested to, the Court declares as unconstitutional the failure of the legislature to fulfill constitutional duties, and by so doing, it creates new rules, which are complete norms and are automatically effective.

Thanks to the ordinary and administrative courts' loyalty in implementing the Constitutional Court's decisions and to the massive support by public opinion, the Court has strengthened its attitude toward judicial activism. Its strong legitimacy in the public mind is because it provides quasi-legislative decisions acting in a judicial manner with the aim of ensuring an impartial and balanced *implementation* of constitutional values. Further, the more parliamentary and governmental decision-making are ineffective and lacking, the more the Court's decisions rise to the people's expectations.

* * *

WILLIAM J. NARDINI, PASSIVE ACTIVISM AND THE LIMITS OF JUDICIAL SELF-RESTRAINT: LESSONS FOR AMERICA FROM THE ITALIAN CONSTITUTIONAL COURT
30 SETON HALL LAW REVIEW 1, 6–11 (1999)

The Constitutional Court's most important duty is to rule on the compatibility of any national or regional law with the Italian Constitution. The bulk of its workload arrives from lower courts, which must certify constitutional questions on an interlocutory basis as they arise in pending cases. As long as the Constitutional Court agrees that the challenge is relevant to the litigation and not manifestly groundless, it is obliged to rule on the constitutionality of the impugned law. The Court assesses the constitutionality of the challenged law in the abstract, not simply as applied to the parties before the Court. In other words, the Constitutional Court reviews laws; it does not decide cases. This distinction is important, because it means that the Court itself cannot tailor a remedy to fit only the parties before it. That is a job for the lower court on re-mand. This centralized system stands in obvious contrast with the American system of diffuse constitutional review, in which both trial and appellate courts must rule on constitutional issues as they arise. Only as a last resort does the United States Supreme Court address constitutional questions, and it enjoys broad discretion under its certiorari jurisdiction to avoid most of them.

With respect to judicial review, the Constituent Assembly that drew up the Italian constitution in 1948 provided the Constitutional Court with a single power: to nullify unconstitutional laws. Article 136 of the Italian Constitution reads: "When the Court declares the constitutional illegitimacy of a norm of a law or of an act having the force of law, the norm ceases to be effective on the day after the publication of the decision." In short, the Constitutional Court has the power of "negative legislation." The Court can wipe off the books any law that conflicts with the Constitution. These decisions are known as *sentenze di accoglimento*, or judgments that "accept" a constitutional challenge. Only these judgments that strike down a law are technically binding because Article 136 of the Italian Constitution provides only for declarations of *unconstitutionality*. Once the Constitutional Court issues its decision, proceedings resume in the lower court. If the Court has struck down the law, the ordinary judge must proceed to decide the case without reference to the nullified law. The Constitutional Court has no power to review how its decisions are implemented in particular cases.

When the Constitutional Court *declines* to strike down a law, by contrast, its decision lacks formal finding authority because neither the Italian Constitution nor the implementing legislation makes any mention of declarations of *constitutionality*. Technically, then, the Court never actually upholds a law; it merely declines to invalidate it. These judgments refusing to annul a statute, known as *sentenze di rigetto* because they "reject" a challenge to the law, have only one formal consequence: The judge who certified the constitutional question must apply the challenged law in the pending litigation. Beyond that, the decision has only persuasive force, insofar as it indicates how the court is likely to rule on a similar challenge in a future case.

This distinction between binding and nonbinding decisions is quite meaningful in practice because lower courts may ask the Constitutional Court to review a law that it has already declined to strike down. For example, consider the Italian statute that criminalized blasphemy against the "State religion," that is, Catholicism. In a 1973 case, the Court turned away a challenge to that law based on the principle of equality, concluding that the legislature was entitled to take into consideration the religious affiliation of a majority of the Italian population. Because this decision was not binding precedent, however, lower courts were able to continue challenging the blasphemy law in later cases. Accordingly, in 1988, a similar question was referred to the Court. It again rejected the argument that the law was unconstitutional, but noted that recent official recognition of other religions had undercut the rationale for singling out blasphemy against Catholicism as a crime. Reconsidering the issue in 1995 when yet another lower court certified the question for review, the Court finally decided that the blasphemy law was unconstitutional. The Court rested its decision on the equality provision of the Constitution, reasoning that blasphemy must be forbidden either as to all religions, or as to none.

At this point, the Court's judgment was final and binding, and it nullified the blasphemy law....

The drafters of the Italian Constitution thought the power of negative legislation would give the nascent Constitutional Court all the tools it needed to fulfill its most important task: to guard against laws that curtailed civil and political rights. Memories of the fascist era and its clampdowns on political dissent were still fresh. The drafters believed that the Court, as the guardian of individual liberty, needed only the power to strike down oppressive laws. One speaker at the time of the Constituent Assembly described the proposed Court simply as an institutionalization of the popular right of resistance against tyranny, of civil disobedience of unjust laws. By erasing those unjust laws, the theory held, the court could restore liberty and put the constitutional house back in order.

* * *

MARIO COMBA, CONSTITUTIONAL LAW,
IN JEFFREY LENA AND UGO MATTEI, EDS.
INTRODUCTION TO ITALIAN LAW 31, 34, 36–40 (2002)

[The] section of the Constitution [devoted to constitutional rights and duties] follows the classical divide between liberty and welfare rights, though upon deeper analysis this division emerges as deceptively complex. The classical example of this difficult divide is provided by freedom of the press. Is freedom of the press merely a liberty right that provides everyone the right to publish what he or she wishes, or is it also cognizable as a welfare right that binds the State to offer everyone the opportunity to publish his or her thoughts for free? ...

[O]ne has to deal with the problem of the interpretation of constitutional rights: can they be expanded by the Constitutional Court, or is it necessary to adhere to the original meaning of the constitutional wording? In strict legal terms, the question is whether the "inviolable rights of man" mentioned in art. 2 are only those analytically described and protected in the subsequent articles of Part 1 of the Constitution, or whether art. 2 is an "open formula," allowing for the "discovery" of new fundamental rights by the Constitutional Court through a sort of evolutionary process, and assuming that the rights provided for in the Constitution are only those which were felt to be fundamental in 1948.

In its first phase, the Constitutional Court followed an interpretation based on the notion of "original intent" (such was the decision no. 29 of 1962): an extensive construction of constitutional rights was adopted only when strictly necessary and stemming from the text. The case of the right to life, not mentioned in the Constitution but presupposed by all other rights (decision no. 26 of 1979), and the case of sexual identity (decision no. 98 of 1979) provide two examples. But by the early 1970s, the Constitutional Court had recognized a new right, the right to privacy (decision no. 38 of 1973). Even though it did so through the application of the European Convention of Human Rights, this nevertheless constituted an initial step towards an "open" interpretation of art. 2 protecting the "inviolable rights of men," which has led, among other things, to the recognition of a right to housing (decision no. 404 of 1988).

Civil Rights (Negative Rights). Civil rights are also referred to as *diritti negativi*, or "negative rights," because they prohibit the State from regulating or intervening in certain areas of private life. These negative rights are listed in arts. 13 to 28 and are consistent with the tradition of western liberal democracies dating back at least to the French Declaration of Rights of 1789.

Space limitations prevent examination of each constitutionally protected freedom in detail....Because freedom of religion (arts. 19–20) and speech (art. 21) are commonly considered the core liberty rights in a liberal democracy, they deserve a slightly more thorough analysis....

Freedom of religion, which is considered the root of all modern liberties and democracies, is a particularly hot issue in Italy due to Italy's deep link with the Catholic Church. This link is based not only on the cultural and religious history of the Italian Peninsula but also on Italy's 1929 Lateran Treaty with the Holy See. Article 19 provides that "[a]ll shall be entitled to profess their religious beliefs freely in any form, individually or in association with others, to promote them, and to celebrate their rites in public or in private, provided that they are not offensive to public morality." This language represents a significant shift towards a secular state when compared with art. 1 of the *Statuto Albertino* [the previous constitution], which provided that "[t]he Catholic, Apostolic, Roman Religion is the only Religion of the State. Other religions presently existing are tolerated according to the Law."

Freedom of religion is protected in all its facets—the right to promote it, the right to change it, and the right not to participate in religious activities at all. On this last point the Constitutional Court struck down clauses in the Codes of Criminal and Civil Procedure requiring witnesses to swear "before God" before testifying in court (decision no. 117 of 1979).

Article 20, which protects religious associations, is a specification of art. 18, but its wording is constructed only in a negative sense: the religious nature of an association cannot be considered a valid reason for burdening it with any kind of negative provision. The Constitution lacks an explicit provision forbidding any "establishment" of religion, meaning any positive provision *in favor* of a religious association. This is probably due to a need to maintain harmony with arts. 7 and 8 of the Constitution, which allow the State to regulate its relationship with the Catholic Church (art. 7) and with other religions (art. 8) on the basis of special agreements, thus leaving open the possibility of more favorable treatment for religious associations that have signed those agreements.

The interpretation of art. 20 noted above, read together with the wording of art. 33 para. 2 ("The Republic shall lay down general rules for education and shall establish public schools of all kinds and grades. Public and private bodies shall be entitled to establish schools and educational institutions *without financial burdens on the State*") (emphasis added) is at the core of one of the most striking debates presently dividing constitutional lawyers and political parties over freedom of religion in Italy. The question posed is whether or how private schools will be financed (where "private" means not established by the State or any other public body). Because private schools are in large measure Catholic, their public financing is commonly perceived as the funding of Catholic schools. The special language of art. 33 para. 3, "without financial burdens for the State," has been interpreted in various ways. It has been construed by the mainstream of constitutional lawyers to mean that the State cannot spend money to finance private schools. It has also been construed to mean that the State cannot be forced to do so, but can if it wishes....

Article 21 protects the freedom of expression of everyone's thoughts, by any means of communication. It also provides that freedom of the press can be limited only by subsequent seizure, and not by prior restraints like authorization or censorship. These limitations may be imposed only by judicial order and only in cases expressly provided for by the law regulating the press or for offense to public morality.

The jurisprudence of the Constitutional Court has expanded the substantial limitations of freedom of the press based on the principle of balancing constitutional rights. If a law in conflict with the principle of freedom of the press is rooted in another constitutional value and the balance weighs in favor of the latter, that law can be upheld, notwithstanding the limitation imposed on the press. The most common countervailing constitutional value is that of a person's reputation and privacy. Rules set forth by the Italian Supreme Court (*Corte di Cassazione*, decision no. 5259 of 1984) provide that a defamatory statement published in the press is legitimate only if (1) the fact reported is true (and not merely likely to be true), (2) the fact is correctly described, and (3) there is a social interest in knowing the fact (e.g., the defamed person is a "public figure")....

Welfare Rights ("Positive Rights"). The constitutional foundation of social rights can be traced to art. 3 para. 2, which states that "[i]t is the duty of the Republic to remove all economic and social obstacles which, by limiting the freedom and equality of citizens, prevent the full development of the individual and the participation of all workers in the political, economic, and social organization of the country." Welfare rights are thus considered a necessary instrument for the implementation of civil rights. The Republic must remove economic and social obstacles that may prevent citizens from fully enjoying civil rights like liberty and equality and, in particular, the right to participate in those social organizations which are so crucial in the Italian Constitution's idea of what "rights" are.

Following a tradition that dates back to the 1919 Weimar Constitution and to the 1946 Preamble to the French Constitution, the main welfare rights granted by the Italian Constitution are health (art. 32), education (art. 34), and social assistance (art. 38). These are all "expensive rights," in the sense that in order to be granted, they require the appropriation of funds from the State budget.

Health is defined as a fundamental right to be granted to anyone who cannot afford to pay for it. Law no. 833 of 1978 created the National Health Service, providing health assistance to all persons, notwithstanding their wealth. Judicial interpretation of art. 32 expanded it by awarding damages to a person for the violation of his constitutional rights to health, even if actual damage was not proved.

Education must be given to everyone for at least eight years. It is compulsory and free. But the Constitutional Court has declined to broadly interpret art. 34, holding that books and transport are not affected by art. 34 and therefore that the State is not obliged to provide them to everyone for free (decision no. 7 of 1967).

Social assistance is twofold: it consists of social security payments to people who are unable to work or who, for some reason, cannot make a living on their own; it also consists of mandatory insurance for workers in order to pay for their retirement pensions, accidents, healthcare, and so on. The Constitutional Court, while acknowledging statutory discretion of the law in defining the level of social assistance, has stated that a minimum level of assistance must be granted by the State (decision no. 80 of 1971).

The cost of social rights is embedded in these same articles of the Constitution. Article 41 recognizes the freedom of contract, but it also says that such contracts cannot be executed against the common good. Article 42 recognizes private property, but no longer considers it a fundamental right. On the contrary, private property can be limited in consideration of its "social function." Article 43 allows the State to expropriate private enterprises "of primary common interest that concern essential public services or energy sources, or act as monopolies." Private property and freedom of enterprise are thus subordinated to the social interest, an interest mainly represented by the granting of social rights.

Note

1. "Some of the provisions of the Italian Constitution are said to be enforceable (*precettive*) and others to be programmatic (*programmatiche*). Many of the social goals of the Constitution impose a duty upon Parliament to act, but create no legally enforceable right in the individual. Consequently, for example, the right to employment guaranteed by the constitution, has been held not to create the right of unemployed individuals to undertake public works not authorized by competent public organs. Thus, in a sense, the "right" to employment is merely a platform plank elevated to constitutional status. Despite often unwieldy political coalitions, however, the programmatic provisions are slowly being acted upon.... [P]re-constitutional legislation requiring that judges and many other civil servants be male continued to be enforced until 1963, when equal civil-service rights for women were granted by law. This constitutional progress was induced by social and economic progress. Socially, it is now deemed proper for women of all classes to seek employment. Economically, civil-service positions no longer attract a sufficient number of qualified male applicants; industry has made rapid progress and pays higher salaries. The times, in this case, have caught up to the Constitution." Mauro Cappelletti, John Henry Merryman, and Joseph Perillo, The Italian Legal System 56–59 (1967).

1. Abortion

THE CONSTITUTION OF ITALY[7]

Article 31. The Republic supports, economically and otherwise, the formation of the family and the achievement of related ends, with particular regard for large families. It protects motherhood, infancy, and youth, favoring those institutions necessary to such ends.

---

7. Translation by the editor of provisions from the version of the 1948 Italian Constitution (updated as of May 30, 2003) published online at <http://www.senato.it/funz/cost/home.htm> .

Article 32. The Republic protects health as a fundamental right of the individual and a public concern, and guarantees free care to the indigent. No one is obliged to accept a particular medical treatment except where required by legislation. Legislation may not ever violate limits imposed by respect for the human person.

* * *

THE ITALIAN PENAL CODE OF 1930[8]

Article 54. Anyone who has committed an act having been compelled to do so by the necessity of saving himself or others from the present danger of serious bodily harm, a danger not voluntarily caused by him, nor otherwise avoidable, shall not be punishable, provided the act is proportionate to the danger....

Article 546. Whoever causes a woman to miscarry, with her consent, shall be punished by imprisonment for from two to five years. The same punishment shall apply to the woman who has consented to the abortion....

* * *

CARMOSINA ET AL., CORTE CONSTITUZIONALE, DECISION OF FEBRUARY 18, 1975, NO. 27
[1975] 43 RACCOLTA UFFICIALE DELLE SENTENZE E ORDINANZE DELLE CORTE COSTITUZIONALE 201

[Facts and argument:][9]

In the course of a criminal trial against Minella Carmosina and others, the investigating judge of the tribunal of Milan raised the incidental question of the constitutionality of article 546 of the criminal code, in particular that part which provides for the punishment of whoever causes an abortion in a consenting woman, even if it has been ascertained that the pregnancy was dangerous to the physical well-being or the psychological equilibrium of the expectant mother, in the absence of those extremities to which the state of necessity of article 54 speaks. The judge in the case observed that, according to the common legal interpretation, the so-called therapeutic abortion occurs only when an actual and inevitable danger of serious injury to the person is present, and abortion practiced with the medical aim of avoiding aggravation of a preexisting physical deterioration of the woman is sanctioned criminally. That criminalization would, according to the judge's order (*ordinanza*) of referral, conflict with article 31, paragraph 2, and article 32, paragraph 1, of the Con-

---

8. From Edward M. Wise, The Italian Penal Code 18, 183 (1978).

9. Summary of facts and argument from the Italian report of the case, translated by the editor.

stitution, according to which the Republic 'protects motherhood, infancy, and youth, favoring those institutions necessary to such ends,' and 'protects health as a fundamental right of the individual and a public concern.' The declaration of the unconstitutionality of the law would permit many women to have recourse to sanitary operations, instead of resorting to quacks.

The President of the Council of Ministers intervened in the matter, represented and defended by the Advocate General of the State, with a brief filed February 13, 1973, asking [the Court] to declare the question without foundation.

Defending the law, the State observes that the existing penal system, if correctly interpreted, does not conflict with the constitutional provisions invoked, inasmuch as the only exemption available (article 54 of the criminal code) permits abortion (even if the life of the pregnant mother is not in danger) any time that there is in prospect the danger of a serious injury to the health of the woman, an injury proportional to the corresponding seriousness of the abortion. That system is therefore fully compatible with article 31, paragraph 2, of the Constitution which, protecting motherhood and infancy, would permit the woman to carry the child to term and to raise children in the best physical, psychological, and environmental conditions possible; and likewise with article 32 of the Constitution, it would permit the avoidance of any danger of a serious injury to the health of the pregnant woman.

OPINION [10]

The *ordinanza* by the examining judge of the *Tribunale* of Milan raises a serious problem which is the subject of debate and legislative activity in many nations.

This is not the place to retell the legislative history of voluntary abortion as a crime, a history which is linked with the development of religious thought and with the evolution of moral philosophy as well as social, legal, political and demographic doctrines. Not punished in certain epochs, punished in others sometimes lightly, sometimes very severely, voluntary abortion was considered violative of disparate values, such as life, family order, common morality, and the growth of the population.

In the present penal code voluntary abortion is termed "crime against the integrity of the progeny" (book II, title X of the penal code). According to the background materials and the report to the King which accompanied the [1931] code, the value protected is "the demographic interest of the State." The preceding [pre-fascist] code, on the other hand, considered abortion

---

10. English translation published in Mauro Cappelletti and William Cohen, Comparative Constitutional Law: Cases and Materials 612 (1979).

among the "crimes against the person," seemingly a fairer and more correct way of putting it.

The product of conception was from time to time held to be simply a part of the woman's body, the hope of a person, and a thing alive from the beginning, or after a more or less long period of gestation.

The Court holds that the protection of conception—which already figures prominently in the law (articles 320, 339, 687 of the civil code)—has constitutional foundation. Article 31, 2nd paragraph, of the Constitution, expressly imposes the "protection of motherhood" and, more generally, article 2 of the Constitution recognizes and guarantees the inviolable rights of man, among which must be placed, although with the particular characteristics unique to it, the legal situation of the foetus.

What has just been said—which in itself justifies legislative intervention resulting in penal sanctions—must however be accompanied by the further consideration that the constitutionally protected interest of the foetus may conflict with other values which are themselves constitutionally protected. Consequently, the law cannot place a total and absolute priority on the first interest, denying adequate protection to the others. Herein lies the reason why, in the opinion of the Court, the present criminal legislation concerning abortion is unconstitutional.

The *ordinanza* under consideration specifically challenges only that part of article 546 of the penal code, in reference to articles 31 and 32 of the Constitution, which prescribes punishment both for anyone who performs an abortion for a consenting woman, and for the woman herself, "even when it has been ascertained that there are pregnancy dangers to the physical well-being and to the psychological equilibrium of the pregnant woman, but without the occurrence of all of the elements of 'necessity' prescribed in article 54 of the penal code."

Within this scope, the question is well-founded. The condition of the pregnant woman is particular in every way and does not receive adequate protection in a law of general character like article 54 [of the penal code], which requires not only the gravity and the absolute inevitability of harm or of danger, but also its imminence, whereas injury or danger resulting from continuation of a pregnancy may be foreseen, but is not always imminent.

Moreover, the exemption contained in article 54 [of the penal code] is based on the presupposed equivalence of the infringed value to another value which this very infringement was meant to safeguard. Yet, there is no equivalence between the right not only to life but also to health of one who—like the pregnant woman—is already a person, and the safeguard of an embryo which has yet to become a person.

The legislature appropriately prescribed that in some particular cases, in addition to the general cause of exemption from the criminal sanction foreseen by article 54 of the criminal code, other kinds of "necessity" may exempt from the criminal sanction (article 384 of the penal code). Not less worthy of consideration is the unique state of necessity of the pregnant woman in grave danger of compromising her health.

Therefore, it seems inevitable that part of article 546 of the penal code must be declared unconstitutional.

It should be added, however, that the exemption from any punishment of anyone who, in the situation described above, procures the abortion, and of the woman who consents, does not at all exclude the requirement, already under present law, that the operation should be in such a way as to save, when possible, the life of the foetus. But this Court also holds that it is the legislators' obligation to set up the necessary legislative safeguards intended to forbid the procuring of an abortion without careful ascertainment of the reality and gravity of injury or danger which might happen to the mother as the result of the continuation of pregnancy: therefore the lawfulness of abortion must be anchored to a preceding evaluation of the existence of the conditions which justify it. For these reasons the Constitutional Court declares the unconstitutionality of that part of article 546 of the penal code which does not recognize that pregnancy may be interrupted when further development of the gestation could imply injury or danger which is grave, medically ascertained in the manner indicated above, and not otherwise avoidable, for the health of the mother.

2. Capital Punishment

THE CONSTITUTION OF ITALY[11]

Article 2. The Republic recognizes and guarantees the inviolable rights of man, as an individual and in those social groups in which his personality develops, and it requires the fulfillment of inderogable obligations of political, economic, and social solidarity.

Article 27. (1) Criminal responsibility is personal.

(2) The accused is not considered guilty until convicted in a court of law.

(3) Punishment may not consist in treatment contrary to the sensibilities of mankind and should promote the reeducation of the convict.

(4) The death penalty is not permitted, except in cases prescribed by military laws during wartime.

---

11. Translation by the editor of provisions from the version of the 1948 Italian Constitution (updated as of May 30, 2003) published online at <http://www.senato.it/funz/cost/home.htm> .

* * *

ANDREA BIANCHI, INTERNATIONAL DECISION: VENEZIA V. MINISTERO DI GRAZIA E GIUSTIZIA, ITALIAN CONSTITUTIONAL COURT, JUNE 27, 1996, (EDITED BY BERNARD H. OXMAN)

91 AMERICAN JOURNAL OF INTERNATIONAL LAW 727 (1997)

This case concerns a successful challenge before the Italian Constitutional Court to the decree of the Italian Ministry of Justice allowing the extradition to the United States of Pietro Venezia, indicted for capital murder in Dade County, Florida. The Court held that the prohibition on the death penalty in the Italian Constitution is absolute and precludes extradition for a capital offense on the basis of an evaluation by government officials or the courts of the sufficiency of assurances from the requesting state that the death penalty will not be imposed in that case.

Following an unsuccessful appeal to the Court of Cassation and the intervention of the European Commission on Human Rights, Venezia brought a challenge before the Regional Administrative Tribunal regarding the constitutionality of Article 698 of the Italian Code of Criminal Procedure, as well as the domestic statute that incorporated the 1983 U.S.-Italy Extradition Treaty and gave effect to Article IX of the Treaty. Both Article 698 of the Code of Criminal Procedure and Article IX of the Extradition Treaty, on which the extradition decree is based, provide that

> when the offense for which extradition is requested is punishable by death under the laws of the requesting Party, extradition shall be refused, unless the requesting Party provides such assurances as the requested Party considers sufficient that the death penalty shall not be imposed, or, if imposed, shall not be executed.

Venezia argued that the statutes violated several provisions of the Italian Constitution, including Article 2, which protects fundamental human rights, and Article 27(4), which prohibits the death penalty. The administrative tribunal suspended the operation of the extradition decree, stayed the proceedings, and referred the matter to the Constitutional Court.

The Constitutional Court delivered its judgment on June 27, 1996. It held that Article 698 of the Code of Criminal Procedure and the act of incorporation of the U.S.-Italy Extradition Treaty, as far as the incorporation of Article IX is concerned, are unconstitutional. The extradition of a fugitive indicted for a crime for which capital punishment is provided by the law of the requesting state would violate Articles 2 and 27 of the Italian Constitution, regardless of the sufficiency of the assurances provided by the requesting state that the death penalty would not be imposed or, if imposed, would not be executed.

In its judgment, the Court first addressed the issue of the preeminence of the values embodied in Articles 2 and 27 of the Italian Constitution. In particular, the Court stressed that the drafters of the Constitution had deemed the prohibition of the death penalty and inhuman forms of punishment laid down in Article 27 to be derived from the right to life, which is one of the fundamental human rights protected by Article 2. The absolute character of the protection granted by Article 2 to fundamental human rights affects the exercise of powers by all public authorities, including those in charge of international judicial cooperation. The Court had already held in its judgment No. 54 of 1979 that participation by Italy in the enforcement of penalties "which in no hypothesis, and for no kind of crime, would be inflicted in Italy in time of peace" amounts to a violation of the Constitution.

The Court found that the relevant issue in the case at hand was to determine whether the assurances provided by the requesting state could be an appropriate means to protect the values enshrined in the Italian Constitution. The Court held that the very concept of "sufficient assurances" that the death penalty shall not be imposed or executed is constitutionally inadmissible. This is so because the prohibition of Article 27 and its underlying values such as the right to life require absolute protection. Such protection cannot be made to depend on the discretion of public authorities who, on a case-by-case basis, would have to decide whether the assurances given by the requesting state were effective and reliable.

The assurances given by U.S. authorities had been reviewed by both the judiciary and the executive. The Ministry of Justice signed the extradition decree for Venezia after the Court of Cassation rejected his appeal. The Court of Cassation, in its ruling of October 12, 1995, relied on the prior case law of the Constitutional Court and held that, in principle, Article 27 does not prohibit the extradition of fugitives when the offense for which their extradition is requested is punishable in the requesting state by death. The constitutional requirement is met when sufficient assurances are given that the death penalty shall not be inflicted. The Court of Cassation held that the assurances given by the United States Embassy in Rome in its note *verbale* of August 24, 1995, on behalf of the Department of State, that "the death penalty will not be imposed or inflicted upon Mr. Venezia for his offense" were to be deemed appropriate and sufficient for the purpose of Article IX of the Extradition Treaty, as they had emanated from the federal government. This fully satisfied the quest, by the Court of Cassation, for certain, objective and binding parameters concerning the validity of the pledge by the U.S. Government. In these circumstances, in the wording of the Court of Cassation, "the sanction of the death penalty is non-existent or, at least, non-effective."

With respect to the effectiveness of the assurances given by the United States, a letter of the U.S. Department of Justice, forwarded by the U.S. Embassy in Rome to the Italian Ministry of Justice, explained that Article VI of the U.S. Constitution provides that international treaties are the supreme law of the land and, as such, prevail over conflicting state law. This argument, later also used by the Italian Government before the Constitutional Court, was meant to give further strength, in terms of effectiveness, to the assurances presented by the U.S. Government. The Constitutional Court, in its sweeping assertion that the prohibition laid down in Article 27(4) has an absolute character, quickly dismissed the argument based on Article VI of the U.S. Constitution as irrelevant.

The question arises whether the Constitutional Court has ruled out altogether the extradition of fugitives charged with crimes punishable by death under the municipal law of the requesting state. The answer is probably in the negative. The Court held that the discretionary appraisal by the courts and the Ministry of Justice of the assurances given by the requesting state is inadmissible in the Italian legal system. For an offense punishable by death, the extradition treaty with Morocco, for example, requires the requesting state to substitute the penalty provided for the same offense under Italian law. Such a treaty implies no discretion to evaluate the nature and effectiveness of assurances given by the requesting state. Moreover, the petitioner argued that, contrary to the clear obligation undertaken by Morocco in the Extradition Treaty with Italy, no reliable assurance could ever be given by the United States under the terms of its Extradition Treaty with Italy. It is not clear whether the Constitutional Court accepted this reasoning. In terms of international law, the binding nature of an international obligation undertaken by the United States Government by means of the note *verbale* presented by the American Embassy in Rome to the Italian Government can hardly be questioned.

....[G]iven the strong mutual interests underpinning such instruments of international judicial cooperation as extradition treaties, Italy will undertake negotiations to revise not only this Extradition Treaty but others that contain provisions similar to its Article IX. The ruling of the Court seems to compel the choice of different wording for provisions like Article IX. One model, as previously noted, may be found in Article 31 of the 1971 Extradition Treaty between Italy and Morocco....

C. Germany and the Constitutional Appeal

Germany's postwar constitution—its Basic Law—also provided for a constitutional court with the power of abstract review upon the request of government actors, and incidental review in concrete cases, by judicial referral. Germany's important innovation, however, was the constitutional complaint, provision for which was made first by implementing legislation, and then by constitutional amendment in 1969.

DAVID S. CLARK, SELECTION AND ACCOUNTABILITY OF JUDGES IN WEST GERMANY: IMPLEMENTATION OF A *RECHTSSTAAT*

61 SOUTHERN CALIFORNIA LAW REVIEW
1795, 1808–1814 (1988)

The structure of German courts is defined by four characteristics: (1) political division into federal and state courts; (2) appeal through unitary hierarchies; (3) geographical decentralization so that even small towns have civil and criminal courts; and (4) specialization by subject matter.

Figure 1 illustrates these characteristics. The first three features also describe the system of courts in the United States, although the federal state division is almost totally different. In Germany the unitary judicial hierarchies are more thoroughly integrated so that most kinds of litigation may find its way into a federal court of last resort. These federal courts, except for the Federal Constitutional Court (Bundesverfassungsgericht), have almost no original jurisdiction; they primarily hear cases appealed from lower state courts. There is nothing comparable to the United States district courts, which have important concurrent subject matter jurisdiction that would allow the same cases to be heard in state trial courts.

The dominance of federal courts in the German system is accentuated because about 95 percent of the law involved in litigation is federal. The five principal codes—civil, commercial, criminal, civil procedure, and criminal procedure—promulgated by the end of the nineteenth century were nationwide in scope. Federal law established the network of state and national courts and today prescribes the status, duties, and compensation for all judges. The responsibility of state governments is to appoint and promote state judges and to provide for their financial support.

The primary distinguishing feature of the German court structure, however, is its specialization by subject matter. The most important jurisdiction in terms of caseload...is the hierarchy of ordinary courts (*ordentliche Gerichte*) for civil and criminal matters....A court of appeals (*Oberlandesgericht*) is the highest ordinary court maintained by states; its decisions based on purely state law are final and not subject to review. Nevertheless, since national law dominates

State Constitutional Courts

9 courts

Federal Social Security Court

State Courts of Social Security Appeals

11 courts

State Social Security Courts

51 courts

Federal Constitutional Court

Federal Tax Court

State Tax Courts

14 courts

Federal Administrative Court

State Courts of Administrative Appeals

11 courts

State Administrative Courts

35 courts

Federal Labor Court

State Courts of Labor Appeals

12 courts

State Labor Courts

96 courts

● = Professional judge on a panel

○ = Lay judge on a panel

▲ = Appeal

Federal Supreme Court

Federal Patent Court

1 court

State District Courts

Criminal

93 courts

State District Courts

Criminal

551 courts

State Courts of Appeals

20 courts

Civil

Commercial

Civil

Family

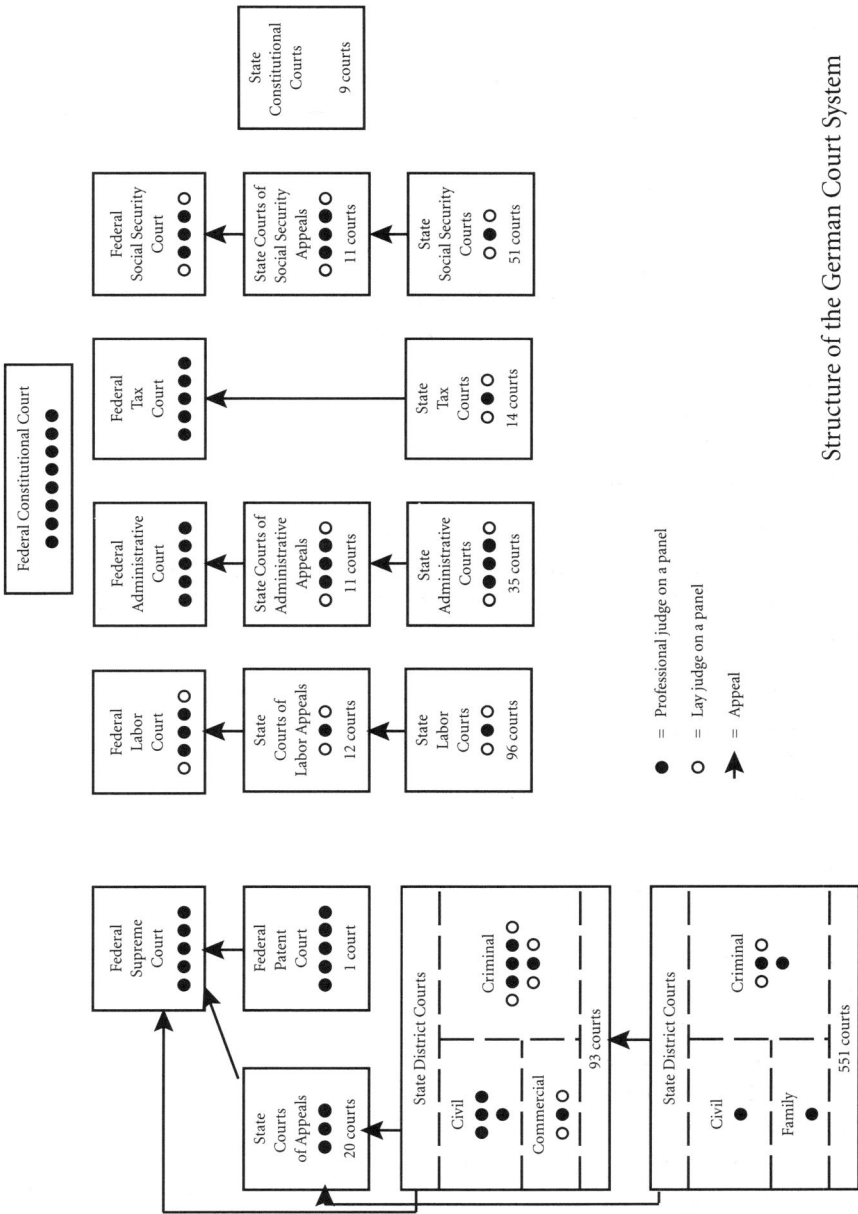

Structure of the German Court System

most fields, appeals are common to the Federal Supreme Court *(Bundes-gerichtshof)*, which also can review decisions made by the Federal Patent Court *(Bundespatentgericht)*....

Besides the *Bundesgerichtshof*, there are five specialized federal courts that are the final arbiters of disputes within their subject matter competence.... Controversies between employees and management, including complaints about a voice in a firm's operation, go to labor courts *(Arbeitsgerichte)*, with de novo appeal to a state court of labor appeals *(Landesarbeitsgericht)* and final appeal on legal issues to the Federal Labor Court *(Bundesarbeitsgericht)*. Lay judges, selected from labor and management groups, vote on a court's decision.

A series of administrative courts adjudicate public law controversies. When one has a complaint about executive action or inaction that has not been satisfactorily resolved with an agency, a lawsuit may be filed in an administrative court *(Verwaltungsgericht)*, appealed de novo to a state court of administrative appeals *(Oberverwaltungsgericht)*, and finally appealed on the legal issues to the Federal Administrative Court *(Bundesverwaltungsgericht)*. A parallel system of courts exists for social insurance and other welfare matters culminating in the Federal Social Security Court *(Bundessozialgericht)* that, like the high labor court, uses two lay judges on its five judge panels. For tax litigation, there is a two tier system with a right of appeal to the Federal Tax Court *(Bundesfinanzgericht)*....

At the apex of this system of courts and jurisdictions in terms of prestige and ultimate authority is the Federal Constitutional Court *(Bundesverfassungs-gericht)*. This Court only adjudicates issues of national constitutional law; it is the guardian of institutional boundaries and the protector of fundamental human rights....Each of the states, except for Berlin and Schleswig-Holstein, also has a constitutional court that hears cases raising purely state constitutional issues.

Note

1. At the 1948 constitutional conference four different models were in play. Start with the German idea of specialized courts: judicial courts, administrative courts, tax courts and so on. At the head of each of these hierarchies, as we have seen, is a federal court: the *Bundesgerichthof*, the *Bundesverwaltungsgericht*, the *Bundesfi-nanzgericht*, and so on. The first question is whether there should be yet another federal court to stand above and review the work of all these specialized courts, a so-called "High Federal Court." If no such high court was added to the scheme, we would have a one-level model of federal courts; with the high court added, it would be a two-level model. The second question, given that there was to be constitutional review, is whether that review would take place in an independent constitutional court, or in one of the federal courts (the High Federal Court, in

the two-level model, one of the other federal courts, probably the Bundes-gerichthof, in the one-level model. Thus there were four possibilities: (1) a two-level model with independent constitutional court; (2) a one-level model with in-dependent constitutional court; (3) a two-level model with judicial review in the High Federal Court; and (4) a one-level model with judicial review in one of the federal courts. The third and fourth were ruled out because constitutional review is inevitably political, and would lead to the political infiltration of the judiciary. "This, however, is incompatible with the required 'absolute purity of the legal sphere.'" Eventually the second of the four possibilities was chosen. *See* Martin Borowski, The Beginnings of Germany's Federal Constitutional Court, 16 Ratio Juris 155, 164–165 (2003).

* * *

THE GERMAN BASIC LAW[12]

Article 93. (1) The Federal Constitutional Court decides:

1. on the interpretation of this Basic Law in the event of disputes concerning the extent of the rights and duties of a highest federal body or of other parties concerned who have been vested with rights of their own by this Basic Law or by rules of procedure of a highest federal body;

2. in case of differences of opinion or doubts on the formal and material compatibility of federal law or State law with this Basic Law, or on the compatibility of State law with other federal law, at the re-quest of the Government, of a State government, or of one third of the House of Representatives [Bundestag] members;

2a. in case of differences of opinion on the compatibility of federal law with Article 72 II [a provision allocating legislative authority be-tween the federal government and the States], at the request of the Senate [Bundesrat], of a State government, or of a State parliament;

3. in case of differences of opinion on the rights and duties of the Federation and the States [Länder], particularly in the execution of fed-eral law by the States [Länder] and in the exercise of federal supervision;

---

12. These provisions of the German Basic Law are taken from the 2002 translation of the International Constitutional Law project, published by Jurisprudentia Verlag, Wuerzburg, and found at <www.jurisprudentia.de>. Where that translation uses the word "Constitution," I have substituted the words "Basic Law," which is still the correct literal translation from the original.

4. on other disputes involving public law, between the Federation and the States [Länder], between different States [Länder] or within a State [Land], unless recourse to another court exists;

4a. on complaints of unconstitutionality, being filed by any person claiming that one of his basic rights or one of his rights under [specified provisions] has been violated by public authority;

4b. on complaints of unconstitutionality filed by communes or associations of communes on the ground that their right to self-government…has been violated by a statute other than a State statute open to complaint to the respective State constitutional court;

5. in the other cases provided for in this Basic Law.

(2) The Federal Constitutional Court also acts in such other cases as are assigned to it by federal legislation.

Article 94. (1) The Federal Constitutional Court consists of federal judges and other members. Half of the members of the Federal Constitutional Court are elected by the House of Representatives [Bundestag] and half by the Senate [Bundesrat]. They may not be members of the House of Representatives [Bundestag], the Senate [Bundesrat], the Government, nor of any of the corresponding bodies of a State [Land].

(2) The constitution and procedure of the Federal Constitutional Court are regulated by a federal statute which specifies in what cases its decisions have the force of law. Such statute may require that all other legal remedies must have been exhausted before a complaint of unconstitutionality can be entered, and may make provision for a special procedure as to admissibility.

Article 100. (1) Where a court considers that a statute on whose validity the court's decision depends is unconstitutional, the proceedings have to be stayed, and a decision has to be obtained from the State court with jurisdiction over constitutional disputes where the constitution of a State [Land] is held to be violated, or from the Federal Constitutional Court where this Basic Law is held to be violated. This also applies where this Basic Law is held to be violated by State law or where a State statute is held to be incompatible with a federal statute.

(2) Where, in the course of litigation, doubt exists whether a rule of public international law is an integral part of federal law and whether such rule directly creates rights and duties for the individual (Article 25), the court obtains a decision from the Federal Constitutional Court.

(3) Where the constitutional court of a State [Land], in interpreting this Basic Law, intends to deviate from a decision of the Federal Constitutional Court or of the constitutional court of another State [Land], it obtains a decision from the Federal Constitutional Court.

* * *

DONALD P. KOMMERS, GERMAN CONSTITUTIONALISM: A PROLEGOMENON

40 EMORY LAW JOURNAL 837, 837, 845–847 (1991)

Germany's written constitution is known as the Basic Law (*Grundgesetz*), so labeled because it was conceived in 1949 as a transitional document pending national unification. The more dignified term "constitution" (*Verfassung*) would be reserved for a governing document applicable to the nation as a whole and designed to last in perpetuity. Yet, over the years, having survived the test of time, the Basic Law has taken on the character of a genuine constitution. In fact, following the bloodless coup of March 18, 1990—the day on which East Germans voted to end Germany's division—a new and freely elected East German government chose to accede to the Federal Republic of Germany within the framework of the Basic Law. This decision and the Unification Treaty signed later by East and West Germany transposed the Basic Law from a temporary instrument of governance for one part of Germany into a document of force and permanence for the entire German nation....The Basic Law marks a radical break with Germany's past. Previous constitutions in the democratic tradition were easily amended and not regarded as binding in all respects. By contrast, the Basic Law is a binding document. As several of its provisions make clear, it controls the entire German legal order, in which respect Articles 1, 19, 20, and 79 are particularly relevant. Article 1, paragraph 3, declares that the fundamental rights listed in the Basic Law, including the inviolable principle of human dignity, "shall bind the legislature, the executive, and the judiciary as directly enforceable law." In reinforcing this provision, Article 20 subjects "legislation" to the "constitutional order" and binds "the executive and the judiciary to law and justice."

In binding executive and judicial authority to "law" (*Gesetz*) and "justice" (*Recht*), the Basic Law's founders were recreating the formal *Rechtsstaat*—a state based on the rule of positive law (i.e., *Gesetz* or *Rechtspositivismus*)—but now, unlike the situation under previous constitutions, positive law is subject to the supra-positive notion of justice or *Recht*, a notion that appears to include unwritten norms of governance. In one of its landmark decisions the Federal Constitutional Court declared that laws "must also conform to unwritten fundamental constitutional principles as well as to the fundamental decisions of the Basic Law, in particular the principles of the rule of law and the social welfare state." In short, the Rechtsstaat, far from being an end in itself, now serves the constitutional state (*Verfassungsstaat*).

Articles 19 and 79 carry the principle of the Basic Law's supremacy even further. Article 19, paragraph 2, bans any law or governmental action that invades "the essential content of [any] basic right." But this is not all. Article 79, paragraph 3—the so-called "eternity clause"—bars any amendment to the Basic Law that would tamper with the principle of federalism or impinge upon "the basic principles laid down in Articles 1 and 20." Article 1, as already noted, sets forth the principle of human dignity and imposes upon the state an affirmative duty "to respect and protect it," whereas Article 20 proclaims the basic principles governing the polity as a whole—i.e., federalism, democracy, republicanism, separation of powers, the rule of law, popular sovereignty, and the social welfare state. The Basic Law's framers believed, quite clearly, that the best way to realize human dignity, now and in the future, is to freeze certain principles of governance into the constitutional structure itself.

Finally, the authority conferred upon the Federal Constitutional Court, as well as upon the judiciary as a whole, assures every person that the Basic Law will prevail over all legal rules or state actions that would subvert or offend it. Accordingly, Article 19, paragraph 4, grants a judicial hearing to any person whose rights the state violates. Indeed, "recourse shall be to the ordinary courts" in the event that some other judicial remedy is not specified by law. In addition, Article 80 (1) helps to insure the protection of the rule of law against the decisions of executive officials. It requires that any law delegating the power to make legally enforceable regulations specify the "content, purpose, and scope of the authorization." The right of administrative judges—and indeed all judges—to refer constitutional questions to the Federal Constitutional Court in cases where they seriously doubt the constitutionality of a statute under which an action is brought backs up this guarantee. Failing these protections, the individuals affected have the option, once their legal remedies have been exhausted, of filing a complaint with the Constitutional Court....

* * *

WOLFGANG ZEIDLER, THE FEDERAL CONSTITUTIONAL COURT OF THE FEDERAL REPUBLIC OF GERMANY: DECISIONS ON THE CONSTITUTIONALITY OF NORMS

62 NOTRE DAME LAW REVIEW 504, 504–511, 519–520 (1987)

1. Categories of Disputes. Nearly all of the Federal Constitutional Court's jurisdiction, covering fourteen types of disputes, is defined in the Basic Law. The most significant areas of review involve abstract and concrete judicial review and constitutional complaints. There are no statutory provisions for a preventative or an advisory judicial review of legal norms. The Law Concerning the Federal Constitutional Court originally provided for the possibility of obtaining advisory opinions. The provision was soon dropped, however, in view of the difficulties that arose in conjunction with the binding nature of such decisions.

Abstract Judicial Review. The federal government, a state government, or one-third of the *Bundestag* may require the Federal Constitutional Court to determine the compatibility of federal or state law with the Basic Law as well as the compatibility of state law with any other federal law....In practice, the party requesting an abstract judicial review is frequently the political opposition in the *Bundestag* or a state government ruled by the opposition party. Commentators critically note that it is only the political disputes which were unsuccessfully resolved in the *Bundestag* that are continued in the courtroom. Because an abstract judicial review forces the Federal Constitutional Court to decide the constitutionality of a legal norm without access to sufficient information regarding the implementation of the norm or its implications, this review procedure has been subject to criticism.

Concrete Judicial Review. Any court that employs a legal norm, upon which its decision depends, must first examine the compatibility of this norm with a higher norm, especially the Basic Law. If a court reaches the conclusion, mere doubts will not suffice, that a law passed by Parliament, a formal law, is not compatible with the Basic Law then the court must discontinue the proceedings and certify the question of compatibility to the Federal Constitutional Court. The Court will only decide whether or not the submitted legal norm is compatible with the Basic Law. Subsequently, a concrete ruling on the matter must be made by the proper specialized court. The exclusive power of the Federal Constitutional Court to proclaim a formal law unconstitutional is intended to foreclose a lower court from bypassing the will of the democratic legislature by means of declaring a law unconstitutional.

Constitutional Complaints. Unlike the other methods of judicial review, a constitutional complaint can be lodged by any person asserting a violation by a public authority of either basic rights or certain other constitutional rights (such as the right to be heard). The constitutional complaint can be lodged against any act of public authority, including measures taken by administrative agencies or court decisions. However, available legal recourse must be exhausted prior to any such review by the Federal Constitutional Court. A constitutional complaint lodged directly against a law or legal norm is only admissible if certain restrictive conditions are met. The complainant himself must above all be presently and directly affected by the law. [In extreme cases, the complainant will be heard even if he has not exhausted available legal recourses. However], the Court increasingly requires that it must be unreasonable for the complainant to first seek relief by following the ordinary recourse of law....

Other Methods of Procedure. The incidental review of legal norms has arisen in the context of judicial disputes between public bodies concerning the respective rights and duties of not only the highest federal bodies but also of parliamentary groups and parties as well. For example, the authority of the Federal Constitutional Court to rule on complaints against decisions by the *Bundestag* pertaining to the validity of elections led to a review of the constitutionality of the Federal Election Laws.

Legislative Omissions. Legislative omissions can also be the subject of a ruling by the Federal Constitutional Court. Such cases pose many problems, including the determination of the unconstitutionality of a present legal condition and appeals to the legislature. Although not intended to be exhaustive, the following examples may serve as illustrative: Constitutionally required mandates, the constitutional duty to regulate by law the basic rights and duties of a certain group of people, the constitutional duty of the legislature to take into consideration changes in actual conditions, as well as disparities which are incompatible with the principle of equality. These examples range from cases involving genuine omission (the legislature does not act in defiance of a specific constitutional mandate) and lack of implementation (the legislature has not acted for a long time) to discrimination (the legislature acted, but failed to consider a certain group)....

2. Subject Matter of the Decisions: Nullity-Compatibility. If the Federal Constitutional Court comes to the conclusion that a law is not compatible with the Basic Law, the Court "nullifies the law." This legal regulation is based on the traditional German doctrine which states that a norm which violates a higher norm is void *eo ipso* and *ex tunc.* The law also provides the Federal Constitutional Court with the opportunity to nullify particular provisions of the same law as long as these are incompatible with the constitution for the same reasons. The Law Concerning the Federal Constitutional Court already restricts the effects of the nullity of an unconstitutional norm. For example, a new trial is permissible in a criminal case if the final decision was based on an unconstitutional legal norm. In all other cases, however, incontestable decisions are sustained although they can no longer be enforced.

In the event the Federal Constitutional Court determines that the law subject to its review is compatible with the Basic Law, the Court proclaims the constitutionality of the contested legal regulation. Even in the context of constitutional complaint procedures, the Federal Constitutional Court may hold that a law is constitutional. Frequently, a determination of constitutionality by the Court is stated only in the reasons which refute a constitutional complaint.

Partial Nullity. Rarely is there a need for the complete nullification of a law or other legal norm. Nullification would be proper, however, when the authority to decree a law is completely absent from the public body (for example, the Federal Republic or a state) and/or if the remaining, constitutionally compatible provisions no longer possess any individual significance. Such would be the situation where the unconstitutional provision is so intimately connected with the entire law that it forms a comprehensive, inseparable unit which cannot be divided into individual components without losing its meaning and its justification.

Even an individual legal provision must not always be entirely proclaimed unconstitutional and void. Restrictions on judicial review may result from the issue of constitutional procedures. In the context of concrete judicial review, the limited range of the introduced issues — which are often more clearly specified by the Federal Constitutional Court — restricts the Court's ability to nullify an entire law. The Federal Constitutional Court may arrive at the conclusion that only part of a linguistically divisible provision is unconstitutional.

Finally, partial nullity may be assumed in the case of a requirement not specifically mentioned in a particular law, or with respect to a particular application of the law. In 1982, for example, the Federal Constitutional Court nullified legal provisions which conditioned "admission to medical school for the purpose of studying medicine as a second academic major on the requirement that the study of medicine meaningfully compliment the first academic major, even in the case of applicants who had begun their studies prior to the 1974–75 winter semester in the belief that the possibility for such a second academic major existed."

Interpretations which Conform with the Constitution. Ever since the Federal Constitutional Court was impaneled, it practiced interpretations which conformed to the Basic Law. Such interpretations are functionally similar to partial nullification of a norm; they specifically avoid the declaration of nullity. By engaging in this type of interpretation, the legislature is spared from having the Federal Constitutional Court pronounce the unconstitutionality of a provision — an act which is often excessively valued by the political public.

If the wording of a law permits several interpretations, then the Federal Constitutional Court must choose the one which produces results harmonious with the Basic Law. There is no room for any interpretation that would lead to an unconstitutional result. The constitutionally acceptable interpretation also must not conflict with the wording and the clearly expressed intent of the legislature. Accordingly, the normative content of the law to be interpreted must not be determined anew and the essential legislative goals must not be missed in the process. Admittedly, this applies only to those basic principles, determinations of value and regulative purpose, which are recognizably expressed by the law.

The statements by legislative committees or individual members of the legislative bodies concerning the significance of a normative component or concept (or scope of an individual provision), its handling, and result do not constitute binding guidelines for the courts, no matter how illuminating they might be in determining meaning. The existence of adverse legislative history, however, occasionally proves problematic. In 1980, such a quandary resulted in a fairly rare decision by the plenum session of the Federal Constitutional Court[13]. Rather briefly, the full court found that restricting the language of a statutory provision which revised the legal recourse to the Federal High Court of Justice in its function in civil matters as a Court of Appeals was proper, in light of the de minimus restriction on legislative intent.

In another decision, the Federal Constitutional Court interpreted as constitutionally conforming, a provision in the tax laws which afforded unwed mothers and foster parents certain special benefits. The Court concluded that fathers of illegitimate children—who are not specifically covered by the wording of the law—could, in certain circumstances, be considered "foster parents," in view of the constitutional requirement of equality of illegitimate children. The Court premised its decision on the assumption that the legislature would have augmented the provision accordingly if it had recognized the omission.

By comparison, the Federal Constitutional Court rejected as an interpretation which did not conform with the constitution, a National Socialist administrative order—that is, an order that reflected a totalitarian administrative philosophy—which did not meet the constitutional requirement of definiteness. It was deemed impossible to reinterpret such a vague regulation without simultaneously examining whether the subsequent effect agreed at all with the intentions of the democratic legislature. A constitutionally conforming interpretation would have essentially redefined the normative content, and to do so would not have been within the purview of the Federal Constitutional Court. Indeed, by employing a constitutionally acceptable interpretation one must not disregard the danger of shouldering the legislature with results it did not intend.

Equally, and only slightly less problematical, is the functional relationship between the Federal Constitutional Court and the specialized courts, especially the highest. In certain instances, the Federal Constitutional Court may prescribe a constitutionally conforming interpretation of a provision which a specialized court did not support in an earlier decision despite careful deliberations. Furthermore, the Federal Constitutional Court's specific mission authorizes it only to proclaim that a certain interpretation is incompatible with the Basic Law. To do so, the Court must demonstrate that an interpretation which is different from the one held unconstitutional is indeed possible. The Court, however, must leave undecided whether only the speci-

---

13. The Federal Constitutional Court is divided into two chambers, called senates, which have exclusive memberships and exclusive jurisdiction over certain constitutional cases. The plenum, an en banc session of the Court, meets only to address matters concerning the internal administration of the court as a whole, the disputes arising out of the wish of one senate to depart from a formal ruling by the other, or the transfer of jurisdiction from one senate to another. [Footnote in original text.]

fied interpretation is possible or whether there is the possibility for additional constitutional interpretations. Also, the Federal Constitutional Court is not authorized to decide for the specialized courts whether only one of several differing interpretations is legitimate.

Recent Variations in the Decisions. The Federal Constitutional Court went beyond these *quasi*-classic decision techniques by creating an additional set of instruments which make it possible to avoid the often undesirable *ex tunc* effect of nullity without having to accept for any period of time a condition which would be considered unconstitutional. For example, the Court has proclaimed a law or legal situation not "yet" unconstitutional, and therefore still tolerable, while appealing to the legislature for change, possibly within a specified period of time. In other circumstances, the Court merely determined that a law was incompatible with the Basic Law but not simultaneously void....

4. Binding Nature of the Decisions: Res Judicata and Legal Force. Like the decisions of any other court of law those of the Federal Constitutional Court also become res judicata. Res judicata applies only to the holding and not to the reasoning employed by the Court, even though such reasoning may be the basis for determining the meaning of the holding. An earlier decision will have res judicata effect on an issue in a subsequent proceeding only if the matter in dispute is the same and not merely when only essential legal questions are identical. The principle of res judicata not only has an effect *inter pares* but also binds the Federal Constitutional Court itself.

The legal force of a decision by the Court may be either negatively nullifying, in the case where incompatible provisions are voided, or positively determining, in the case where the Court rules on the compatibility of a law with the Basic Law. The Minister of Justice is obligated to publish the holding in the Federal Law Gazette. This also applies to cases where a specific declaration concerning the constitutionality of a norm has been made within the context of a constitutional complaint. Thus the Court determines simultaneously for itself the possible legal force of its decisions.

Binding Nature. The Law Concerning the Federal Constitutional Court explicitly requires that the decisions of the Court bind the constitutional bodies of the Federal Republic and the Federal states, as well as all courts and public authorities. In an early decision, for example, the Court held that the principles governing the allocation of air time by radio and television stations for political campaigns are binding on all stations (not merely those involved in the original lawsuit) and with respect to all political parties. Once the Court declares a norm unconstitutional, the legislature is prevented from repromulgating the same provision.

The binding effect extends to the holding and its essential reasoning but not to every single statement made by the Court in its often comprehensive explanations. Accordingly, canonizing individual sentences, possibly taken out-of-context, from the decisions of the Federal Constitutional Court is inappropriate. In one instance, however, the Court stipulated that all the arguments of a particular opinion were essential. The case involved the Basic Treaty with the German Democratic Republic and was strongly criticized in legal literature. Since then, the Court has refrained from making such stipulations....

Is the Federal Constitutional Court Bound by Its Own Decisions? The decisions of the Federal Constitutional Court are not binding on the Court itself. The Court has explicitly declared that it is permitted to dismiss legal opinions stated in earlier decisions, whether essential to the earlier decision or not. Realistically, however, the Court departs from its own precedent only with great reluctance. Because of its unique ability to establish binding interpretations of the Basic Law, the Federal Constitutional Court, as the highest court, must be authorized to correct legal opinions which are later found inappropriate, excessively far reaching, or based on false precepts. In accord with this authority, the Court recently corrected fixed guidelines for building development plans which were too general. After a detailed analysis of the res judicata effect in each individual case, the Court arrived at a more differentiating solution, explicitly stating that it would no longer adhere to earlier case law.

* * *

DONALD P. KOMMERS, GERMAN CONSTITUTIONALISM: A PROLEGOMENON
40 EMORY LAW JOURNAL 837, 855–862 (1991)

The Primacy of Rights. The West German Basic Law takes rights seriously. It leads off by proclaiming that "[t]he dignity of man is inviolable" and then, in the very next sentence, commands the state to respect and protect it (Article 1). All of the ensuing rights enumerated in the remaining eighteen articles of the Bill of Rights are designed to actualize this crowning principle of human dignity. Human dignity, as the Constitutional Court repeatedly emphasizes, is the highest value of the Basic Law, the ultimate basis of the constitutional order, and the foundation of guaranteed rights. All other rights proceed in logical succession, moving from the general to the particular. Article 2 secures to every person "the right to the free development of his or her personality" and the right to personal inviolability. Article 3 contains a general equality clause together with provisions forbidding discrimination based on gender, race, national origin, language, religion, and political affiliation. The remaining articles guarantee all the rights and liberties commonly associated with liberal constitutionalism. These include the freedoms of religion, speech, assembly, association, and movement as well as the rights to property, privacy, and petition. Conscientious objection to military service and the right to choose a trade or occupation round out this list of fundamental rights.

The Bill of Rights, however, includes more than these personal liberties. It also protects communal interests such as marriage and the family and the right of parents to decide whether their children shall receive religious instruction in public schools. In sharp contrast to the United States Constitution, the German Bill of Rights speaks of duties and responsibilities as well as rights. Article 6, for example, tells parents that it is their "natural right" and "duty" to care for their children while simultaneously instructing the "national community" to "watch over their endeavors in this respect." Article 14 declares that the right to property "imposes duties" and should "serve the public weal." Under Article 12a, finally, all men eighteen years or older are subject to military service or, if a male citizen refuses induction because of conscience, he may be required to serve society in an alternative civilian capacity for a period equal to the time he would have spent in the military. While Article 20 is not part of the Bill of Rights it nevertheless incorporates the concept of the social welfare state in terms of which basic rights are often interpreted. German constitution-makers thus believed—and have always believed—that any realization of human dignity implies a fusion of individual rights and social responsibilities.

A close look at the Basic Law discloses an interesting hierarchy of rights. Some are cast in unqualified language, others in conditional language. In actuality, however, no right under the Constitution is absolute. A right framed in unconditional language may conflict with another express constitutional right in which case the task of the Court is to apply a balancing test consistent with the interpretive principle of concordance. The broad principle of human dignity, for example, which under the explicit terms of Article 1 (1) binds all state authority, may also serve to limit the exercise of a so-called unconditional right.

In addition, all rights, including those cast in more absolute terms, are limited by the architectonic political principle that informs the Basic Law as a whole, namely, the "free democratic basic order."...[T]his normative view of constitutionalism—contrary to the theory of the Weimar Constitution—implies a sturdy defense of certain principles of political obligation. And so, as Article 5 (3) declares, "[a]rt and science, research and teaching, shall be free," but "[f]reedom of teaching shall not absolve [one] from loyalty to the Constitution." The right to association, couched in otherwise unconditional terms, is similarly restricted to activities consistent with the constitutional order.

All other rights are conditional, and they fall into three categories. First are those rights which can only be limited by the terms of the Basic Law itself. These rights, like those framed in unconditional terms, are the object of the Constitutional Court's special vigilance. The state has the burden of showing that any limitation upon such rights falls within the explicit exceptions mentioned in the Constitution, examples of which may be drawn from the rights of speech and personality. Article 5 (2) declares that speech rights "are limited... by the...provisions of law for the protection of youth and by the right to the inviolability of [one's] personal honor," just as Article 2 secures the general right to the development of one's personality so long as "he [or she] does not violate the rights of others or offend the constitutional order or the moral code." These reservation clauses also have the distinctive merit of providing the Federal Constitutional Court with interpretive guidelines.

The second category of conditional rights are those whose contours are to be defined by law. For example, the right to life and to the inviolability of one's person, under the terms of Article 2 (1), "may only be encroached upon pursuant to a law." Numerous other rights (e.g., the rights to privacy of posts and telecommunications, open-air assemblies, practice of a trade, conscientious objection to military service, inviolability of the home, and property) can only be limited by means of a special legislative enactment. Here too the Basic Law seeks to circumscribe legislative power, for under Article 19 (1), any basic right "restricted pursuant to a law...must apply generally...and name the basic right, indicating the Article concerned." Finally, certain rights may be restricted by the "general laws." The reference here is to the general provisions of the civil and criminal code. No specific legislation is required here to restrict the applicable right, but in the case of speech rights, for example, they "are limited by provisions of the general laws" (e.g., libel and slander), just as the right to association—to take another example—is limited by general criminal law.

An Objective Order of Values. In its search for constitutional first principles, the Constitutional Court has seen fit, as noted earlier, to interpret the Basic Law in terms of its overall structural unity. Perhaps "ideological" unity would be the more accurate term here, for the Constitutional Court envisions the Basic Law as a unified structure of substantive values. The centerpiece of this interpretive strategy is the concept of an "objective order of values," a concept that derives from the gloss the Federal Constitutional Court has put on the text of the Basic Law. According to this concept, the Constitution incorporates the "basic value decisions" of the founding fathers, the most basic of which is their choice of a free democratic basic order—i.e., a liberal, representative, federal, parliamentary democracy—buttressed and reinforced by basic rights and liberties. These basic values are objective because they are said to have an independent reality under the Constitution, imposing upon all organs of government an affirmative duty to see that they are realized in practice....Value theory is controversial among constitutional scholars because the enforcement of a basic value may curtail the exercise of a basic right. Professor Ernst-Wolfgang Böchenförde, who is also a Justice of the Federal Constitutional Court, has written:

> The particular liberty enshrined in the basic right is qualified in a special way by relating all basic rights to values. As a result of this value dimension it is aimed at realising and fulfilling the value expressed in and through such rights. This makes possible and justifies the drawing of a legally relevant distinction between uses of liberty that realise and

uses that jeopardise that value. The particular liberty is thus qualified and made subject to the logic of fluctuating values. In the event, therefore, of a conflict between a subjective right and an objective value, the latter is often likely to trump the former.

The Justices of the Federal Constitutional Court have not only postulated an objective order of values; they have also arranged these values in a hierarchical order crowned by the principle of human dignity. It was precisely this principle of human dignity that prompted the Court in 1975 to strike down a liberalized abortion statute. Not all of the justices—or constitutional scholars—are comfortable with the value theory of constitutional interpretation....Wolfgang Zeidler, a former President of the Federal Constitutional Court, strongly criticized the Court's tendency "to superimpose 'a higher order of values' on the positive constitutional order." In his opinion, the notion of a basic value order—a "tyranny of values" according to some commentators—is often used as a tool to incorporate religious and philosophical views into the meaning of the Constitution. In any event, by advancing the notion of an objective value order, the Court seemed clearly to reject the legal positivism (*Rechtspositivismus*) and moral relativism presumed to have been at the basis of the Weimar constitutional order. That the Basic Law is a value-oriented—not a value-neutral—constitution is a familiar refrain in the Constitutional Court's case law. Early on its jurisprudence the Court spoke of certain "unwritten" or "supra-positive" norms that presumably govern the entire constitutional order. Justices intellectually rooted in the Christian natural law tradition adhered to this view. Today the Court is more inclined to speak of the value system inherent in the Basic Law itself. The objective values of the Basic Law define a way of life to which the German people, as a nation, are committed. The task of the Court in adjudicating constitutional controversies is one of integrating these values into the common culture and common conscientiousness of the German people. The task is no less than creating and maintaining a nation of shared values.

Negative and Positive Rights. German constitutional theory posits the dual character of basic rights. These rights are both negative and positive. A negative right is a subjective right to liberty. It protects the individual against the state, vindicating his right to freedom and personal autonomy. A positive right, on the other hand, represents a claim that the individual has on the state. In the German understanding positive rights embrace not only a right to certain social needs but also a right to the effective realization of personal freedoms and autonomy. Yet personal freedom and autonomy are limited by the requirements of human dignity—which the state is duty-bound to respect—and the common good, a principle found to exist in the Basic Law's "social state" clause (*Sozialstaatsprinzip*).

Although closely related, a positive right is not the same as an objective value. An objective value of the Basic Law addresses itself exclusively to the state. The state must create and maintain an environment conducive to the realization of basic values. In short, objective values speak to the organization of the state as a whole. A positive right, on the other hand, is an individual right or, perhaps more accurately, an entitlement that the individual may claim from the state. Reference to the positivity of rights implicates not society as a whole but the particular situation of an individual, an individual who may need the state's help to enjoy a basic right effectively such as, for example, equality. In this respect, the notion of a right under the Basic Law is broader than the concept of a right under the United States Constitution. A right in the German constitutionalist view is not only the right to be left alone, free of state interference, but the right to some form of state assistance in the enjoyment of the right. A positive right, however, cannot be made the object of a constitutional complaint. Here Parliament enjoys broad discretion, given the limited resources of the states, to determine the degree of assistance that individuals shall receive from the state.

* * *

1. Freedom of Speech and the Constitutional Complaint: The Lueth Boycott Case

THE GERMAN BASIC LAW (1949)[14]

Article 5. (1) Everyone has the right to freely express and disseminate his opinion in speech, writing, and pictures, and to freely inform himself from generally accessible sources. Freedom of the press and freedom of reporting by means of broadcast and film are guaranteed. There may be no censorship.

(2) These rights are subject to limitations in the provisions of general statutes, the statutory provisions for the protection of the youth and in the right to personal honor....

* * *

THE GERMAN CIVIL CODE[15]

§826 (1) Whoever intentionally causes injury to another person in a manner contrary to good morals has the duty of compensating for that injury.

* * *

---

14. These provisions of the German Basic Law are taken from the 2002 translation of the International Constitutional Law project, published by Jurisprudentia Verlag, Wuerzburg, and found at <www.jurisprudentia.de>.

15. Translated at page 349 in Peter Quint, Free Speech and Private Law in German Constitutional Theory, below.

PETER E. QUINT, FREE SPEECH AND PRIVATE LAW IN GERMAN CONSTITUTIONAL THEORY
48 MARYLAND LAW REVIEW 247, 252–264, 281–286 (1989)

The first major free speech case decided under the Basic Law of 1949 was a dispute between Erich Lueth, a minor official in Hamburg, and Veit Harlan, a former director of racist films under the Nazis.[16] The factual roots of the dispute lay deep in the history of the Nazi period.

During World War II Veit Harlan had written and directed the notorious anti-Semitic film "The Jew Suess," produced under the general direction of Nazi propaganda minister Josef Goebbels. In 1950, after a period of retirement, Harlan directed his first post-war movie, "Immortal Beloved." Incensed by the re-emergence of this director of the Nazi period, Lueth called for a boycott of Harlan's new film. Lueth believed that a boycott would demonstrate to the world that the new German cinema was not to be identified with this anti-Semitic director.

Suing in a state court, the producer and distributor of "Immortal Beloved" sought an injunction against Lueth, prohibiting him from issuing further calls for a boycott of the film. The plaintiffs sued under section 826 of the German Civil Code (BGB)[17]—one of the famous 'general clauses' of the Code—which provides a remedy against a person who 'intentionally causes injury to another person in a manner contrary to good morals.' Finding that Lueth's statements injured the plaintiffs' business in violation of section 826, the state court issued an injunction prohibiting Lueth from making further calls for a boycott of Harlan's film.

In response, Lueth filed a 'constitutional complaint' in the Federal Constitutional Court—a procedural method through which a litigant can challenge a lower court's decision on constitutional grounds. Lueth claimed that the injunction against his further expression violated article 5, section 1 of the Basic Law, which gives every person 'the right freely to express and disseminate his opinion, orally, in writing, and in pictures.' In a ground-breaking opinion, the Constitutional Court held that Lueth's speech was indeed protected by the guarantees of article 5 and required that the film producers' complaint be dismissed. This result could only be reached, however, after a complicated and difficult doctrinal journey....

In considering the general question of whether constitutional rights are applicable in private law, the Constitutional Court...remarked that it was confronted with two 'extreme' positions. The first was the view...that public and

---

16. 7 BVerfGE 198, 223 (1958).
17. "BGB" abbreviates "Burgerlichesgesetzbuch", which translated literally means "civil statute book," or in other words the Civil Code.

private law are two distinct systems and therefore that public law in general and constitutional law in particular have no bearing on private law.... Because all jurists agreed that constitutional law is a form of public law, it was argued that this form of public law—like any other form of public law—has no bearing on the separate, distinct and autonomous system of private law. Indeed some went so far as to suggest that because constitutional rights were historically directed only against the state, the Parliamentary Council that was convened to draft the Basic Law in 1948 was not even authorized to affect the traditional relationships of private law....

The second 'extreme' view was a diametrically opposed position. Before *Lueth*, a number of scholars had advanced the view that the most important basic rights are not only directed against the state, but are also fully and 'directly' applicable among individuals in private legal relationships. The implication of this theory was that certain constitutional rights should ordinarily be binding on individuals and private groups in approximately the same manner and to the same extent as they are applicable against the government.

In the *Lueth* case the Court took notice of both of these 'extreme' positions and then made clear that it was not prepared to accept either of them fully. Rather, the Court adopted an intermediate theory which permitted a degree—but only a degree—of constitutional control of the relations of private law. The Court began by acknowledging that the basic rights of individuals do indeed apply most fully against the power of the state exercised as 'public law.' This conclusion was implied by the history of the concept of basic rights: certainly after the gruesome events of the Nazi period it was clear that excessive governmental power represented the basic threat to those rights. Nonetheless, the Court also emphasized that the Basic Law establishes an 'objective ordering of values,' and indicated that the introduction of this concept in constitutional doctrine represents a fundamental strengthening of the effectiveness of the basic rights and a certain extension of those rights beyond their traditional realm.

The concept of an 'objective' ordering of values—outlined in the *Lueth* case— was central to the Court's decision in that case and has come to be a central concept in German constitutional doctrine. Generally, in German legal theory, an 'objective' value is a value that is applicable in general and in the abstract, independently of any specified relationship—in contrast with a 'subjective' right, which is the right of a specified individual to some legal result against a specific party. In effect, by stating that the basic rights establish an 'objective' ordering of values, the Court was stating that those values are so important that they must exist apart from any specified legal relationship—that is, in this context, apart from any specific relationship between the individual and the state. These values are not only specified rights of individuals but are also part of the general legal order, benefitting not only individuals who may be in a certain relationship with the state but possessing relevance for all legal relationships....

Moreover, if basic rights are seen as 'objective' values essential for the public good, it is reasonable to suppose that rights may be impaired even under circumstances in which they have not been abridged by the state. If a citizen is guaranteed certain rights of speech, for example, and external pressure is applied that makes it impossible as a practical matter to exercise those rights, it may make little difference as far as the abstract rights are concerned whether that pressure comes from the state or from some other source—for example, from an authoritarian private employer. If the goal of the 'objective' value is to encourage the optimal amount of speech for the good of society, that value can be significantly impaired by repression of speech whether the repression comes from the state or from private individuals or groups. Because the basic rights establish 'objective' value, then, those rights must apply not only against the state exercising its authority under public law; according to the Constitutional Court, basic rights must also have an effect on the rules of private law which regulate legal relations among individuals.

Yet even though the Court acknowledged that the constitution must play a role in private law, it also made clear that constitutional rights do not ordinarily have the same impact in private law disputes as when those rights are asserted against the state in public law controversies. In reaching this conclusion the Court adopted what has come to be known as the doctrine of the 'indirect' effect of constitutional values on private legal relations .... In a public law action between an individual and the state, a constitutional right can directly override an otherwise applicable rule of public law. In private law disputes between individuals, in contrast, constitutional rights were said to 'influence' rules of civil law rather than actually to override them....

Under the 'indirect' theory of *Lueth*, therefore, private law values retain considerable potency even when confronted by a value of constitutional law. This position may reflect the strength of the private law tradition and the persistence of the view that there should be an area of private legal relations that remains free from substantial government control. In this manner the Court may assume that the values of private law make their own important contribution to the autonomy of the individual—and to the public good—and therefore should remain in effect, to some extent at least, even when confronted by the countervailing objective and public values of constitutional law. Consequently, the Court in *Lueth* called for an accommodation of public and private law values when a constitutional value is threatened in a dispute of private law. The Court's 'indirect' theory therefore imposes an obligation on the lower courts to use their powers creatively to alter or adapt a rule of the civil law when a constitutional value is implicated. A substantial tension remains, however, between the force of the private law values and the influence of constitutional norms....

The Court's discussion of the relationship between free speech and private law in *Lueth* could not conclude simply with a finding that constitutional rights 'influence' private law. Language contained in article 5, section 2 of the Basic Law—which qualifies the rights of free expression of opinion contained in section 1—raised a more specific argument that rights of free expression do not as a practical matter apply in disputes of private law. Article 5, section 2 states that the speech rights of section 1—the rights relied on in *Lueth*—'find their limits in the rules of the general laws....'The purpose of this provision clearly was to permit the legislature to place some limits on the expression of opinion, and the basic question was whether section 826 of the Civil Code—and, more generally, all of the rules of private law—are 'general laws' which limit the basic rights of article 5, section 1. If the rules of private law were found to be 'general laws' in this sense, it might follow that the basic right of free expression of opinion would never be applicable to disputes of private law because the 'general law' embodied in the rule of private law—for example, the private law doctrine prohibiting certain boycotts—would always limit the basic right of speech from the outset.

· Perhaps foreseeing this possibility, Lueth argued that in cases involving speech that contributes to public political life, the 'general laws' of article 5, section 2, should include rules of public law only....

In the second part of the *Lueth* opinion, the Constitutional Court rejected this argument without retreating to the position that under article 5, section 2, private law values always prevail over rights of free speech. The Court's first task was to determine which laws are 'general laws,' which would be permitted to limit free expression. Drawing on the interpretation of the same phrase in the Weimar Constitution, the Court asserted that 'general laws' are any laws

> that do not prohibit an opinion as such [and] that are not directed against the expression of opinion as such; [rather, they are laws that] serve to protect a legal value that can be protected without consideration of a particular opinion, [that is, they serve] to protect a community value that has priority over the free expression of opinion.

Under a definition of such breadth, rules of private law certainly could be 'general laws,' and private law rules protecting important personal interests therefore might limit speech under article 5, section 2.

The Court thus found that the basic speech rights of article 5, section 1, can be limited by rules of private law under section 2. This conclusion did not mean, however, that the general rules of private law would always prevail over expressions of opinion. As discussed above, all aspects of the legal order— even the rules of 'private law'—are to be influenced by 'objective' constitutional values. Moreover, according to the Court, this influence is particularly important in the case of the rights of free speech because speech is 'absolutely fundamental'...in a liberal constitutional order. As a result, even general laws that may have the effect of limiting speech—whether they are rules of private law or of public law—must also be influenced by basic constitutional values, including the basic value of free speech itself. Thus, in determining the extent of the limitation of speech effected by the general laws, those laws must themselves be interpreted in light of the basic right of free speech, so that the special values of expression are preserved. In other words, the basic right of free expression can be limited by legislation under article 5, section 2, but because the legislature and the judges are themselves bound by the basic right, any general laws that are enacted and interpreted must in turn be limited by that basic right. As the Court put it, the basic right and the general laws qualify each other through the exercise of a 'reciprocal effect' (Wechselwirkung). In light of this 'reciprocal effect,' the only way in which a result can be reached in any specific case is by deciding whether the values embodied in the general laws or the values embodied in the basic right are more weighty under the circumstances and therefore have the more powerful qualifying effect in the particular case. Thus the Court concluded that an individual balancing of the values of the basic right against the values of the general law must be undertaken in each case under article 5, sections 1 and 2.…

In the final pages of the opinion, the Court undertook the required balancing. Acknowledging that there is a 'presumption' in favor of free expression, the Court remarked that speech should be given heightened protection to the extent that it furthers a discussion of public matters rather than the purely private or economic interests of the individual speaker. The Court also reiterated the point that its task was to interpret the phrase 'contrary to good morals' in section 826 of the BGB in light of the constitutional influence exerted by article 5, section 1 of the Basic Law—an influence that the Court found to be particularly weighty because of the implicit reference to evolving ethical principles contained in the statutory language. The Court thus sought to determine whether Lueth's call for a boycott was 'contrary to good morals' and invoked the speech values of article 5, section 1, in answering that question.

In undertaking the balancing that was required in order to perform this task, the Court considered a somewhat broader range of factors than is ordinarily taken into account in American balancing opinions—focusing with special care on certain aspects of Lueth's activities and career that made the speech particularly justifiable in his case. To determine whether the speech was 'contrary to good morals' in the requisite sense, the Court first considered Lueth's motives and goals in calling for the boycott. First, the Court noted that Lueth was not motivated by economic goals of his own and was not in economic competition with Harlan or the film producers. Moreover, the goal of the speech—to exclude Harlan as a representative of German films—arose from Lueth's fear that Harlan's re-emergence would lead world opinion to believe that Germany had not rejected the national-socialist past. Thus Lueth's speech reflected his general political views concerning an issue that was of essential importance for the German people—the reputation of German cultural life and the German nation after the gruesome events of the Nazi period. Moreover, it was clear that this justification was not merely a pretext subsequently devised by Lueth, because a number of other individuals had protested against Harlan's re-emergence for similar reasons. The Court placed particular emphasis on the fact that Lueth was a person with a particularly 'legitimate' interest in taking a position on Harlan's re-emergence as a director, because of Lueth's involvement in activities furthering understanding between Christians and Jews in Germany and his involvement in matters relating to the cinema in Hamburg. Indeed, in this light, the public probably expected a statement from Lueth on this question and his response accordingly could be seen as an understandable defensive reaction rather than an unprovoked attack.

Against these very powerful interests favoring Lueth's speech, the private economic interests of Harlan and the film producers occupied a distinctly subordinate position. Indeed, the Court did not concede that Harlan had any countervailing constitutional interests of substance. For example, the Court rejected the argument that Lueth's remarks injured Harlan in his 'human dignity'—a right protected by article 1, section 1 of the Basic Law. The Court doubted that the power of Lueth's attack was sufficient to remove Harlan from his chosen sphere of endeavor—activity in the cinema; some such damage would have been necessary, apparently, to constitute an invasion of human dignity. In light of the strength of Lueth's constitutionally protected interests and the minimal nature of Harlan's economic interest protected by the private law, the constitutional interests prevailed over the private law interests and the injunction against Lueth was accordingly dissolved.

* * *

2. Abortion: Abstract *A Posteriori* Review

THE GERMAN BASIC LAW (1949)[18]

Article 1. (1) Human dignity is inviolable. To respect and protect it is the duty of all state authority.

(2) The German People therefore acknowledge inviolable and inalienable human rights as the basis of every human community, of peace, and of justice in the world.

---

18. These provisions of the German Basic Law are taken from the 2002 translation of the International Constitutional Law project, published by Jurisprudentia Verlag, Wuerzburg, and found at <www.jurisprudentia.de>.

(3) The following basic rights are binding on legislature, executive, and judiciary as directly valid law.

Article 2. (1) Everyone has the right to the free development of his personality, so long as he does not violate the rights of others or offend against the constitutional order or morality.

(2) Everyone has the right to life and physical integrity. The freedom of the person is inviolable. Intrusion on these rights may only be made pursuant to a statute.

* * *

PENAL STATUTE ON THE INTERRUPTION OF PREGNANCY [repealed and replaced by the Fifth Statute to Reform the Penal Law (1974) below][19]

Section 218. A pregnant woman who intentionally aborts her fetus or kills it in her womb shall be punished with up to five years in the penitentiary. If extenuating circumstances are present, an incarceration for not less than six months will result. The same penal provisions have application to anyone who, with the consent of the pregnant woman, applies the means for the abortion or killing or supplies them to her.

* * *

THE FIFTH STATUTE TO REFORM THE PENAL LAW (1974)[20]

Section 218. (1) Anyone who interrupts a pregnancy after the 13th day following conception shall be punished by incarceration up to three years or fined....

(3) If the pregnant woman commits the act, the punishment is incarceration up to one year or a fine.

Section 218a. An interruption of pregnancy performed by a physician with the consent of the pregnant woman is not punishable under §218 if no more than twelve weeks have elapsed since conception.

---

19. From page 613 of the translation by Robert Jonas and John Gorby in The West German Abortion Decision: A Contrast to Roe v. Wade, below.

20. From page 611–612 of the translation by Robert Jonas and John Gorby in The West German Abortion Decision: A Contrast to Roe v. Wade, below.

Section 218b. An interruption of pregnancy performed by a physician with the consent of the pregnant woman after the expiration of twelve weeks after conception is not punishable under § 218 if, according the judgment of medical science:

> 1. The interruption of pregnancy is indicated in order to avert from the pregnant woman a danger to her life or the danger of a serious impairment to the condition of her health insofar as the danger cannot be averted in a manner that is otherwise exactable from her, or

> 2. Compelling reasons require the assumption that the child will suffer from an impairment of its health which cannot be remedied on account of an hereditary disposition or injurious prenatal influences which is so serious that a continuation of the pregnancy cannot be exacted of the pregnant woman; and not more than 22 weeks have elapsed since conception.

Section 218c. [This section required the mother to present herself to a counseling center for the purpose of receiving education about resources available to enable the mother to continue the pregnancy. This section was to apply regardless of how much time had elapsed since conception.]

* * *

THE 1975 GERMAN ABORTION CASE
("ABORTION I"), [1975] BVERGE 1[21]

One hundred ninety-three members of the German Parliament as well as the state governments of Baden-Württemberg, Bavaria, Rhineland-Pfalz, the Saarland and Schleswig-Holstein....petitioned for constitutional review of §218a of the Penal Code, in the version of the Fifth Statute to Reform the Penal Law. They considered the provision to be inconsistent with the Basic Law because the availability of abortion made possible thereby during the first twelve weeks after conception runs afoul of Article 2, Paragraph 2, Sentence 1, in connection with Article 1, Paragraphs 1, 2 and 4 of the Basic Law as well as the principle of the just state....The gravity and the seriousness of the constitutional question posed becomes clear, if it is considered that what is involved here is the protection of human life, one of the central values of every legal order. The decision regarding the standards and limits of legislative freedom of decision demands a total view of the constitutional norms and the hierarchy of values contained therein.

---

21. From the translation of Robert Jonas and John Gorby, in Robert E. Jonas and John D. Gorby, West German Abortion Decision: A Contrast to Roe v. Wade, 9 John Marshall Journal of Practice and Procedure 605 (1976). Numerous citations to earlier decisions of the Federal Constitutional Court have been deleted in the interest of conserving space.

I.

1. Article 2, Paragraph 2, Sentence 1, of the Basic Law also protects the life developing itself in the womb of the mother as an intrinsic legal value.

a) The express incorporation into the Basic Law of the self-evident right to life—in contrast to the Weimar Constitution—may be explained principally as a reaction to the "destruction of life unworthy of life," to the "final solution" and "liquidations," which were carried out by the National Socialistic Regime as measures of state. Article 2, Paragraph 2, Sentence 1, of the Basic Law, just as it contains the abolition of the death penalty in Article 102, includes "a declaration of the fundamental worth of human life and of a concept of the state which stands, in emphatic contrast to the philosophies of a political regime to which the individual life meant little and which therefore practiced limitless abuse with its presumed right over life and death of the citizen".

b) In construing Article 2, Paragraph 2, Sentence 1, of the Basic Law, one should begin with its language: "Everyone has a right to life…" Life, in the sense of historical existence of a human individual, exists according to definite biological-physiological knowledge, in any case, from the 14th day after conception (nidation, individuation). The process of development which has begun at that point is a continuing process which exhibits no sharp demarcation and does not allow a precise division of the various steps of development of the human life. The process does not end even with birth; the phenomena of consciousness which are specific to the human personality, for example, appear for the first time a rather long time after birth. Therefore, the protection of Article 2, Paragraph 2, Sentence 1, of the Basic Law cannot be limited either to the "completed" human being after birth or to the child about to be born which is independently capable of living.…

c)…The security of human existence against encroachments by the state would be incomplete if it did not also embrace the [step prior to] "completed life," unborn life.

This extensive interpretation corresponds to the principle established in the opinions of the Federal Constitutional Court, "according to which, in doubtful cases, that interpretation is to be selected which develops to the highest degree the judicial effectiveness of the fundamental legal norm".…

2. The duty of the state to protect every human life may therefore be directly deduced from Article 2, Paragraph 2, Sentence 1, of the Basic Law. In addition to that, the duty also results from the explicit provision of Article 1, Paragraph 1, Sentence 2, of the Basic Law since developing life participates in the protection which Article 1, Paragraph 1, of the Basic Law guarantees to human dignity. Where human life exists, human dignity is present to it; it is not decisive that the bearer of this dignity himself be conscious of it and know personally how to preserve it. The potential faculties present in the human being from the beginning suffice to establish human dignity.

3. On the other hand, the question disputed in the present proceeding as well as in judicial opinions and in scientific literature whether the one about to be born himself is a bearer of the fundamental right or on account of a lesser capacity to possess legal and fundamental rights, is "only" protected in his right to life by the objective norms of the constitution need not be decided here. According to the constant judicial utterances of the Federal Constitutional Court, the fundamental legal norms contain not only subjective rights of defense of the individual against the state but embody, at the same time, an objective ordering of values, which is valid as a constitutionally fundamental decision for all areas of the law and which provides direction and impetus for legislation, administration, and judicial opinions. Whether and, if so, to what extent the state is obligated by the constitution to legal protection of developing life can therefore be concluded from the objective—legal content of the fundamental legal norms.

II.

1. The duty of the state to protect is comprehensive. It forbids not only—self-evidently—direct state attacks on the life developing itself but also requires the state to take a position protecting and promoting this life, that is to say, it must, above all, preserve it even against illegal attacks by others.... The degree of seriousness with which the state must take its obligation to protect increases as the rank of the legal value in question increases in importance within the order of values of the Basic Law. Human life represents, within the order of the Basic Law, an ultimate value, the particulars of which need not be established; it is the living foundation of human dignity and the prerequisite for all other fundamental rights.

2. The obligation of the state to take the life developing itself under protection exists, as a matter of principle, even against the mother.... Were the embryo to be considered only as a part of the maternal organism the interruption of pregnancy would remain in the area of the private structuring of one's life, where the legislature is forbidden to encroach. Since, however, the one about to be born is an independent human being who stands under the protection of the constitution, there is a social dimension to interruption of pregnancy which makes it amenable to and in need of regulation by the state. The right of the woman to the free development of her personality, which has as its content the freedom of behavior in a comprehensive sense and accordingly embraces the personal responsibility of the woman to decide against parenthood and the responsibilities flowing from it, can also, it is true, likewise demand recognition and protection. This right, however, is not guaranteed without limits—the rights of others, the constitutional order, and the moral law limit it. A priori, this right can never include the authorization to intrude upon the protected sphere of right of another without justifying reason or much less to destroy that sphere along with the life itself; this

is even less so, if, according to the nature of the case, a special responsibility exists precisely for this life.... According to the principle of the balance which preserves most of competing constitutionally protected positions in view of the fundamental idea of Article 19, Paragraph 2, of the Basic Law; precedence must be given to the protection of the life of the child about to be born....

3. .... The state must proceed, as a matter of principle, from a duty to carry the pregnancy to term and therefore to view, as a matter of principle, its interruption as an injustice. The condemnation of abortion must be clearly expressed in the legal order. The false impression must be avoided that the interruption of pregnancy is the same social process as, for example, approaching a physician for healing an illness or indeed a legally irrelevant alternative for the prevention of conception....

III.

How the state fulfills its obligation for an effective protection of developing life is, in the first instance, to be decided by the legislature. It determines which measures of protection are required and which serve the purpose of guaranteeing an effective protection of life.

1. .... Regardless of how the state fulfills its obligation to protect, it should not be forgotten that developing life itself is entrusted by nature in the first place to the protection of the mother. To reawaken and, if required, to strengthen the maternal duty to protect, where it is lost, should be the principal goal of the endeavors of the state for the protection of life. Of course, the possibilities for the legislature to influence are limited. Measures introduced by the legislature are frequently only indirect and effective only after completion of the time-consuming process of comprehensive education and the alteration in the attitudes and philosophies of society achieved thereby.

2. The question of the extent to which the state is obligated under the constitution to employ, even for the protection of unborn life, the penal law, the sharpest weapon standing at its disposal, cannot be answered by the simplified posing of the question whether the state must punish certain acts....

The legislature is not obligated, as a matter of principle, to employ the same penal measures for the protection of the unborn life as it considers required and expedient for born life. As a look at legal history shows, this was never the case in the application of penal sanctions and is also true for the situation in the law up to the Fifth Statute to Reform the Penal Law.

a) .... Abortion is an act of killing; this is most clearly shown by the fact that the relevant penal sanction—even in the Fifth Statute to Reform the Penal Law—is contained in the section "Felonies and Misdemeanors against Life" and, in the previous penal law, was designated the "Killing of the Child *en ventre sa mere.*" The description now common, "interruption of pregnancy," cannot camouflage this fact....

b) Punishment, however, can never be an end in itself. Its employment is in principle subject to the decision of the legislature. The legislature is not prohibited, in consideration of the points of view set out above, from expressing the legal condemnation of abortion required by the Basic Law in ways other than the threat of punishment. The decisive factor is whether the totality of the measures serving the protection of the unborn life, whether they be in civil law or in public law, especially of a social-legal or of a penal nature, guarantees an actual protection corresponding to the importance of the legal values to be secured. In the extreme case, namely, if the protection required by the constitution can be achieved in no other way, the lawgiver can be obligated to employ the means of the penal law for the protection of developing life.... It is not a question of an "absolute" duty to punish but rather one of a "relative" duty to use the penal sanction, which grows out of the insight into the inadequacy of all other means.

On the other hand, the objection that a political duty to punish can never be deduced from a norm of the Basic Law which guarantees freedom is not decisive.... In any case, the legislature must resolve the conflict which arises from this situation through a balancing of both of the fundamental values or areas of freedom which are in opposition to each other according to the standard of the ordering of values in the Basic Law and in consideration of the constitutional principle of proportionality....

3. The obligation of the state to protect the developing life exists — as shown — against the mother as well. Here, however, the employment of the penal law may give rise to special problems which result from the unique situation of the pregnant woman. The incisive effects of a pregnancy on the physical and emotional condition of the woman are immediately evident and need not be set forth in greater detail. They often mean a considerable change of the total conduct of life and a limitation of the possibilities for personal development. This burden is not always and not completely balanced by a woman finding new fulfillment in her task as mother and by the claim a pregnant woman has upon the assistance of the community (Article 6, Paragraph 4, of the Basic Law). In individual cases, difficult, even life-threatening situations of conflict may arise. The right to life of the unborn can lead to a burdening of the woman which essentially goes beyond that normally associated with pregnancy. The result is the question of exactability, or, in other words, the question of whether the state, even in such cases, may compel the bearing of the child to term with the means of the penal law. Respect for the unborn life and the right of the woman not to be compelled to sacrifice the values in her own life in excess of an exactable measure in the interest of respecting this legal value are in conflict with each other. In such a situation of conflict which, in general, does not allow an

unequivocal moral judgment and in which the decision for an interruption of pregnancy can attain the rank of a decision of conscience worthy of consideration, the legislature is obligated to exercise special restraint. If, in these cases, it views the conduct of the pregnant woman as not deserving punishment and forgoes the use of penal sanctions, the result, at any rate, is to be constitutionally accepted as a balancing incumbent upon the legislature.

In determining the content of the criterion of non-exactability, circumstances, however, must be excluded which do not seriously burden the obligated party, since they represent the normal situation with which everyone must cope. Rather, circumstances of considerable weight must be present which render the fulfillment of the duty of the one affected extraordinarily more difficult, so that fulfillment cannot be expected from him in fairness. These circumstances are especially present if the one affected by fulfilling the duty is thrown into serious inner conflicts. The solution of such conflicts by criminal penalty does not appear in general to be appropriate, since it applies external compulsion where respect for the sphere of personality of the human being demands full inner freedom of decision.

A continuation of the pregnancy appears to be non-exactable especially when it is proven that the interruption is required "to avert" from the pregnant woman "a danger for her life or the danger of a grave impairment of her condition of health" (§218b, No. 1, of the Penal Code in the version of the Fifth Statute to Reform the Penal Law). In this case her own "right to life and bodily inviolability" (Article 2, Paragraph 2, Sentence 1, of the Basic Law) is at stake, the sacrifice of which cannot be expected of her for the unborn life. Beyond that, the legislature has a free hand to leave the interruption of pregnancy free of punishment in the case of other extraordinary burdens for the pregnant woman, which, from the point of view of non-exactability, are as weighty as those referred to in §218b, No. 1. In this category can be counted, especially, the cases of the eugenic (cf. Section 218b, No. 2, of the Penal Code), ethical (criminological), and of the social or emergency indication for abortion which were contained in the draft proposed by the Federal Government in the sixth election period of the Federal Parliament and were discussed both in the public debate as well as in the course of the legislative proceedings. During the deliberations of the Special Committee for the Reform of the Penal Law, the representative of the Federal Government explained in detail and with convincing reasons why, in these four cases of indication, the bearing of the child to term does not appear to be exactable. The decisive viewpoint is that in all of these cases another interest equally worthy of protection, from the standpoint of the constitution, asserts its validity with such urgency that the state's legal order cannot require that the pregnant woman must, under all circumstances, concede precedence to the right of the unborn.

Also, the indication arising from general emergency (social indication) can be integrated here. Finally, the general social situation of the pregnant woman and her family can produce conflicts of such difficulty that, beyond a definite measure, a sacrifice by the pregnant woman in favor of the unborn life cannot be compelled with the means of the penal law. In regulating this case, the legislature must so formulate the elements of the indication which is to remain free of punishment that the gravity of the social conflict presupposed will be clearly recognizable and, considered from the point of view of non-exactability, the congruence of this indication with the other cases of indication remains guaranteed. If the legislature removes genuine cases of conflict of this kind from the protection of the penal law, it does not violate its duty to protect life. Even in these cases the state may not be content merely to examine, and if the occasion arises, to certify that the statutory prerequisites for an abortion free of punishment are present. Rather, the state will also be expected to offer counseling and assistance with the goal of reminding pregnant women of the fundamental duty to respect the right to life of the unborn, to encourage her to continue the pregnancy and—especially in cases of social need—to support her through practical measures of assistance.

In all other cases the interruption of pregnancy remains a wrong deserving punishment since, in these cases, the destruction of a value of the law of the highest rank is subjected to an unrestricted pleasure of another and is not motivated by an emergency. If the legislature wants to dispense (even in this case) with penal law punishment, this would be compatible with the requirement to protect of Article 2, Paragraph 2, Sentence 1, of the Basic Law, only on the condition that another equally effective legal sanction stands at its command which would clearly bring out the unjust character of the act (the condemnation by the legal order) and likewise prevent the interruptions of pregnancy as effectively as a penal provision.

D.

If the challenged regulation of terms of the Fifth Statute to Reform the Penal Law is examined according to these standards, the result is that the statute does not do justice, to the extent required, to the obligation to protect developing life effectively which is derived from Article 2, Paragraph 2, Sentence 1, in conjunction with Article 1, Paragraph 1, of the Basic Law....

It is constitutionally permissible and to be approved if the legislature attempts to fulfill its duty to improve protection of unborn life through preventive measures, including counseling to strengthen the personal responsibility of the woman. The regulation in question, however, encounters decisive constitutional problems in several respects.

1. The legal condemnation of the interruption of pregnancy required by the constitution must clearly appear in the legal order existing under the constitution. Therefore, as shown, only those cases can be excepted in which the constitution of the pregnancy is not exactable from the woman in consideration of the value decision made in Article 2, Paragraph 2, Sentence 1, of the Basic Law....

2. A formal statutory condemnation of the interruption of pregnancy would, furthermore, not suffice because the woman determined upon abortion would disregard it. The legislature which passed the Fifth Statute to Reform the Penal Law has replaced the penal norm with a counseling system in §218c of the Penal Code on the judgment that positive measures to protect developing life are also required for an interruption of pregnancy performed by a physician with the consent of the pregnant woman. Through the complete repeal of punishability, however, a gap in the protection has resulted which completely destroys the security of the developing life in a not insignificant number of cases by handing this life over to the completely unrestricted power of disposition of the woman....

3. The counseling and instruction of the pregnant woman provided under §218c, Par. 1, of the Penal Code cannot, considered by itself, be viewed as suitable to effectuate a continuation of the pregnancy....

IV.

....Underlying the Basic Law are principles for the structuring of the state that may be understood only in light of the historical experience and the spiritual-moral confrontation with the previous system of National Socialism. In opposition to the omnipotence of the totalitarian state which claimed for itself limitless dominion over all areas of social life and which, in the prosecution of its goals of state, consideration for the life of the individual fundamentally meant nothing, the Basic Law of the Federal Republic of Germany has erected an order bound together by values which places the individual human being and his dignity at the focal point of all of its ordinances. At its basis lies the concept, as the Federal Constitutional Court previously pronounced, that human beings possess an inherent worth as individuals in order of creation which uncompromisingly demands unconditional respect for the life of every individual human being, even for the apparently socially "worthless," and which therefore excludes the destruction of such life without legally justifiable grounds. This fundamental constitutional decision determines the structure and the interpretation of the entire legal order. Even the legislature is bound by it; considerations of socio-political expediency, even necessities of state, cannot overcome this constitutional limitation. Even a general change of the viewpoints dominant in the populace on this subject — if such a change could be established at all — would change nothing. The Federal Constitutional Court, which is charged by the constitution with overseeing the observance of its fundamental principles by all organs of the state and, if necessary, with giving them effect, can orient its decision only on those principles to the development of which this Court has decisively contributed in its judicial utterances. Therefore, no adverse judgment is being passed about other legal orders "which have not had these experiences with a system of injustice and which, on the basis of

an historical development which has taken a different course and other political conditions and fundamental views of the philosophy of state, have not
made such a decision for themselves".

E.

On the basis of these considerations, §218a of the Penal Code in the version
of the Fifth Statute to Reform the Penal Law is inconsistent with Article 2,
Paragraph 2, Sentence 1, in conjunction with Article 1, Paragraph 1, of the
Basic Law to the extent that it excepts interruption of pregnancy from punishability if no reasons are present which, according to the present opinion, having
standing under the ordering of values of the Basic Law....

There is no occasion to declare further provisions of the Fifth Statute to Reform the Penal Law to be invalid....

* * *

Dissenting Opinion... The fundamental legal norms standing in the central part
of our constitution guarantee as rights of defense to the citizen in relation to the
state a sphere of unrestricted structuring of one's life based on personal responsibility. The classical function of the Federal Constitutional Court lies in defending against injuries to this sphere of freedom from excessive infringement by the
state power. On the scale of possible infringements by the state, penal provisions
are foremost: they demand of a citizen a definite behavior and subdue him in the
case of a violation with grievous restrictions of freedom or with financial burdens. Judicial control of the constitutionality of such provisions therefore means
a determination whether the encroachment resulting either from the enactment
or application of penal provisions into protected spheres of freedom is allowable;
whether, therefore, the state, generally or to the extent provided, may punish.

In the present constitutional dispute, the inverse question is presented for
the first time for examination, namely whether the state *must* punish, whether
the abolition of punishment for the interruption of pregnancy in the first three
months of pregnancy is compatible with fundamental rights. It is obvious,
however, that the disregard of punishment is the opposite of state encroachment. Since the partial withdrawal of the penal provision did not occur to benefit interruptions of pregnancies but rather, because the previous penal sanction, according to the unrefuted assumption of the legislature which has been
confirmed by experience, has thoroughly provided itself ineffective, an "attack"
on the unborn life by the state is not even indirectly construable....

Since the fundamental rights as defense rights are from the beginning not
suitable to prevent the legislature from eliminating penal provisions, the majority of this Court seeks to find the basis for this in the most extensive meaning of fundamental rights as *objective value decisions*. According to this, the
fundamental rights not only establish rights of defense of the individual

against the state, but also contain at the same time objective value decisions, the realization of which through affirmative action is a permanent task of state power. This idea has been developed by the Federal Constitutional Court in the laudable endeavor to lend greater effectiveness to the fundamental rights in their capacity to secure freedom and to strive for social justice. The majority of this Court insufficiently considers differences in the two aspects of fundamental rights, differences essential to the judicial control of constitutionality....

The idea of objective value decisions should however not become a vehicle to shift specifically legislative functions in the formation of social order onto the Federal Constitutional Court. Otherwise the Court will be forced into a role for which it is neither competent nor equipped....

Our strongest reservation is directed to the fact that for the first time in opinions of the Constitutional Court an objective value decision should function as a *duty* of the legislature to enact *penal norms*, therefore to postulate the strongest conceivable encroachment into the sphere of freedom of the citizen. This inverts the function of the fundamental rights into its contrary. If the objective value decision contained in a fundamental legal norm to protect a certain legal value should suffice to derive therefrom the duty to punish, the fundamental rights could underhandedly, on the pretext of securing freedom, become the basis for an abundance of regimentations which restrict freedom. What is valid for the protection of life can also be claimed for other legal values of high rank—for example, inviolability of the body, freedom, marriage, and family.

Quite obviously the constitution presupposes that the state can also resort to its power to punish to protect an orderly social life; the thrust of fundamental rights, however, does not go to the promotion of such a utilization but rather to the drawing of its boundaries. In this way the Supreme Court of the United States has even regarded punishment for the interruption of pregnancy, performed by a physician with the consent of the pregnant woman in the first third of pregnancy, as a violation of fundamental rights. This would, according to German constitutional law, go too far indeed. According to the liberal character of our constitution, however, the legislature needs a constitutional justification to punish, not to disregard punishment, because, according to its view, a threat of punishment promises no success or appears for other reasons to be an improper reaction....

Even if one, contrary to our position, agrees with the majority that a constitutional duty to punish is conceivable, no constitutional violation can be charged to the legislature....

Even according to the opinion of the majority a constitutional duty to punish should only come into consideration as *ultima ratio*. If one considers that seriously, such a duty immediately presupposed that suitable means of a milder form are not available or that their employment has proved to be ineffective; moreover, the penal sanction must be suitable and required to achieve the de-

sired goal at all or more effectively....In its adjudication of the factual basis and
the effectiveness of the intended measures, the Court must accept as a basis the
view of the legislature so long as it has not been refuted as obviously erroneous.

The reasoning of the judgment does not satisfy these requirements. It is repeatedly entangled with contradictions and in the end directly shifts the burden of proof: the legislature shall be allowed to forgo penal sanction, only
when it is established without doubt that the milder measures favored by it to
fulfill the duty of protection are "at least" equally effective or more effective....

On the whole therefore, in our opinion, the legislature was not prevented by
the constitution from dispensing with a penal sanction which, according to its
unrefuted view, was largely ineffective, inadequate, and even harmful. Its attempt to remedy through socially adequate means the manifestly developing inability of state and society in the present conditions to serve the protection of
life may be imperfect; it corresponds, however, more to the spirit of the Basic
Law than the demand for punishment and condemnation.

* * *

DEBORAH GOLDBERG, RECENT DEVELOPMENTS: DEVELOPMENTS IN GERMAN ABORTION LAW

5 UCLA WOMEN'S LAW JOURNAL 531, 536–538, 540–544 (1995)

Despite liberalization efforts in West Germany, Section 218 of the 1871
Penal Code, which criminalized abortion, remained largely unchanged until
1974. After a long political battle, the more liberal political parties passed a
radically reformed version of Section 218 which reflected a time-limit model
[Fristenlosung] similar to that of East Germany. The new law decriminalized
abortion in the first twelve weeks of pregnancy. Even in cases where the
woman failed to undertake counseling, only the doctor performing the abortion (and not the woman) was guilty of violating the law. In what would become a pattern, the Federal Constitutional Court held that the time-limit
model was unconstitutional after it was challenged by the Christian Democratic Union (CDU). The Court held that the 1974 legislation did not fulfill the
state's constitutional duty to protect the fetus' right to life and to guarantee the
inviolability of human dignity. Finding that life begins with implantation
(fourteen days after conception), the Court held that the time-limit model did
not provide sufficient protection to the developing fetus. Although the right to
self-determination is also a constitutional right in Germany, the Court held
that the right of the fetus' life to protection prevails even against the will of the
pregnant woman. Although the legislature maintained the prerogative to
choose the appropriate means to protect the developing life, the Court required the law to impose criminal sanctions when the minimum constitutional

standards for protecting developing life could not otherwise be met. However, in cases where continuing the pregnancy would impose an unreasonable burden on the woman, the Court held that the state could no longer compel the woman to carry the fetus to term.

In 1976, in response to the Federal Constitutional Court's order, the West German legislature amended the Penal Code, using what was described as an "indication" model [Indikationslosung]. The legislature technically criminalized all abortions but provided extensive exceptions, or indications, where continuing the pregnancy would constitute an unreasonable burden on the pregnant woman. The German Penal Code was amended to include four indications: the medical indication if the woman's health or life was threatened, the eugenic or embryopathic indication if the child would be born with permanent birth defects, the criminological indication if the pregnancy was the result of rape, and the general emergency or social indication if carrying the child to term would be an unreasonable burden. In addition to requiring the presence of an indication, the 1976 reform provided that abortions performed by a physician were legal if the counseling requirement had been met, the presence of one of the four indications was confirmed by both an independent physician and the physician performing the abortion, the three-day waiting period was complied with, and the abortion was performed within the statutorily prescribed time period. The statutory time allowances for the performance of an indicated abortion were twelve weeks, if the abortion was based on a criminological or a social indication, twenty-two weeks, if it was based on embryonic or embryopathological reasons, and any time during the pregnancy, if it was based on a medical indication. Many scholars considered this indication model to be "pro-life" because it made the woman's choice to have an abortion contingent upon a third party's finding that an emergency situation existed....

The German Unification Treaty of 1990 required the Parliament [Bundestag] to pass new abortion legislation within two years of reunification. The Treaty also required the German parliament to draft legislation that, "in conformity with the Grundgesetz [constitution], would...protect...unborn life while allowing pregnant women to cope with conflict situations."

In July 1992, the legislators of a reunified Germany redrafted the abortion laws of the former East and West Germany with a bill that had broad support in both parts of the legislative branch: the Parliament [Bundestag] and the Council of States [Bundesrat]. This bill, the 1992 Act, represents a compromise between the time-limit and the indication models and is known as the "counseling" model [Beratungslosung]. This amalgam fuses aspects of the other two models. The counseling model is based on the theory that the state can better fulfill its constitutional duty to protect unborn life through counseling the woman and by supporting her decision. Under this model, counselors provide pregnant women with information about the various options available to them. Ultimately, however, the final decision about whether or not to terminate the pregnancy is left with the pregnant woman. This legislative approach was labeled "support instead of punishment" [Hilfe statt Strafe].

The 1992 Act maintained a general prohibition of abortion, but provided that an abortion could be lawful if: (1) the pregnant woman consented to the abortion (an especially problematic issue with minors), (2) she had been counseled at least three days before the procedure, and (3) the abortion was performed by a physician within the first twelve weeks of the pregnancy. Under the 1992 Act, physicians did not need to ascertain the existence of an indication; the woman was free to choose to have an abortion without determining that an indication existed during the first trimester of the pregnancy. An abortion performed after the twelfth week of pregnancy was legal only if it was undertaken "to avert a serious threat to [the woman's] life or a grave impairment of [the woman's] physical or mental health," a requirement similar to the medical indication.

Additionally, the 1992 Act went beyond mere regulation of the abortion procedure and attempted to address the broader issues at the root of the abortion debate. For example, the 1992 Act would have required the state to provide public sex education, family planning, and support during pregnancy. The 1992 Act also attempted to create a child-friendly society [Kinderfreundliche Gesellschaft] by providing more daycare facilities for working mothers and by ensuring that every child over the age of four would be entitled to attend a state-run nursery school by the year 1996.

Despite this successful effort at compromise between the German political parties, the 1992 Act was never implemented. The conservative CDU party petitioned to have the law enjoined by the Federal Constitutional Court and on August 4, 1992, just one day before the law would have gone into effect, the Court issued an injunction. Because the Federal Constitutional Court enjoined the enforcement of the 1992 Act, the old law remained in force until the Court handed down its decision.

Note

1. The decision itself ("Abortion II") was handed down on May 28, 1993. "In a major departure from *Abortion I*, the court declared that non-indicated abortions in the first twelve weeks of pregnancy, while unjustified, need not be punished. A refined system of counseling oriented toward preserving the life of the fetus could now substitute for the criminal penalty. However, sections of the Criminal Code declaring abortions performed during the first trimester of pregnancy "not illegal" were nullified. Non-indicated abortions remain illegal even though unpunished.... Finally, the court said that the

state could not constitutionally deny welfare assistance to poor women who wanted non-indicated abortions but could not afford them....In rejecting the 1992 abortion statute, the court tossed the ball back into parliament's court. Until parliament acted to craft a new statute within the guidelines of *Abortion II*, the court's rulings would prevail in all of Germany. It would take parliament another two years to agree on amendments to the 1992 statute.... A compromise bill that commanded the support of a substantial parliamentary majority provided for compulsory counseling along the lines suggested by the Federal Constitutional Court, but it seemed to require less vigorous pro-life counseling than the court had urged....Although some Christian Democrats felt that the compromise bill fell short of the Constitutional Court's directives, there seemed to be no desire on anybody's part to mount another judicial challenge against the bill should it be enacted into law." Donald Kommers, The Constitutional Jurisprudence of the Federal Republic of Germany 355–356 (1997).

* * *

D. The End of Parliamentary Supremacy in France: *A Priori* Abstract Review

DAVID POLLARD, SOURCEBOOK ON FRENCH LAW
16, (2nd ed. 1998)

From the Third Republic onwards, France had lived under a system of Parliamentary supremacy....However, the emergence of the modern and welfare State, the ever-growing State control of economic and social affairs, and the need for constant legislative change rendered this parliamentary tradition not the most effective constitutional mechanism. In particular, during the Third and Fourth Republics the parliamentary tradition resulted in an instability of government and often an inability for a government to enact the legislation which its policies deemed necessary. Governments were overthrown with alarming regularity.

* * *

1. DeGaulle and the 1958 Constitution

RICHARD J. CUMMINS, THE GENERAL PRINCIPLES OF LAW, SEPARATION OF POWERS AND THEORIES OF JUDICIAL DECISION IN FRANCE
35 INT'L & COMP. L. Q. 594, 596, 602–603 (1986)

The experience of the 1930s and the war showed how fragile was the Enlightenment heritage of respect for individual liberty. The history of the Vichy regime inevitably raised the question whether the hitherto fundamental belief that Parliament was capable of guaranteeing a free and just society without supervision by the judiciary was still justified. At the same time, the increased complexity of modern life and the growing faith (only now diminishing) in detailed regulation of many aspects of life made it inevitable that the legislature would be forced to leave to the courts an increased role in applying legislation. This role, nominally one of interpretation, inevitably came to have a large creative element....

The first of two 1946 Constituent Assemblies proposed a constitution which maintained the parliamentary supremacy of the Third Republic. After the rejection of that constitution by referendum, the Second Assembly adopted a document not greatly different although providing both a Preamble of Rights and a form of constitutional review which turned out to be largely symbolic. Although it was widely recognised that the previous system had proved incapable, when put under great pressure, of protecting civil liberties, the tradition of parliamentary supremacy was not seriously questioned.

Notes

1. "The Fourth Republic was born of the aftermath of World War II and anxiety over the burgeoning political power of the Communist and Socialist Parties. In a speech in Bayeux on June 16, 1946, Gen. Charles de Gaulle argued for a strong presidential regime having a nonpartisan head of state while preserving the parliamentary system. The voters, however, approved a bicameral assembly, with the upper house and the president having limited authority. Politically unstable governing coalitions, a costly war in Algeria, and the real possibility of a civil war, however, doomed the Fourth Republic. On June 1, 1958, de Gaulle, now Prime Minister, was granted emergency powers for six months, and a new constitution was prepared by a committee of experts and ministers. The result, which included a strong president who could select the prime minister and run the government, was adopted by eighty percent of those who voted on September 28, 1958, and was promulgated on October 4, 1958....The preamble to the 1958 constitution of France reaffirms the 1789

Declaration of the Rights of Man and the Citizen and the preamble to the
1946 constitution of the Fourth Republic...." Robert L. Maddox, Constitutions of the World 84 (1995).

* * *

MARTIN A. ROGOFF, THE FRENCH (R)EVOLUTION OF 1959–1998: A REVIEW OF *DROIT ET PASSION DU DROIT SOUS LA VE RÉPUBLIQUE* BY JEAN CARBONNIER,
3 COLUMBIA JOURNAL OF EUROPEAN LAW
453, 455–460 (1997/98)

The Fifth Republic...came into being on October 4, 1958, with the adoption of a new Constitution. The Constitution of 1958 marks a decided break
with the French constitutional tradition, for unlike prior French constitutions,
it did not establish either a *régime bonapartiste* or a *régime d'Assemblée*[22]. Rejecting both authoritarianism and extreme democracy, the framers of the Constitution of the Fifth Republic opted instead for a middle way, one which combined a strong executive with a government responsible to Parliament. It also
established a mechanism, the *Conseil constitutionnel*, to assure in practice the
supremacy of the Constitution over acts of Parliament, and it recognized and
made accommodation for international legal obligations undertaken by the nation. It is this Constitution which has provided the framework within which
the passion for law, described by Dean Carbonnier, has developed.

The Constitution as polestar of the legal system is something quite new and
revolutionary in the history of French law. Since 1804, for more than a century
and a half, that role had been played by the *Code civil*. Although dealing for the
most part with private law, the *Code civil* (along with other codifications of the
Napoleonic era), "provided a context. The historical influence of that context,
because of the majesty of its title and the solemnity attending its launching, extended well beyond the civil law: it in fact defined the domain of the law itself"....

The *Code civil* of 1804 (and, one might add, the tradition of constitutional instability—the constitution as a "contested" document, so to speak)
was the legal legacy of the Revolution. Revolutionary periods often give rise

---

22. In a *régime bonapartiste* power is concentrated in a single person. The *régime
bonapartiste* has the capacity to act firmly and decisively but is not necessarily representative of differing views or interests. In a *régime d'assemblée*, power resides in the popularly
elected legislative chamber to which the government (i.e., the Prime Minister and other
ministers) is responsible. The *régime d'assemblée* has often been characterized by factious-
ness, indecisiveness and instability. [Footnote in original text.]

to new conceptual and structural points of departure for legal and political systems. The 1789–1815 period certainly did for France. For the United States, the period from 1776–1788 (from the Declaration of Independence, through the period of the Articles of Confederation, to the ratification of the Constitution) represents a similar phenomenon. This was a period during which new ways of viewing law and government took shape in the crucible of traumatic political and social change. To appreciate fully what the 1958 Constitution means for the French, it is instructive to view it as the legal culmination of another period which was truly revolutionary for the French people: the period from 1940 through 1958. Following the overthrow of the parliamentary Third Republic and its replacement by the collaborationist Vichy regime in 1940, the forces of the extreme right took power in France. The liberation of France and the reconstruction of French political life in late 1944, 1945 and 1946 can truly be described as a period of extreme political turmoil. The Constitution of the Fourth Republic, adopted in 1946, represented only a momentary truce. Serious social, economic, and political problems — the loss of colonial empire abroad, and the threat of international communism at home — persisted and continued to embroil and divide French society.

Like the American Constitution of 1788 and the French *Code civil* of 1804, the French Constitution of 1958 represents the accommodation of both revolutionary forces (or the forces of change) and the forces of stability and continuity — those sober second thoughts after revolutionary excesses. As such, the 1958 Constitution speaks to a broad segment of French society as an acceptable social and political compromise.

Symbolic of this historic compromise is the preamble to the 1958 Constitution which (in a document establishing a strong executive) incorporates by reference both the Declaration of the Rights of Man and the Citizen of 1789, with its focus on individual and political rights, and the preamble to the Constitution of 1946, with its concern for economic and social rights. An analogous compromise was achieved in the United States with the addition of the Bill of Rights to the Constitution in 1791, thus affording legitimacy to at least some of the concerns and according protection to certain interests of those who had previously opposed the ratification of the Constitution....

The principal feature of the Constitution of 1958 was the establishment of a strong executive. The President is charged with certain affirmative responsibilities. According to article 5:

> The President of the Republic shall secure respect for the Constitution. He shall ensure, by his arbitration, the regular functioning of the governing authorities (*pouvoirs public*) as well as the continuity of the State. He is the guarantor of national independence, territorial integrity, and respect for Community agreements and treaties.

The President appoints the Prime Minister (article 8), he presides at meetings of the Council of Ministers (article 9), he can dissolve the National Assembly (article 12), he conducts foreign affairs (articles 14 and 52), he is commander-in-chief of the armed forces (article 15), and he can exercise emergency powers in certain grave situations (article 16). The office of President was further enhanced by a 1962 amendment providing for the direct election of the President by universal suffrage.

The Prime Minister in turn directs the activities of the Government (article 21), which is charged with determining and directing the policy of the nation (article 20). The Prime Minister also exercises the executive rule-making power (*pouvoir réglementaire*) (article 21), he may seek delegation of parliamentary law-making power for a designated period (article 38), and he has the power to initiate legislation (*projets de loi*) (article 39).

In its practical operation since 1958, this system has resulted in the concentration of governing power in the hands of the President. Except for three brief periods (1986–1988, 1993–1995, and June 1997 to the present), called *cohabitations*, the President and the Prime Minister have been members of the same political party, and it has been that party and its coalition allies that have controlled the National Assembly. Since in most cases the National Assembly has the last word on legislation if it is deadlocked with the Senate (article 45), the normal situation in France since 1958 has been the conjunction of executive and legislative power.

As a result of this concentration of governmental power, combined with the Gaullist propensity to action (*"d'agir sur la société"*) without a sense of "either the constraints of past history or the obstacles of future ineffectiveness," and later (1981–1995) with the Socialist desire to carry out its economic and social program, a great deal of law, of all sorts, has been produced-*lois* enacted by Parliament, *décrets-lois* of the Government pursuant to delegations under article 38, *décrets* of the Government within the scope of its autonomous regulatory power under article 37, and international obligations having the effect of domestic law pursuant to article 55....

The institution created by the Constitution of 1958 which may ultimately have the most significant impact on contemporary French law and ways of thinking about law is the *Conseil constitutionnel*. Originally intended as a body to assure that Parliament did not encroach on the executive's autonomous regulatory power and to handle a number of other matters (like assuring the regularity of elections and referenda and passing on the constitutionality of organic laws), the *Conseil constitutionnel* has emerged as an institution of tremendous power, both for the practical operations of government and symbolically, as principal interpreter of the Constitution.

* * *

2. Executive Legislation and Constitutional Review in the Administrative Courts

As Rogoff points out, under the 1958 constitution a great deal of law-making power was specifically shifted to the executive branch (in the form of the autonomous power to make regulations and ordinances without legislative delegation), and the powers of the legislature were for the first time limited to specific categories.

CONSTITUTION OF FRANCE (1958)[23]

Title V. On Relations Between Parliament and the Government.

Article 34. Statutes [*lois*] shall be passed by Parliament.

Statutes shall determine the rules concerning :

-civic rights and the fundamental guarantees granted to citizens for the exercise of their public liberties ;

-the obligations imposed for the purposes of national defence upon citizens in respect of their persons and their property ;

-nationality, the status and legal capacity of persons, matrimonial regimes, inheritance and gifts ;

-the determination of serious crimes and other major offences and the penalties applicable to them ; criminal procedure ; amnesty ; the establishment of new classes of courts and tribunals and the regulations governing the members of the judiciary ;

-the base, rates and methods of collection of taxes of all types ; the issue of currency.

Statutes shall likewise determine the rules concerning :

-the electoral systems of parliamentary assemblies and local assemblies ;

-the creation of categories of public establishments ;

-the fundamental guarantees granted to civil and military personnel employed by the State ;

-the nationalization of enterprises and transfers of ownership in enterprises from the public to the private sector.

Statutes shall determine the fundamental principles of :

---

23. The full Constitution in English (updated as of October 2, 2000) can be found at <http://www.assemblee-nationale.fr/english/8ab.asp>.

-the general organization of national defence ;

-the self-government of territorial units, their powers and their resources ;

-education ;

-the regime governing ownership, rights in rem and civil and commercial obligations ;

-labour law, trade-union law and social security....

Article 37. Matters other than those that fall within the ambit of statute shall be
matters for regulation.

Acts of Parliament passed concerning these matters may be amended by decree issued after consultation with the Conseil d'Etat. Any such Acts which are
passed after this Constitution has entered into force shall be amended by decree only if the Constitutional Council has declared that they are matters for
regulation as defined in the preceding paragraph.

Article 38. In order to carry out its programme, the Government may ask Parliament for authorization, for a limited period, to take measures by ordinance
that are normally a matter for statute.

Ordinances shall be issued in the Council of Ministers, after consultation
with the Conseil d'Etat. They shall come into force upon publication, but shall
lapse if the bill to ratify them is not laid before Parliament before the date set
by the enabling Act.

At the end of the period referred to in the first paragraph of this article, ordinances may be amended only by an Act of Parliament in those areas which are
matters for statute.

* * *

Who would keep the legislature and the executive each on its own side of
the constitutional fence? If it was important to transfer some powers to the executive that had previously been held by the legislature, then it would be important to insure that the legislature knew its place and kept to it. For that purpose the 1958 constitution made provision for a special forum, the
Constitutional Council. But it made no provision for a check on the executive.
The slack was taken up by the Council of State, which had previously reviewed
executive and administrative action only for exceeding the limits of enabling
legislation, or for violating the "general principles of law" we read about in
Chapter One. Now that the executive was authorized directly by the constitution to take over certain areas of lawmaking, the Council of State took upon itself the responsibility for constitutional control of the executive.

In 1959 the Council of State broke this new ground with the *Syndicat-Gen-
eral* case. The French Minister of Overseas Territories had ordered that certain

sorts of building designs for buildings in the French colonies were to be made only by licensed architects. A group of engineers and contractors protested, claiming that this violated the general principle of liberty of contract. In its decision the Council for the first time made reference to the Preamble to the Constitution as governing administrative action.

CONSTITUTION OF FRANCE (1958)[24]

Preamble. The French people solemnly proclaim their attachment to the Rights of Man and the principles of national sovereignty as defined by the Declaration of 1789, confirmed and complemented by the Preamble to the Constitution of 1946. By virtue of these principles and that of the self-determination of peoples, the Republic offers to the overseas territories that express the will to adhere to them new institutions founded on the common ideal of liberty, equality and fraternity and conceived with a view to their democratic development.

* * *

THE *SYNDICAT-GÉNÉRAL* CASE, DECREE OF THE COUNCIL OF STATE, JUNE 26, 1959
RECUEIL LEBON 394[25]

Considering that on June 25, 1947, while the transitional period mentioned in Article 104 of the Constitution of October 27, 1946[26] had not come to an end, the president of the Council of Ministers held under Article 47 of that Constitution the power of regulating by decree in the territories under the authority of the French overseas ministry,... those questions which in the mother country belong to the province of statutory law, in the exercise of those powers, he was nevertheless obliged to respect, on one hand, the statutory regime applicable in the overseas territories, and, on the other, the general principles of law which, resulting notably *from the preamble* of the Constitution [of 1958], control the whole rulemaking authority even in the absence of legislative authorization;... [nevertheless the decree does not conflict with any legislation or general principle of law, and the appeal is rejected.] [Emphasis added.]

---

24. The full Constitution in English (updated as of October 2, 2000) can be found at <http://www.assemblee-nationale.fr/english/8ab.asp>.

25. Translation by the editor. The case may be found in French, with commentary, in M. Long *et al., Les grands arrets de la jurisprudence administrative* 555–563.

26. Article 104 of the 1946 Constitution temporarily suspended the effect of provisions that would bring legislation for the overseas territories under the control of Parliament.

Notes

1. The Preamble of the 1958 Constitution is capable of being considered binding by the courts "because, unlike the 1946 Preamble, it appears after words of adoption and because the 1958 Constitution has no counterpart of Article 92 of the Constitution of 1946 which distinguished between its preamble and its first ten titles to which it assigns normative value." George D. Haimbaugh,Jr., Was It France's Marbury v. Madison?, 35 Ohio State Law Journal 910, 924 (1974).

2. "In finding the decree was subject to the 'general principles,' the *Conseil* was in a sense not deciding anything new as it has long taken the position that such regulations were subject to its review. The importance of the case is therefore found in the conclusions of the *Commissaire du gouvernement* Fournier, who, while noting that the status of autonomous regulations under the 1958 Constitution was not at issue [this decree was autonomous under the 1946 Constitution, as involving a territory], nevertheless implicitly anticipated dealing with them by stating that certain of the "general principles" are derived from constitutional texts and therefore may have constitutional status. This would be important under the 1958 Constitution since a lower than constitutional status would arguably be insufficient to subject the autonomous regulations to the 'general principles' as they are the highest form of lawmaking in their domain." Richard J. Cummins, The General Principles of Law, Separation of Powers and Theories of Judicial Decision in France, 35 International and Comparative Law 594, 606–607 (1986).

3. If the 1958 Preamble is positive law for the Council of State (and, by the same reasoning, for the Constitutional Council), then it incorporates into the law both the Declaration of the Rights of Man and the 1946 Preamble. The Declaration of 1789 is a statement of what were called "negative rights" in Section C above, and the 1946 Preamble consists largely of what were called "positive rights."

* * *

RICHARD J. CUMMINS, THE GENERAL PRINCIPLES OF LAW, SEPARATION OF POWERS AND THEORIES OF JUDICIAL DECISION IN FRANCE
35 INTERNATIONAL AND COMPARATIVE LAW
594, 605–608 (1986)

Three cases, *Syndicat Général des Ingénieurs-Conseils* of 1959 and the *Ruben de Servens* and *Canal* cases in 1962, illustrate the range and limits of application [of "general principles"].

Despite the central place given to the parliamentary statute (*loi*), all French constitutional regimes have recognised, in addition to various kinds of regulation clearly derived from and subsidiary to laws, a form of administrative enactment given status virtually equal to that of a law. It may be described as a decree-law or an *ordonnance*, or otherwise.

The 1958 Constitution introduced a form of "super-regulation" which depended not on legislative delegation but directly on the constitution, the so-called autonomous regulation. For the first time in a French constitution, the powers of Parliament were enumerated, in Article 34, and limited to those listed. As Article 37 of the Constitution states: "Matters other than those which are in the domain of the law have a regulatory character." The regulations adopted under Article 37 in areas not covered by Article 34 are thus the highest form of law-making related to those matters.

The *Conseil d'Etat* had in the past uniformly taken the position that anything less than a law was subject to its review. The *Syndicat-Général* case involved a challenge to a regulation defining the profession of architect in the overseas colonies on the ground that that profession's monopoly was defined too broadly and thus rights of other professionals under the general principle of liberty and commerce and industry were violated. The regulation had been adopted in 1947 under a provision of the 1946 Constitution which, following a long tradition with respect to colonial legislation, authorised the President of the Council of Ministers to adopt by decree regulations which would have the force of law in the colonies.

In finding the decree was subject to the "general principles," the *Conseil* was in a sense not deciding anything new as it had long taken the position that such regulations were subject to its review. The importance of the case is therefore found in the conclusions of the *Commissaire du Governement* Fournier, who, while noting that the status of autonomous regulations under the 1958 Constitution was not at issue, nevertheless implicitly anticipated dealing with them by stating that certain of the "general principles" are derived from constitutional texts and therefore may have constitutional status. This would presumably be important under the 1958 Constitution since a lower than constitutional status would arguably be insufficient to subject the autonomous regulations to the "general principles" as they are the highest form of law-making in their domain. In its decision the *Conseil d'Etat* itself does not, of course, deal with this question on which, as we shall see, much scholarly ink has been spilled. The administration had, nevertheless, been warned that autonomous regulations would not necessarily be accorded the same status as laws.

The two 1962 decisions, related to the Algerian crisis, show the difficulties of distinguishing reviewable regulations from those not reviewable. After the attempted putsch of the French army generals in Algeria in the spring of 1961, General de Gaulle as president of the Republic, after making the necessary consultations, declared Article 16 of the Constitution applicable. That controversial article provides that: "When the institutions of the Republic, the independence of the Nation, the integrity of its territory or the execution of its international undertakings are threatened in a grave and immediate manner and the regular functioning of the constitutional public powers is interrupted, the President of the Republic may take the measures required by the circumstances...." Although the rebellion fizzled out rather quickly, de Gaulle kept Article 16 in force for several months, decreeing a series of measures which would normally have required laws. These included the creation of a special court to try Ruben de Servens and others accused of committing crimes against the state during the uprising. The *Conseil* decided in response to various arguments made by the complainants that neither the act of proclaiming Article 16 effective nor the decision to keep it in effect after the severe crisis had arguably passed were reviewable acts. They were "government acts" under a doctrine the *Conseil* had long used as a way to avoid dealing with "political questions." The decision to establish a special tribunal was not described as a "government act" but escaped review because it was a measure explicitly within the legislative power under Article 34 of the Constitution. As a "law" it was unreviewable by the *Conseil d'Etat*. The *Conseil* took the President to be exercising constitutionally established legislative power and thus acting in a field beyond its jurisdiction.

Later in the year a defendant named Canal and others, threatened with execution, complained of a similar action as an abuse of presidential power. The settlement with the rebellion in Algeria had been approved by referendum in the form of a law (law of 13 April 1962) which conferred on the President of the Republic the power "to take...all regulatory measures relative to the application of the governmental declarations of 19 March 1962." As in *Ruben de Servens*, the President had established a special tribunal before which Canal and others had been tried. Many of the aspects of the procedures of the court were unusual including the fact that all appeals were barred. The *Conseil* annulled the action taken by de Gaulle in establishing the special court, finding that "it results from its very terms that this text has for its object not to enable the President of the Republic to exercise the legislative power himself but only to authorise him exceptionally to use his regulatory power to take measures which are normally within the area of the statute." The measure could thus be attacked as an administrative one and as such fell short of standards set by "the general principles of the criminal law."

The *Canal* case shows the *Conseil* will go very far to avoid letting measures taken by anyone other than Parliament escape review. *Ruben de Servens* and *Canal* present an interesting contrast as in the two cases the grant of power and the way it was exercised were similar. Attempts to explain the difference in result are not entirely satisfactory. Each case involved the exercise of a power which was legislative in nature under the terms of Article 34. In *Canal*, as the grant of power was by a law, it was perhaps easy to regard the exercise of the power as of lesser or regulatory status. *Reuben de Servens* involved a constitutional grant of power. An exercise of that grant which came normally within the legislative domain would have the status of a law and thus be beyond review by the *Conseil d'Etat*.

* * *

3. The Constitutional Council

CONSTITUTION OF FRANCE (1958)[27]

Title VII - The Constitutional Council

Article 56. The Constitutional Council shall consist of nine members, whose term of office shall be nine years and shall not be renewable. One third of the membership of the Constitutional Council shall be renewed every three years. Three of its members shall be appointed by the President of the Republic, three by the President of the National Assembly and three by the President of the Senate.

In addition to the nine members provided for above, former Presidents of the Republic shall be ex officio life members of the Constitutional Council.

The President shall be appointed by the President of the Republic. He shall have a casting vote in the event of a tie.

No sitting member of Parliament may be a member of the Constitutional Council; The Council oversees popular referendums and the election of the President of the Republic, and it has jurisdiction in case of a dispute over the election of national legislators. Review of legislation for constitutional conformity is governed by the following article:

Article 61. Institutional Acts, before their promulgation, and the rules of procedure of the parliamentary assemblies, before their entry into force, must be referred to the Constitutional Council, which shall rule on their conformity with the Constitution.

To the same end, Acts of Parliament may be referred to the Constitutional Council, before their promulgation, by the President of the Republic, the Prime Minister, the President of the National Assembly, the President of the Senate, [or sixty deputies or sixty senators]....

Article 62. A provision declared unconstitutional shall be neither promulgated nor implemented.

No appeal shall lie from the decisions of the Constitutional Council. They shall be binding on public authorities and on all administrative authorities and all courts.

Notes

1. What was the intended role of the Constitutional Council? Here is the prevailing view of that role as of 1960: "The sole justification for [the Constitu-

---

27. The full Constitution in English (updated as of October 2, 2000) can be found at <http://www.assemblee-nationale.fr/english/8ab.asp>.

tional Council's] existence, apart from a few purely housekeeping responsibilities, such as assuring the regularity of elections, and determining the constitutionality of treaty texts, is to define the relationship between separate instruments of government—and thus presumably by its decisions to clarify these divisions and enforce their existence." Edwin D. Godfrey, The Government of France 31 (1968). "In contrast to the American practice, the Constitutional Council is the guardian of the constitutional provisions regarding executive-legislative relations with particular reference to lawmaking rather than the ultimate court of appeal for the protection of the law of the land at the request of an individual against legislative or administrative infringements." Roy C. Macridis and Bernard E. Brown, The De Gaulle Republic: Quest for Unity 173 (1960).

2. The 1958 Constitution restricted "standing" before the constitutional court to the President, the Prime Minister [or Premier], and the President of either house of the Parliament. An amendment of 1974 allowed sixty members of either house to bring a bill before the Council. The reason for this extension is not difficult to see. The four offices mentioned were very likely to be occupied by the same political party, so that it would never happen that a minority group would manage to get an issue before the Council. The President was generally of the same party as the Prime Minister ("cohabitation" was still some distance in the future), and the Prime Minister was of course of the prevailing party in the Assembly. At most the President of the Senate might be of a different party, and thus be inclined to seek review of legislation for constitutionality. With the 1974 amendment, parties with at least sixty members in either house could get a hearing. "Still, clearly 'if the legislature and the executive *together* attempt to violate the Constitution, the *Conseil constitutionnel* is helpless' since no private parties have standing." Mauro Cappelletti and William Cohen, Comparative Constitutional Law 47 (1979).

3. The Council has jurisdiction only over legislation—that is, parliamentary action falling under Article 34—to see that the legislature has not overstepped its bounds. It has nothing to say about the constitutionality of executive or administrative action. (That is, it may say that the legislature has overstepped into executive (Article 37) territory, but not that the executive has overstepped into Article 34 territory. The latter determination falls within the exclusive domain of the Council of State.)

4. The Council's reach extends only to legislative enactments that have not yet been promulgated. Once an act has been promulgated, it is forever beyond the constitutional control of the Council. To underline these limitations on the Council's capacity for constitutional control of legislation, we should put them together: *Only certain political actors* may bring *only legislation* before the Council, and *only after enactment and before promulgation*.

5. The ordinary courts, of course, still refuse (despite some scholarly urging) to consider the constitutionality of legislative acts. Indeed some scholars have

taken the creation of the Constitutional Court as support for this position. "It seems…that the essential coherence of the constitutional system is not changed and that the fundamental role of the courts remains the same under the 1958 Constitution as under previous regimes. The Council, playing an essentially legislative rather than judicial role, does not change this.…The creation of a specialized organ of review indeed reaffirms the essential correctness of the position of the courts…in refusing to consider constitutional arguments." Richard J. Cummins, General Principles of Law, Separation of Powers and Theories of Judicial Decision in France 601 (1986).

* * *

a. Separation of Powers

The job of the Constitutional Council is to keep the legislature from overstepping its constitutional bounds under the 1958 constitution. In the early years the Council was occupied only with making sure that the legislature did not infringe on the legislative powers guaranteed to the executive by Article 37. For example, in the *Agricultural Orientation Act* case of 1962, the Government brought before the Council a legislative act which proposed to fix agricultural prices. The same question had been before the Council in 1961 in relation to two agricultural acts, and the Council had ruled that the power to fix prices was within the authority reserved to the executive under Article 37. Instead of ruling again in the 1962 case, the Council simply declared that the issue was foreclosed by its earlier rulings. The case stands not only for this limitation upon the legislature then, but establishes the extent of the binding effect of the Council's decisions.

THE AGRICULTURAL ORIENTATION ACT CASE, DECISION 62-18L (16 JANUARY 1962)
RECUEIL DES DÉCISIONS DU CONSEIL CONSTITUTIONNEL 31.[28]

The Constitutional Council, petitioned by the Premier on January 8, 1962, pursuant to article 37, paragraph 2 of the Constitution, to consider the juridical nature of the provisions of article 31, paragraph 2 of the Law of Agricultural Planning dated August [5], 1960;

In view of the Constitution, in particular articles 34, 37 and 62;

---

28. This translation is from Henry P. deVries, Civil Law and the Anglo-American Lawyer 110–111 (1975). The case may be found in French, with commentary, in L. Favoreu and L. Philip, Les grandes décisions du Conseil constitutionnel 165–183 (1999).

In view of the Ordinance of November 7, 1958 containing the organic law on the Constitutional Council, in particular articles 24, 25 and 26;

Considering, on the one hand, that under the terms of article 62 of the Constitution, 'the decision of the constitutional Council...are binding on the governing authorities and all administrative and judicial authorities'; that the authority of the decisions to which this provision refers concerns not only the decision (*dispositif*) but the reasons (*motifs*) which supply the necessary support and which constitute its very basis;

Considering that, in a decision dated September 8, 1961, the Constitutional Council declared that a bill determining the conditions under which future price supports of certain agricultural products would be fixed by decree had an executive character for the reason that the provisions of this bill constituted an intervention by the legislature in a matter (that of prices) which is not among those reserved to its jurisdiction by article 34 of the Constitution; [...] that the above-cited decision—reaffirmed by a decision of October 8, 1961, establishing the executive character of the provisions of an amendment to the bill on the fixing of agricultural prices—is therefore binding on the public authorities and all administrative and judicial authorities with the same effect that the aforementioned reasons (*motifs*) which are its necessary support give it; [...]

Considering that it results from the above that the petition of the Premier for a consideration by the Constitutional Council of the juridical nature, with respect to article 34 of the Constitution, of the provision of article 31 of the Law of Agricultural Planning dated August 5, 1960, must be regarded as moot;

Decides,

Art. 1. There is no reason for the Constitutional Council, for the reasons (*motifs*) given above, to make a pronouncement upon the petition presented by the Premier under article 37 (paragraph 2) of the Constitution for a consideration of the juridical nature of article 31 of the Law of Agricultural Planning dated August 5, 1960.

* * *

JOHN BELL, FRENCH CONSTITUTIONAL LAW
49–50 (1992)

The scope of such binding authority extends to any provision with the same effect as one on which the Conseil has already ruled. Thus, in the case of the *Amnesty Law of 1989* a provision was introduced both to amnesty and to make eligible for reinstatement those who had been guilty of serious fault during industrial disputes. A clause to this effect had already been struck down in the case of the *Amnesty Law of 1988* because it would impose an excessive burden on the victims of the fault. Although the legislature had tried to modify the

1988 provision by making an exception for employers thus affected, the Conseil did not consider that this had cured the problem, particularly in relation to the burdens that reinstatement would place on fellow employees. Relying on its previous decision, the Conseil struck down the new provision because it "violates the authority that attaches, by virtue of article 62 of the Constitution, to the decision of the Conseil constitutionnel of 20 July 1988."

The private and administrative courts have used techniques similar to those known in common law to distinguish decisions of the Conseil constitutionnel that they have not wished to follow. The first technique is to confine the decision to the test that was before the Conseil. This is often combined with a second technique of restrictive interpretation of the reasoning. Thus, in a decision of 1977 the Conseil held as unconstitutional a *loi* that intended to confer on the police an unlimited power to search vehicles on the highway even where no crime had been committed and there was no threat to public order, on the ground that the imprecise nature of the grounds of intervention by the police threatened individual liberty. In 1979 the Chambre criminelle of the Cour de cassation held that the police could search vehicles belonging to any person under the general provisions relating to the investigation of "flagrant offences." While formally consistent, the latter decision did much to undermine the effect of the decision of the Conseil constitutionnel.

The third technique is to draw a distinction between the necessary reasons for the decision and other points that may be raised (in other words, between the *ratio decidendi* and mere *obiter dicta*). This again arose with regard to criminal penalties. These are divided in French law between *crimes*, *délits*, and *contraventions*. Article 34 of the Constitution states that *loi* should lay down the rules for "the determination of *crimes* and *délits* and the penalties applicable thereto." A provision of the Rural Code established the fines for illegal joinder of agricultural properties (an offence in the nature of a *contravention*). In declaring this to be within the competence of the executive to amend by way of *règlement*, the Conseil constitutionnel ruled that "the determination of *contraventions* and the penalties applicable to them falls within the province of *règlement* when those penalties do not include measures depriving a person of their liberty." The *procureur général*, Touffait, sought to argue in a subsequent case that the proviso relating to measures for the deprivation of liberty did not bind the criminal courts, because "the Conseil constitutionnel stressed its reasoning by inserting a general principle, which in this case was incidental, not to say superfluous." The necessary reasons were only those most directly concerned with disposing of the case before the Conseil, namely, the classification of those provisions submitted to it, and Touffait was followed by the Cour de cassation in thinking that the proviso did not fall within that specific category.

b. *Constitutional Rights: Freedom of Association*
JAMES BEARDSLEY, CONSTITUTIONAL REVIEW IN FRANCE
[1975] SUPREME COURT REVIEW 198 (1975)

Entirely apart from the importance of the 'general principles' as a precursor and perhaps essential support to judicial review of the constitutionality of *administrative acts* in the Fifth Republic, it is also important to recognize that this preexisting body of law had already consecrated the principles which have so far been applied by the *Conseil constitutionnel* in its substantive constitutional decisions. The *Conseil* had only to add the label 'constitutional.' Moreover, the attribution of legal force to the preamble by the *Conseil constitutionnel* was certainly made a good deal easier by the *Conseil d'Etat*'s earlier veiled recognition of the Preamble's constitutional force.

* * *

BARRY NICHOLAS, FUNDAMENTAL RIGHTS AND JUDICIAL REVIEW IN FRANCE
[1978] PUBLIC LAW 82, 86–87 (1978)

The Constitution of 1946 had expressly provided that its Preamble should not have constitutional force, and though the Constitution of 1958 contained no equivalent provision, many would have said before 1971 that so vague and sweeping a text was unsuited to be an instrument of judicial review and that the Conseil Constitutionnel was too unadventurous a body to attempt to use it for that purpose. And yet the decision of July 16, 1971, and its successors did precisely that.

The decision of July 16, 1971. The case in which the conseil decided to set out on its "activist" path was well calculated to appeal to liberal, anti-authoritarian sentiments. In May 1970 the Council of Ministers, acting under powers conferred by a *loi* of 1936 (directed originally against the then increasing number of private militias) dissolved *La Gauche Prolétarienne*, a small political party. As a riposte to this Jean-Paul Sartre, Simone de Beauvoir and others announced the formation of the *Association des Amis de la Cause du Peuple* (provocatively adopting the title of a paper which had been published by the dissolved party). The Government sought to meet this challenge by an administrative device. The Law on Associations of July 1, 1901, provides that before an association can obtain legal capacity certain information must be declared to the *Préfecture* and then published in the *Journal Officiel*. In this case the requisite declaration was made, but the Prefect, acting of course on the orders of the Government, refused to issue the usual receipt (on the ground that the new association was no more than a reincarnation of *La Gauche Prolétarienne*). The requisite publication in the *Journal Officiel* was thereby made impossible and *L'Association des Amis de la Cause du Peuple* was left in limbo, neither illegal nor yet enjoying any legal capacity. An administrative court, however, annulled the Prefect's refusal on the ground of *excès de pouvoir*, declaring that the function of the Prefect was merely to receive the information, not to decide on the desirability of the association which filed it. The Government reacted to this rebuff by introducing a parliamentary Bill to amend the law of 1901 by *inter alia* empowering the Prefect, if he thought that an association had an illicit or immoral purpose or that it amounted to a revival of an illegal association, to withhold his receipt and refer the matter to the *Procureur de la République* with a view to its being tested in court. This Bill raised a political storm, but was eventually forced through by the Government. Before promulgation, however, it was referred to the Conseil Constitutionnel under Article 61 by the President of the Senate, M. Poher....He was unhappy with the Bill. He could not see the need for it and was surprised at the absence of any reference to the rights of man. He wanted the Conseil "in a sense to lay down the law, as is its role." ...

* * *

CONSTITUTION OF FRANCE (1958)

Preamble. (See above, Section 2.)

* * *

THE SIMONE DE BEAUVOIR CASE
DECISION 71-44DC (16 JULY 1971), RECUEIL DES DÉCISIONS DU CONSEIL CONSTITUTIONNEL 29.[29]

The Constitutional Council:

Pursuant to Article 61 of the Constitution the President of the Senate initiated this proceeding on July 1, 1971 for review of the text of the law, passed by the National Assembly and the Senate, completing Articles 5 and 7 of the Law of July 1, 1901 relating to the contract of association.

In view of the Constitution and particularly its Preamble;-

In view of the Ordinance of November 7, 1968 pertaining to the organic law of the Constitutional Council, notably chapter II of Title II of the said Ordinance;-in view of the law of July 1, 1901 relating to the contract of modified association;-in view of the Law of January 10, 1936 relating to groups of combat and private militia.

---

29. This translation is from Henry P. deVries, Civil Law and the Anglo-American Lawyer 115–116 (1975). The case may be found in French, with commentary, in L. Favoreu and L. Philip, Les grandes décisions du Conseil constitutionnel 252–271 (1999).

Considering that the law submitted to examination of the Constitutional Council was submitted to a vote by both assemblies pursuant to the procedure set down by the Constitution, in the course of the session of Parliament which opened April 2, 1971;-

Considering that among the fundamental principles recognized by the laws of the Republic and solemnly reaffirmed by the Preamble of the Constitution there is reason to place the principle of freedom of association; that this principle underlies the general provisions of the law of July 1, 1901 relating to the contract of association; that by virtue of this principle associations are freely constituted and can be given public status subject to the sole requirement of filing of a prior declaration; that thus, except for measures taken with respect to special categories, of associations, the organization of associations even if they would appear to be tainted with nullity, or have an illicit purpose, cannot be submitted for validity to the previous intervention of the administrative authority or even of judicial authority;

Considering that if nothing was changed with respect to the organization of undeclared associations, Art. 3 of the law whose text is submitted to the Constitutional Council has as purpose to institute a procedure pursuant to which the acquisition of juridical capacity of declared associations is subjected to previous control by the judicial authority as to conform to law;

Considering, consequently, that there is reason to declare as not conforming to the Constitution the provisions of Art. 3 of the law submitted to the Constitutional Council's decision; [...]

Considering finally that the other provisions of the text are not contrary to any provision of the Constitution.

Art. 1-The provisions of Art. 3 of the law submitted to decision by the Constitutional Council completing provisions of Art. 7 of the Law of July 1, 1901, as well as the provisions of Art. 1 of the law submitted to the Council referring thereto, are declared not to conform to the Constitutions.

Art. 2-The other provisions of the said text of law are declared to conform to the Constitution.

* * *

MARTIN A. ROGOFF, THE FRENCH (R)EVOLUTION OF 1959–1998: A REVIEW OF *DROIT ET PASSION DU DROIT SOUS LA Vᴱ RÉPUBLIQUE,* BY JEAN CARBONNIER

3 COLUMBIA JOURNAL OF EUROPEAN LAW 453, 460 (1997/98)

Although the Kelsenian notion of a hierarchy of norms had made headway in France after the Second World War, it was decisions of the *Conseil constitutionnel* that gave operational form to the acceptance of that idea by the French people. In a bold stroke in a case decided in 1971, the *Liberté d'Association* case, the *Conseil constitutionnel* held that the Preamble to the Constitution of 1958 had substantive constitutional status, and that therefore its references to the Declaration of the Rights of Man and the Citizen of 1789 and to the Preamble to the Constitution of 1946 (which in turn made reference to "the fundamental principles recognized by the law of the Republic") conferred constitutional status (*une valeur constitutionnelle*) on these texts, too. Taken together, the Declaration of 1789, the Preamble to the Constitution of 1946, and the open-ended "fundamental principles of the laws of the Republic" furnish a multitude of substantive constitutional principles which the *Conseil* can now employ to evaluate the constitutionality of parliamentary enactments.

While the competence of the *Conseil constitutionnel* to review legislation is severely limited in that it does not extend to reviewing laws and treaties once they have entered into force (or the legislative or decisional products of institutions established by treaty) or to reviewing executive *décrets,* the importance of its jurisprudence cannot be underestimated. For by engaging in substantive review of legislative enactments and by arrogating to itself the power to define "general principles," it has overthrown the revolutionary legacy of the de facto supremacy of statutory law over the constitution.

The existence of even the limited form of judicial review that now exists in France may be even more important to the felicitous operation of the political process than judicial review is in the United States. This is so because in the United States, at least for the past fifty years, divided government and weak party discipline have been the rule. Given the many centers of power (the President, the Senate, the House of Representatives, the Supreme Court, the 50 state governments) and the need, mandated by the Constitution, for the cooperation of two, three or more institutions to reach a workable decision, most political conflict is resolved through the interactions of different parts of the government itself. A constitutional override is needed only in those cases where there is long-term political deadlock regarding matters of great national importance (e.g., racial relations or the reform of the electoral system) or when the rights of individuals or minorities are threatened.

In France, on the other hand, the constitutional scheme of the Fifth Republic is a blueprint for the concentration of power.... There is a compelling political need, therefore, for a counterweight to that power—to prevent the existing majority from running roughshod over the rights and interests of individuals, minority groups, or minority political parties. The *Conseil constitutionnel*, as it has evolved since 1971, is now in the position to fulfill that role. Therefore, looking at the present system as a whole, the President-Prime Minister-National Assembly are empowered to take affirmative, decisive action, with few, if any, institutional restraints of a political nature, while at the same time the *Conseil constitutionnel* is there to assure conformity to the Constitution and to prevent abuse.

* * *

c. Constitutional Rights: Abortion, Liberty, and Respect for Persons

DECLARATION OF THE RIGHTS OF MAN AND OF THE CITIZEN (1789)[30]

Article 1. Men are born and remain free and equal in rights. Social distinctions can only be based upon the common good.

Article 2. The aim of all political association is the preservation of the natural and imprescriptible rights of Man. These rights are liberty, property, security, and the right to resist oppression.

* * *

PREAMBLE OF THE 1946 CONSTITUTION[31]

Paragraph 11: [The nation] guarantees to all, especially to children, to mothers, and to older workers, protection of their health, material security, rest and leisure. Any human being who, by reason of his age, his physical or mental state, or his economic condition is unable to work has the right to obtain from society the means of subsistence.

* * *

---

30. Translation by the editor.
31. Translation by the editor.

THE 1975 ABORTION DECISION,
DECISION 74-44DC (15 JANUARY 1975)
RECUEIL DES DÉCISIONS DU
CONSEIL CONSTITUTIONNEL 19[32]

The *Conseil Constitutionnel*, seized the 20th of December, 1974, by M.M....
under the terms provided by Article 61 of the Constitution, with the issue concerning the constitutionality of the text of the law adopted by Parliament relative to the voluntary interruption of pregnancy;

Considering the observations produced in support of this issue;

Considering the Constitution, and notably its Preamble;

Considering the *Ôrdonnance* of November 7, 1958 (the organic law of the
Conseil Constitutionnel), in particular Chapter II of Title II of the *ôrdonnance*;

Having heard the Reporter's report;

Considering that Article 61 of the Constitution does not confer on the *Conseil Constitutionnel* a general power of evaluation and decision identical to that
of Parliament, but rather gives it competence solely to pronounce the conformity to the Constitution of the laws referred to its scrutiny;

Considering in the first place, that, according to the terms of Article 55 of
the Constitution, "The treaties or [international] accords regularly ratified or
approved have, from their publication, an authority superior to that of the
laws, upon the reservation, for each accord or treaty, of its application by the
other party";

Considering that, even though these provisions, under the conditions which
they define, confer on treaties superiority over the laws, they neither prescribe
nor imply that the respect of this superiority principle must be enforced within
the framework of the control of the conformity of laws to the Constitution
provided by Article 61;

Considering that, in effect, the decisions taken on the basis of Article 61 of
the Constitution assume an absolute and definitive character, as is made clear by
Article 62, which prevents the promulgation and application of all provisions
once declared unconstitutional [by this *Conseil Constitutionnel*]; that, in contrast, the superiority of the treaties over the laws, which principle is posed by the
aforementioned Article 55, has a character at the same time relative and contin-

32. This translation is from Mauro Cappelletti and William Cohen, Comparative
Constitutional Law 577–578 (1979). The case may be found in French, with commentary,
in L. Favoreu and L. Philip, Les grandes décisions du Conseil constitutionnel 313–337
(1999).

gent, since such superiority is limited to the scope of the application of the treaty and is subordinated to a condition of reciprocity, and the realization of this condition may vary according to the behavior of one or more of the signatory States at the time when one must judge the respect of the condition;

Considering that a law contrary to a treaty would thus not be, for that reason only, contrary to the Constitution;

Considering that, therefore, the control of the respect of the principle of Article 55 of the Constitution would not be exercisable under the framework of review provided by Article 61, by reason of the difference in nature of the two controls;

Considering that, under these conditions, it is not the task of this *Conseil Constitutionnel*, when it is seized [with issues of constitutionality] under the terms of Article 61 of the Constitution, to examine the conformity of a law to the provisions of a treaty or an international accord;

Considering, in the second place, that the law relative to the voluntary interruption of pregnancy respects the liberty of the persons who have recourse to or participate in an interruption of pregnancy, whether they do so in a situation of distress or for a therapeutic reason; that, therefore, that law does not infringe upon the principle of liberty posed by Article 2 of the Declaration of the Rights of Man and of the Citizen;

Considering that the law referred to this *Conseil Constitutionnel* does not authorize any violation of the principle of respect for every human being from the very commencement of life, a principle stated in Article 1, except in case of necessity and according to the conditions and limitations which it defines;

Considering that none of the provisions of the law are, as it now appears, contrary to the fundamental principles recognized by the laws of the Republic, nor do they disregard the principle stated in the Preamble of the Constitution of October 27, 1946, according to which the nation guarantees the protection of children's health, nor any of the other provisions given constitutional value by the same text;

Considering, in consequence, that the law relative to the voluntary interruption of pregnancy does not contradict any of the texts to which the Constitution of October 4, 1958 made reference in its Preamble, nor any of the articles of the Constitution itself;

Therefore [this *Conseil Constitutionnel*] DECIDES that:

1. The provisions of the law concerning the voluntary termination of pregnancy, referred to the *Conseil Constitutionnel*, are not contrary to the Constitution.

* * *

LOUIS M. AUCOIN, JUDICIAL REVIEW IN FRANCE: ACCESS OF THE INDIVIDUAL UNDER FRENCH AND EUROPEAN LAW IN THE AFTERMATH OF FRANCE'S REJECTION OF BICENTENNIAL REFORM

15 BOSTON COLLEGE INTERNATIONAL & COMPARATIVE LAW REVIEW 443, 450–452 (1992)

Mindful of the potential backlash from other branches of French government, the *Conseil* has carefully limited its own jurisdiction. An example of such judicial restraint is one of the *Conseil's* early rulings addressing a law adopted by referendum.[33] In this ruling, the *Conseil* reasoned that a law adopted through the referendum process had the force and effect of a constitutional provision because it directly reflected the people's views. Given this superior status, the *Conseil* decided that it lacked jurisdiction to rule on the referendum's compatibility with other constitutional provisions.

The *Conseil* has also exercised judicial restraint in defining its role *vis-à-vis* Parliament. In 1975, exercising the jurisdiction conferred by the 1974 constitutional amendment for the first time, Parliament referred France's abortion law to the *Conseil*. The law granted a woman the right to obtain an abortion under certain, enumerated conditions. In its decision, the *Conseil* ruled not only on the law's constitutionality, it also decided for the first time the question of its own jurisdiction under Article 55 of the 1958 Constitution.

Prior to the abortion law decision, some French constitutional authorities had assumed that Article 55 implicitly conferred authority on the *Conseil* to rule on the conformity of parliamentary laws with the terms of treaties and international agreements. In the abortion law case, however, the *Conseil* refused to rule on the abortion law's conformity to the terms of the European Convention on Human Rights. The *Conseil* ruled that the Constitution limited its jurisdiction to the review of parliamentary laws for their conformity with the Constitution, and not for their conformity with international treaties and agreements. Even in deciding the main constitutional question, however, the *Conseil's* decision limited its own power. The *Conseil* held that the abortion law was constitutional, and that it was thus otherwise powerless to rule on it. The *Conseil* stated that the Constitution had not conveyed upon the *Conseil* a decision-making power identical to that of Parliament. The effect of the *Conseil's* decision was to affirm itself as an institution with specific

---

33. [Footnote in original.] Décision 62-20 of Nov. 6, 1962, Con. const., 1962 Dalloz, *Jurisprudence* [D. Jur.] 398 (Fr.). The referendum is entirely a creature of the French Constitution. Article 89 contains provisions for amending the Constitution by referendum. *See* FR. CONST. arts. 11, 89.

jurisdiction conferred by the Constitution, but not as a political institution
with the power to second-guess the legislature.

* * *

CYNTHIA VROOM, EQUAL PROTECTION VERSUS THE PRINCIPLE OF EQUALITY: AMERICAN AND FRENCH VIEWS ON EQUALITY IN THE LAW

21 CAPITAL UNIVERSITY LAW REVIEW 199, 214–221 (1992)

Much of the *Conseil constitutionnel's* jurisprudence on the principle of
equality relates to economic or social legislation, the very area avoided by the
American Supreme Court. French jurisprudence falls into five general and
often overlapping categories: equality before the law, equality before justice,
equality before the public charge, equality in public employment, and equality
of suffrage.

A. Equality Before the Law

This category, found in article 6 of the Declaration of the Rights of Man,
includes four principle elements: (1) absence of differential treatment; (2)
unjustified differential treatment; (3) differential treatment justified by differences in situation; and (4) differential treatment permitted due to exceptional considerations of the general interest.

Absence of differential treatment. A law prohibiting companies that provide
local radio service from collecting advertising revenue was held not to be discriminatory because it applied to all those companies which held the same license. A prohibition against cumulation of advertising revenues and public
funding by those authorized to use radioelectric frequencies was held nondis-
criminatory because all such parties could choose the financing method of
their choice.

Authorization of political advertising on television outside of electoral campaigns was found not to be discriminatory because such advertising was open to
all parties and groups. However, recognizing the danger of unequal access to the
media, the *Conseil constitutionnel* made one of its very rare references to the factual inequalities which may distort application of a law, directing the *Conseil national de la commission et des liberts* to establish rules guaranteeing the democratic
expression of diverse ideas and opinions, and additional rules preventing political
advertisements from giving the advantage to those of greater financial means.

Unjustified differential treatment. The *Conseil constitutionnel* has on occasion
found that the legislature had adopted impermissible criteria for differential

treatment. For example, a law excluding only profit-making enterprises from the right of response in cases of slander was held to be discriminatory, on the ground that differential treatment of businesses was not justified in view of the law's goal. The *Conseil* also struck down a budget law provision on government estimation of taxes (*taxation* d'office) for "visible or notorious expenditures." The provision would have disallowed the right of rebuttal for those whose tax base was in the very top bracket. The *Conseil* held this to be unjustified discrimination among citizens.

The *Conseil constitutionnel* struck down a law excluding employees and workers' union organizations from tort responsibility in case of damage caused by a strike, except where the damage was caused through a criminal infraction or actions clearly unrelated to the exercise of the right to strike. The *Conseil* held that this differentiation in assigning tort responsibility was not justified by the desire to assure effective exercise of the right to strike, and that it violated the principle of equality.

Differential treatment justified by a difference in situation. In a variety of areas, differential treatment has been justified by a difference in the situation of those to whom the law is applied. In 1980, the *Conseil constitutionnel* reviewed a criminal law punishing acts of indecent exposure against minors of fifteen years or younger and "immodest or unnatural acts" with a minor of the same sex eighteen years or younger. The differentiation between homosexual and nonhomosexual acts, and the different protection of female minors according to their age, were found not to violate the principle of equality among offenders, on the ground that the legislature had the right to differentiate between offenses of a different nature as long as all offenders incurred the same punishment.

In a decision on freedom of the press, the *Conseil* held that the greater legal protection accorded to national daily papers, in comparison to that given the regional dailies, was justified by the fact that the two categories of publications are different.

A law maintaining university presidents and department heads in office until the expiration of their normal term, even though the composition of the university councils was changed, was found not to violate the principle of equality, in view of the special nature of the functions involved.

The *Conseil* held that a law authorizing the government to take certain economic and social measures, which provided for favorable treatment for certain categories of disadvantaged persons, did not violate the principle of equality.

Differential treatment justified by considerations of general interest. Differential treatment based on considerations of general interest is rare in the jurisprudence of the *Conseil constitutionnel.* One important example, however, is found in the decision of January 16, 1982. The 1982 law nationalizing certain

French businesses designated for appropriation only banks with capital of over one billion francs in deposits held by French residents. This effectively excluded from nationalization banks whose majority capital was held by nonresidents. The *Conseil constitutionnel* held that the legislature "could, without violating the principle of equality, exclude [these banks] from nationalization, in view of the risk of problems their nationalization could pose on an international level, which in the legislature's view could compromise the general interest in light of the goals of the law of nationalization."

B. Equality Before Justice

Equality before justice is generally included in the broader principle of equality before the law, but it has given rise to a specialized jurisprudence. Equality before justice has been prominent in three important decisions of the *Conseil constitutionnel*.

In its decision of July 23, 1975, the *Conseil constitiutionnel* struck down the provision of a proposed law which would have given the presiding judge of a criminal court the discretionary authority to assign cases to a single judge, instead of the three judges normally required in France. The *Conseil* held that this provision violated the principle of equality before justice: "Respect for this principle prevents citizens in the same circumstances and pursued for the same infractions from being judged by courts composed under different rules."

Eight *years later, in the well-known "Scurit et libert" decision of January 19–20, 1981, the Conseil constitutionnel* voided a provision allowing the civil party in a case to bring up new demands for the first time on appeal if it could justify its failure to do so earlier. The *Conseil* declared that this provision would violate the principle of equality before justice because all parties would not benefit from the "two-level review" (*double degr de juridiction*) found in French law.

In a noncriminal context, a provision allowing the public prosecutor to appeal where civil parties could not, and allowing lower court decisions to become final if the appellate court did not review the case within two months, was found to violate the principle of equality before justice. That principle, according to the *Conseil*, has two components: equality of the parties within a proceeding, and equality of all those judged in court. The first component was not violated because of the public prosecutor's special position as a defender of public order. The second component was violated, however, because those in the appeal process would be placed in different situations through no fault of their own, depending on whether the appellate court reviewed the case within the statutory time period.

Equality Before the Public Charge. This principle is derived from two sources: the principle of equality before the law in article 6 of the Declaration of the Rights of Man, and the principle in article 13 of the Declaration. Article 13 reads, "For the maintenance of public defense, and for the expenses of administration, a common contribution is necessary: it must be equally divided among all citizens, according to their means." It has traditionally been applied in the area of taxation, and only recently extended to nontax areas. There is an abundant jurisprudence in the area of taxation. The legislature is responsible for establishing the tax base within the limits of constitutional principles. It may promulgate fiscal rules, taking into account the particular activities of diverse categories of independent workers. Financial institutions, for example, may have a special contribution imposed on them because their particular status distinguishes them from other kinds of businesses.

A law aimed at creating and developing a sector of activity benefitting the general interest by giving tax breaks to foundations and companies engaged in cultural activity in the general interest was held not to violate the principle equality of taxation.

The legislature's discretion in fiscal matters is not unlimited, however. The *Conseil constitutionnel* verifies that the criterion of differentiation used by the legislature is related to the goal it has established. In this context, it held that rules for taxing large fortunes were not discriminatory, as the legislator had evaluated the contributive capacity of a usufructuary with respect to the total value of the property. The *Conseil* noted that the rules were justified by the fact that the legislature had targeted the contributive capacity conferred by the holding of property and resulting from revenues brought in by such property.

The *Conseil* reserves the right to censure an "obvious error of judgment." The budget law for 1984 exempted from the tax on large fortunes, as professional assets, shares of a company that represented at least twenty-five percent of the company's capital, if the stockholder was a director of the company. The *Conseil* held that the choice of twenty-five percent of the capital as the threshold over which these shares would be considered as professional assets was not an obvious error of judgment.

In this same decision, the *Conseil constitutionnel* held that the fight against tax fraud is a necessary corollary to the principle of equality of taxation contained in article 13 of the Declaration of the Rights of Man. The legislature has the discretion to choose the methods of fighting tax fraud, within constitutional limits. In the case before it, the *Conseil* struck down a provision of the law authorizing the issuance of search warrants to agents of the tax administration, on the ground that the warrant process was not accompanied by sufficient guarantees to assure the protection of individual liberty. The *Conseil* declared that the need to fight fiscal fraud must be balanced against constitutional guarantees of individual rights.

Equality in Public Employment. Equal access to public employment and equal treatment of public employees (*fonctionnaries*) in the advancement of their career are guaranteed by article 6 of the Declaration of the Rights of Man.

1. Equal access to public employment. In France, competitive recruitment (*concours de recrutement*), the traditional method of choosing employees for public service, has long been considered the most egalitarian way of deciding among applicants. The *Conseil constitutionnel*, however, has said that this is not the only permissible method of recruitment. In its decision of January 14, 1983, the *Conseil* upheld a law allowing the possibility of entry into the *Ecole Nationale d'Administration* of persons who had eight years of experience as a local elected official or as a director of a union, public service company, or mutual insurance organization. The following year, the *Conseil* ruled that the legislature could even authorize certain public entities to recruit noncompetitively.

2. Equality in career advancement. The goal of this principle is to eliminate career privileges; equal rules must apply to all public employees in the same service. However, the legislature may fix the appropriate rules for each entity. In its decision of September 12, 1984, the *Conseil constitutionnel* ruled that age limits may be established for the Vice President of the *Conseil d'Etat*, the *Premier prsident*, and the *Procureur gnral de la Cour des Comptes*, with no violation of the principle of equality of career advancement in view of the special functions of these positions.

Career privileges are especially frowned upon. In its decision of January 16, 1986 on the integration of ambassadors into the corps of plenipotentiary ministers, the *Conseil constitutionnel* struck down a provision assuring these persons a grade and rank corresponding to the level they had attained as ambassador, on the ground that this career advantage constituted a privilege with respect to other individuals who had entered the same service before them.

Equality of Suffrage. This principle applies to local as well as national elections. It was applied to a law revising the procedures for electing labor judges in the *Conseils des Prud'hommes* (specialized labor courts), which would have given larger employers a greater number of votes.

The *Conseil constitutionnel* ruled that, in view of the objectives of the law (the election of judges), the fact that certain employers have more employees than others does not justify giving them a greater number of votes.

The principle of equality in suffrage has also been applied to gender quotas in candidate lists. The law governing the election of municipal council members was amended in 1982 to provide that no more than seventy-five percent of those on the candidate list could be of the same sex (the goal was to increase the number of female candidates). The *Conseil constitutionnel* declared this amendment contrary to the principle of equality in suffrage, in that all citizens are eligible both to vote and to be candidates; candidate lists may not be limited through gender quotas, even if the goal is a desirable one.

The principle of equality in suffrage has been used in the review of reapportionment plans. It was applied for the first time to the election of members of the territorial congress of New Caledonia, and has been the subject of several decisions since. In a controversial decision of November 18, 1986, the *Conseil constitutionnel* approved a much-disputed redistricting plan passed by Parliament after the President of the Republic refused to endorse the plan as drafted. The *Conseil constitutionnel* declined to void the plan, stating that it could not substitute its own judgment for that of Parliament, and that it could not evaluate whether the reapportionment plan was the fairest one possible in view of the complexity of local demographics.

This very brief overview of the jurisprudence of the *Conseil constitutionnel* on the principle of equality reveals a clear emphasis on economic and social issues, and an almost total absence of decisions on discrimination based on the inherent characteristics of an individual or group.

Chapter Four

State Sovereignty and Judicial Review

When we talk about judicial review of domestic legislation in domestic courts under domestic constitutions, the primary concern is whether such review interferes with basic democratic principles. In Chapter 4 we raise a new concern: Does judicial review of domestic legislation under international law conflict with principles of national sovereignty? We will trace three steps in the development of judicial review under international law.

First of all, when a nation enters into a treaty, a question arises as to whether the provisions of that treaty take precedence over national law within the state's own legal system. Whether they do or not depends upon the constitutional law of the nation concerned. If the national constitution so provides, then treaty provisions will dominate legislation, and the ordinary courts of the nation will review legislation for consistency with treaties. For legal systems in which the judges of the ordinary courts have traditionally been forbidden from judging the validity of legislation, such review sits uneasily within the system. Nevertheless, for those who worry about national sovereignty there is some reassurance in the fact that it is compatriot judges doing the review, judges who will at least tend to interpret treaty provisions in line with national interests.

The same thing cannot be said about the second development that we will look at here: review of domestic legislation in *international* courts. The international court exacerbates the sovereignty issue. On top of the fact that the rules to be enforced against domestic legislation are not domestic rules, the judges who will be enforcing those rules are not domestic judges. They may have no reason to support what nationals perceive as the national interest. To the standard complaint about a dictatorship by judges, then, may be added the complaint that the laws and the judges who apply those laws are foreign.

It is true that the national legislature must ordinarily approve entering into the treaty. But is that sufficient insurance that those who interpret the treaty will be in any way accountable to the citizens of the nation? Or that once the nation is locked into a treaty the interpretation of its provisions will continue to be consistent with the national will? And all of this is of even greater concern when the international rules to be enforced are not provisions of the treaty, but subsidiary rules adopted under the treaty, rules that may require the consent only of a majority of parties to the treaty.

There is some consolation in the fact that the international court typically has no means to enforce its judgments, and even if individuals are granted standing before the international court, they typically have no way to force local officials to conform to a favorable ruling from the international tribunal. Nevertheless the rulings of such courts are obeyed surprisingly often.

Finally, these two developments may work together to create another, more striking possibility: the possibility that domestic courts will be required to apply international rules *as interpreted by an international court*. If national courts are authorized and required to enforce treaty provisions against national legislation, and if the interpretation of those provisions is dictated by an international (or supranational) court—and if, furthermore, the treaty provisions can be relied upon by individuals complaining of violations—then an alien court's interpretation of non-domestic rules becomes enforceable in local courts. It cannot be ignored by national officials, even in theory. And when the international law to be enforced includes not only treaty provisions but also subordinate rules enacted by an international organization operating under the treaty, the existence of judicial review under the treaty in domestic courts makes it difficult to distinguish between advanced international cooperation and the birth of a new legal system with a tendency toward federalism.

We will look first at the traditional rules governing international law in domestic courts, then at judicial review of domestic legislation in an international court, the Council of Europe's Court of Human Rights, and then at the development of judicial review in the domestic courts of the European Union.

A. Review of Legislation Under International Law in Domestic Courts

Nations are bound by the treaties they enter into, and the provisions of a treaty can be invoked by the parties to the treaty in their dealings with one another in any international forum that may have been created under the treaty. However, it is up to the individual nation whether treaties are also to have *internal effect*, so that their provisions can be invoked in domestic courts. A nation is called "monist," in this respect, when treaties that have been ratified by the nation are considered part of the national legal system, and can be relied on in the courts of that nation. Where that is so, treaty provisions are said to be directly applicable. A nation is called "dualist," on the other hand, if the internal effect of treaties in the courts of the nation depends upon some national institution, perhaps the legislature, translating the treaties into national law. Whether a nation is dualist or monist is ordinarily a constitutional question.

Where, in a dualist system, a treaty is implemented by statute, a later statute will usually take precedence. The general rule for legislation, including legislation implementing treaties, is *lex posterior derogat priori*: The later law takes precedence over the earlier. Nevertheless, the national constitution may provide otherwise, even in a dualist system, so that treaties will take precedence even over later statutes.

JOHN H. JACKSON, STATUS OF TREATIES IN DOMESTIC LEGAL SYSTEMS: A POLICY ANALYSIS
86 AM. J. INT'L L. 310, 313–315, 317–320 (1992)

Monism and Dualism. [L]et us first examine the broad outlines of the existing international situation with respect to the direct applicability of a treaty, using a simple paradigmatic hypothetical to illustrate it. Suppose nations M and D have entered into a treaty that includes the following obligation:

> With respect to the right to own property within the territory of either contracting party [nation M or D], the citizens of the other contracting party shall have equal and nondiscriminatory treatment as compared to treatment received by the citizens of that contracting party within which the property is located.

The intent of this language is to equalize the property ownership rights of both countries' citizens within the territory of each contracting party, a traditional expression of "national treatment" obligations found in many bilateral and multilateral treaties, although the subject of the obligation may differ widely.

In traditional explanations of the effect of treaties (going back a century or more), a distinction is made between "monist" and "dualist" states. This terminology has been criticized, and clearly it is too "dichotomous" in flavor, since there are various degrees of direct application of treaties, to say nothing of the considerable confusion about it. Nevertheless, even though not precise, these terms are used and may help to demonstrate the major alternative approaches.

Let us assume that state M is considered "monist" and state D is considered "dualist," and in each state a citizen of the other has been refused rights to own property by the national government even though that state's citizens possess those rights. What is the national legal situation?

Traditionally, the "monist" state's legal system is considered to include international treaties to which M is obligated. Thus, a citizen of D can sue as an individual in the courts of M to require that he be treated in accordance with the treaty standard.

On the other hand, the term "dualist" has been used to describe the contrary result in state D. In a dualist state, international treaties are part of a separate legal system from that of the domestic law (hence a "dual" system). Therefore, a treaty is not part of the domestic law, at least not directly. Without further facts, a citizen of *M* who is refused the property ownership privilege in *D* that *D*'s citizen has there, has no way to sue in the courts of *D* because those courts apply the law of D, which does not include the rule expressed in the treaty (at least not yet). The citizen of *M*'s only recourse is to persuade his own government to use diplomatic means to encourage *D* to honor its obligation and assure him equal property ownership rights.

It is generally said that for the treaty rule to operate in the domestic legal system of a dualist state, there must be an "act of transformation," that is, a government action by that state incorporating the treaty norm into its domestic law. This may be a statute duly enacted by the parliament that uses all or part of the treaty language and incorporates it as a statutory matter into domestic law. Sometimes such a statute may paraphrase the treaty language, or "clarify" or elaborate on the treaty language. In all these cases, the domestic law is that of the act of transformation, but the treaty language usually has "relevance" in interpreting the statutory language, under various theories of domestic jurisprudence. Other legal instruments can also serve as an act of transformation, including a regulation of an administrative body (if its authority so permits), and possibly even an action or decision of a court or tribunal....

Issues of Treaty Application. [O]ne of the questions posed by this article [is] whether the treaty is "directly applicable" or, more generally, what role the treaty plays in the domestic legal system of a state party. Obviously, if a treaty is "invalid" under either international law or national law, this issue would usually never be reached. In some circumstances, direct application of a treaty might be one form of "implementation" of certain types of treaties. Here again, we refer to "statutelike" application, and note that there may be other types of internal effects of treaties that are not directly applicable.

[Next], comes the important, but often misunderstood, question that can be called "invocability." This term can refer to a group of concepts, one of which is similar, but not necessarily identical, to "standing"; even though a treaty is directly applicable in the domestic legal system, in a specific case a determination may need to be made as to who is entitled to invoke or rely on the treaty norms. In some jurisdictions this concept may be expressed as "partial direct application" or may be governed by the idea that a treaty is directly applicable for some purposes but not others. For example, a treaty might be directly applicable in disputes between different units or levels of government, or between the government and a private person ("vertically"), but not between private citizens or enterprises ("horizontally"). One way to analyze this is to conclude that the treaty as such is directly applicable, that is, becomes part of the domestic jurisprudence. Then the applying institution (e.g., the courts) must determine which parties/entities are entitled to "invoke" or rely on the treaty norms. Alternatively, it may be determined that only portions of a treaty are directly applicable (sometimes depending on the precision and other attributes of the language of specific portions), while the rest of the treaty is not.

In some cases courts or governments have confused (or fused) these two questions…, judging "direct application" or "self-executing" partly by reference to whether a party may invoke the treaty. This author believes that it is analytically preferable (to avoid confusion and potential error) to separate these concepts, particularly since the policies that relate to each one differ considerably. For example, direct application may primarily be a question of intent of one or more of the treaty parties, while invocability may depend on the precision of the language, definitions of categories of persons (e.g., "citizen," "adult male"), or concepts of justiciability or "political question."

[The third question], hierarchy of norms, relates closely to the two previous questions, and it is therefore these three issues…that are central to this article. Hierarchy of norms refers to the questions that arise when a directly applicable and invocable treaty norm is unavoidably inconsistent with other norms in the national legal system. Those other norms may include the constitution, prior national-level statutes, subsequent national-level statutes, various regulatory acts, and laws of subordinate governmental units (states in a federal system) and, among other things, may be either prior or subsequent to the treaty. In fact, a fairly elaborate matrix of possible clashes can be worked out, and the answers for each "cell" can differ in different legal systems. With only one or two exceptions, constitutions generally are deemed superior to treaties, but a key question is usually the status of a treaty norm that clashes with a later national legislative enactment. In the United States, the later in time prevails. In some other countries, the treaty will prevail even over such later enactments, and this is the crux of the most important policy issue (in the view of this author) concerning direct application.

It should be noted that for this issue…to arise, a few other issues must be determined. That is, the treaty must be valid both internationally and domestically, it must be applied directly, and it must be invocable. Unless all these conditions are met, a hierarchy of norms does not arise as a matter of domestic law. Of course, issues remain under both international law and internal law. For example, a treaty may be internationally and domestically valid but not directly applied, and thus a domestic system may perform a legal act or make a legal determination that violates the treaty. In that case the acting nation is still "liable," as a matter of international law, to the contracting parties of the treaty. However, international processes would have to be invoked to "enforce" the treaty obligation. Furthermore, the treaty (even though not directly applicable) may still have a variety of internal law effects, such as influencing the interpretation of municipal statutes and laws, operating through a statutory provision that makes reference to "international law" or a treaty standard, or influencing an appraisal of "public policy"....

The Approach of Various Countries. The United Kingdom is generally considered the prime example of a dualist system. Treaties never have direct "statutelike" application in the United Kingdom, but of course may have other internal effects. Many national systems derived from that of the United Kingdom, such as the Canadian and Australian systems, follow similar approaches. The legislature may enact laws that incorporate ("transform") treaties or treaty norms into domestic law.... Sometimes (such as with the UK European Communities Act of 1972) a parliament can make provision for the "transformation" in advance. Variations on this approach are found in many other countries, for example, Germany and Italy.

At the other extreme, perhaps, is the Constitution of the Netherlands, which could generally be called "monist" since it expressly provides that certain treaties are directly applied and that in such cases these treaties are deemed superior to all laws, including constitutional norms! The 1958 Constitution of France also calls for direct application and a higher status for treaties than later legislation. With a variety of nuances, such provisions are found in the Constitutions of Belgium, Switzerland, Japan and other nations.

The United States stands somewhere in between. Under U.S. jurisprudence, some treaties can be found to be self-executing, in which case they will be directly applied. To determine "self-execution," U.S. courts look at a series of factors, but (it seems) primarily at the intent of the drafters, including intent implied or expressed in the treaty itself. When that language is sufficiently precise and indicates that no further government action is needed to apply the treaty norms, a U.S. court will be willing to conclude that the treaty is self-executing. However, under a long string of precedents over a hundred years, U.S. courts have ruled that a directly applied treaty has the same status as federal laws (statutes, etc.) and that the latest in time therefore prevails. Thus, for internal law purposes, a later U.S. statute will prevail over the international agreement (which sometimes causes the United States to violate its international obligations).....

Note

1. The question of precedence is obviously relevant to the issue of judicial review of legislation. If treaties are on the same level as legislation, but are trumped by later legislation, then judges are not asked to strike legislation when it conflicts with a treaty, but merely to apply the later rule, whichever it may be.

* * *

COMMITTEE OF UNITED STATES CITIZENS LIVING IN NICARAGUA V. REAGAN

859 F.2D 929 (D.C. CIR. 1988)

MIKVA, Circuit Judge:

Appellants, comprising organizations and individuals who oppose United States policy in Central America, claim to have suffered physical, economic and other injuries from the war in Nicaragua. These facts form the backdrop to this lawsuit.

The suit finds its genesis, however, in a 1986 decision by the International Court of Justice (ICJ), which held that America's support of military actions by the so-called "Contras" against the government of Nicaragua violated both customary international law and a treaty between the United States and Nicaragua. The ICJ concluded that the United States "is under a duty immediately to cease and to refrain from all such acts as may constitute breaches of the foregoing legal obligations." Included among those acts were the "training, arming, equipping, financing and supplying the *contra* forces."

Prior to the ICJ's decision, the United States withdrew from the merits phase of the court's proceedings, contending that the court lacked jurisdiction over Nicaragua's application. Since the decision, the President has requested and Congress has approved continued funding for the Contras of the sort that the ICJ found illegal. In addition, the U.S. used its veto power in the United Nations (U.N.) Security Council to block consideration of a resolution enforcing the ICJ decision.

Unhappy with their government's failure to abide by the ICJ decision and believing that continued funding of the Contras injures their own interests, appellants filed suit in the United States District Court for the District of Columbia. The suit sought injunctive and declaratory relief against the funding of the Contras on grounds that such funding violates [among other things] Article 94 of the U.N. Charter and customary international law....

The effect of subsequent statutes upon prior inconsistent treaties. Although appellants' complaint alleges that Congress' funding of the Contras violates Article 94 of the U.N. Charter,...appellants seem to concede here that such a claim is unavailing. They acknowledge, as they must, that "[o]rdinarily, treaty obligations may be overridden by subsequent inconsistent statutes"....Nonetheless, allegations concerning the violation of Article 94 resurface at several points in appellants' arguments, and we therefore briefly canvass the precedents that foreclose such claims. [The court then discusses the *Head Money Cases,* 112 U.S. 580, 5 S.Ct. 247, 28 L.Ed. 798 (1884), and *Diggs v. Shultz,* 470

F.2d 461 (D.C.Cir.1972), *cert. denied,* 411 U.S. 931, 93 S.Ct. 1897, 36 L.Ed.2d 390 (1973)]

These precedents dispose of any claim by appellants that the United States has violated its treaty obligation under Article 94....The claim could succeed only if appellants could prove that a prior treaty—the U.N. Charter—preempts a subsequent statute, namely the legislation that funds the Contras. It is precisely that argument that the precedents of the Supreme Court and of this court foreclose. We therefore hold that appellants' claims based on treaty violations must fail.

Our conclusion, of course, speaks not at all to whether the United States has upheld its treaty obligations under international law....

Finally, we note that even if Congress' breach of a treaty were cognizable in domestic court, appellants would lack standing to rectify the particular breach that they allege here. Article 94 of the U.N. Charter simply does not confer rights on private individuals. Treaty clauses must confer such rights in order for individuals to assert a claim "arising under" them. *See* U.S. Const. art. III, § 2, cl. 1; 28 U.S.C. § 1331 (1982). Whether a treaty clause does create such enforcement rights is often described as part of the larger question of whether that clause is "self-executing"....

This court has noted that, in "determining whether a treaty is self-executing" in the sense of its creating private enforcement rights, "courts look to the intent of the signatory parties as manifested by the language of the instrument." *Diggs v. Richardson,* 555 F.2d 848, 851 (D.C.Cir.1976)....Applying the same test to Article 94 of the U.N. Charter, we reach a similar conclusion.... The words of Article 94 "do not by their terms confer rights upon individual citizens; they call upon governments to take certain action." *Diggs v. Richardson,* 555 F.2d at 851. We conclude that appellants' attempt to enjoin funding of the Contras based on a violation of Article 94 would fail even if Congress' abrogation of treaties were cognizable in domestic courts.

Customary international law and subsequent inconsistent statutes. In addition to relying on Article 94 to challenge continued funding of the Contras, appellants also invoke the rule "of customary international law that nations must obey the rulings of an international court to whose jurisdiction they submit." We accept that some version of this rule describes a norm of customary international law.... Even so, it is far from clear that this rule governs situations like the present one, in which a nation that has consented in advance to the Court's jurisdiction disputes whether the terms of that consent extend to a particular case. *Cf.* ICJ Statute art. 36, para. 6 ("dispute as to whether the ICJ has jurisdiction...shall be settled by decision of the Court")....For the moment, we assume *arguendo* that Congress' decision to disregard the ICJ judgment violates customary international law.

The question is whether such a violation is cognizable by domestic courts. Once again, the United States' rejection of a purely "monist" view of the international and domestic legal orders shapes our analysis. Statutes inconsistent with principles of customary international law may well lead to international law violations. But within the domestic legal realm, that inconsistent statute simply modifies or supersedes customary international law to the extent of the inconsistency....

There is no question that, in the second half of the twentieth century, the protections afforded individuals under international law have greatly expanded. At one time, international law concerned itself chiefly with relations among states, occasionally with relations between a state and citizens of other states, and almost never with a nation's treatment of its own citizens. *See, e.g.,* Sohn, *The New International Law: Protection of the Rights of Individuals Rather than States,* 32 Am.U.L.Rev. 1, 9 (1982). That has now changed, *id.* at 9–11, and government officials can be held responsible for certain egregious violations of their own citizens' rights. *See, e.g., Filartiga v. Pena-Irala,* 630 F.2d 876 (2d Cir.1980) (international law proscribes "official torture"). Notwithstanding these changes, however, the expanded law of nations does not encompass the principles that appellants advance in this lawsuit....

Note

1. Is there any difference between Jackson's use of the term "self-executing," in the first selection in this chapter and Mikva's use of it in the case above? Has Mikva "fused" together (to use Jackson's word) direct applicability and invocability?

*   *   *

JOHN H. JACKSON, STATUS OF TREATIES IN DOMESTIC LEGAL SYSTEMS: A POLICY ANALYSIS
86 AM. J. INT'L L. 310, 330–331 (1992)

.... [S]uppose the legal system of nation M requires direct application of treaty norms and its constitution provides that such norms will trump all other laws except the constitution, even laws enacted later at the highest legislative level. Suppose further that M is party to a treaty.... Ten years after M's accession to the treaty, its legislature, citizenry and government leaders wish to enact a special rule giving M's poor citizens preferential property ownership rights (but they argue that to give these rights to noncitizens would attract an influx of poor persons from other countries who would exploit the rule and make it unacceptably expensive). The envisioned rule may accord purchasing preference to poor citizens when the government disposes of property it owns or has validly seized or repossessed. Yet the treaty norm (sometimes unexpectedly) may seem to preclude this act or be determined internationally to prevent it. Since the domestic application of the norm trumps later legislation, the government's hands are tied. It must either renegotiate the treaty (or terminate it) or refrain from enacting the desired legislation.

For the purposes of our discussion, we will assume that at least some treaty norms are directly applied, since it makes no sense to be concerned about higher status in domestic law unless the norm is part of domestic law. We now consider whether it is wise policy for treaty norms to be both directly applied and given higher status in domestic legal systems than most other laws.

Higher Status as "Constitutionalization." In essence, DAHS (the acronym for "directly applicable with higher status,"...) means that the treaty norm has been "constitutionalized," or given a sort of "constitutional status" almost equivalent to the nation's own constitution. It occurs through a procedure that often falls short of the rigor or democracy of constitutional amending procedures, which may surprise certain interest groups that did not focus on the treaty issues years ago. In these circumstances, what are some of the policy considerations?

argument against DAHS [margin annotation]

....In the absence of higher status, a later statute or other law might correct some of the problems...(e.g., a legislative desire to "interpret" the treaty or to reallocate internal decision-making power), albeit perhaps with some additional trouble and shifting of the political burden of taking the necessary initiative. When higher status is added, however, the problems become much more difficult. For example, the asymmetrical situation noted above, in which some nations do not directly apply treaty norms while others do, is even more anomalous when some that do, do so with a higher status. Those nations find themselves more locked into the norms than the other parties.

Once again, the issue of the "democratic deficit" arises, but more acutely. If the procedures for treaty making do not permit adequate democratic participation, the DAHS treaty norm can be criticized as imposing an elite's vision of control on a society (or worse, that of a special interest group). Indeed, it can be seriously doubted whether such a norm would be truly effective; governmental units, including courts, would struggle to attenuate the norm or avoid it altogether.

Usually, this is not an either-or question, for the degree of democratic input varies and in many cases may be said to be sufficient, even for a "constitutionalized" norm like a DAHS. Yet a series of other concerns can be raised that should at least be understood by policy makers who wish to oppose or to accept the DAHS idea. The most significant of these was noted in the hypothetical above, that the DAHS norm imposes considerable rigidity (almost equal to a constitutional rule) on future government action. Arguably, a constitution should generally contain norms deemed so essential to government that they need to impose rigidity: norms that preserve human rights, allocate power among governmental branches or entities, specify the rules for democratic governance (elections, terms of office), and the like. To constitutionalize the whole body of potential treaty relations is quite another matter. A government with DAHS would need to be very restrained in accepting treaty obligations, or it could find itself hamstrung at many turns by thousands or tens of thousands of treaty norms (especially on economic subjects).

Treaty making, incidentally, can also mean the development of "secondary" treaty rules, i.e., regulations or decisions by international bodies pursuant to treaty authorization. Thus, a nation with DAHS could find its legal system bound both by rules that only a few of its own diplomats (maybe instructed by an elite or small group within the executive part of their government) participated in drafting, and by the majoritarian or other (sometimes defective) voting procedures of multilateral bodies. A nation in that position could refuse to accept such treaties, or it might work toward building international institutions that avoid secondary norm making, but this approach could substantially inhibit the progress of the world legal system.

Note

1. Note that even where treaty provisions can be directly applicable under a constitutional provision, they are usually still subservient to the constitution, which can be changed. Under those conditions, is it fair to say that entering into a treaty amounts to giving away part of the nation's sovereignty? What if treaty provisions trump even the constitution—what is left of sovereignty then?

* * *

B. Judicial Review of Legislation in International Courts: The European Court of Human Rights

1. The European Convention on Human Rights

This section introduces the European Convention on Human Rights and the court created by the Convention, the European Court of Human Rights. The procedure described in the following selection has been modified somewhat since the 1980s—in particular it is no longer necessary to go through the Commission to get to the Court—but knowing something about the older procedure is essential to understanding the pre-1990 cases.

J. A. ANDREWS, THE EUROPEAN
JURISPRUDENCE OF HUMAN RIGHTS
43 MD. L. REV. 463, 465–467, 468–470,
471–472, 479–481, 487 (1984)

.... [O]n November 4, 1950, the European Convention for the Protection of Human Rights and Fundamental Freedoms (the Convention) was signed—the first convention concluded under the auspices of the Council of Europe.

The Convention recognises certain basic rights and freedoms as "the foundation of justice and peace in the world," which the states party to it (the High Contracting Parties) "shall secure to everyone within their jurisdiction." It provides that everyone whose rights under the Convention have been violated "shall have an effective remedy before a national authority," and that the rights and freedoms it guarantees "shall be secured without discrimination on any ground." The obligations of the states party to the Convention may be derogated from "[i]n time of war or other public emergency threatening the life of the nation," but the rights guaranteed by the Convention may be restricted only for prescribed purposes.

One aspect of the Convention was entirely unique at the time of its drafting, and is responsible for the special character of the Convention as an international agreement protecting human rights: It does not stop at imposing obligations upon the states party to it, but goes on to provide a structure by means of which those obligations may be enforced. "To ensure the observance of the engagements undertaken by the High Contracting Parties" under the Convention, the European Commission of Human Rights and the European Court of Human Rights were created. Article 25 provides that each state signatory to the Convention, if it chooses, may recognize the competence of the Commission to receive petitions from "any person...or group of individuals claiming to be the victim of [that state's] violation" of rights guaranteed by the Convention. Article 46 further provides that the High Contracting Parties may "recognis[e] as compulsory...the jurisdiction of the Court in all matters concerning the interpretation and application of the...Convention."

The enforcement mechanism thus built into the Convention was an important innovation. Because of it the Convention has been characterised as sui generis, a law transcending traditional boundaries between international and domestic law and establishing "a new legal order." It ought to be noted, however, that the Convention was not entirely without precedent. In determining what substantive rights should be guaranteed, those responsible for proposing and drafting the Convention primarily looked to the Universal Declaration of Human Rights.

The Universal Declaration of Human Rights was signed on December 10, 1948. At the time of its proclamation it was said to have "a moral value and au-

STATE SOVEREIGNTY AND JUDICIAL REVIEW   197

thority…without precedent in the history of the world," and in fact it has been enormously influential. It was adopted by the General Assembly of the United Nations by a vote of forty-eight in favour and none against, with eight abstentions. Among those who abstained was the delegate from the USSR. Behind his abstention lay an old problem: the difficulty of giving human rights a universally acceptable content. The Soviet Union objected to the Universal Declaration both because it included a defence of property rights and because it failed to include protection of the social and economic rights regarded as fundamental in Marxist ideology.

Unlike the members of the General Assembly in 1948, the founding members of the Council of Europe had a long common historical association and shared cultural, economic, and social values. The members were able to agree fairly quickly, therefore, as to which human rights were to be protected by the Convention (and by the first protocol to the Convention, which followed shortly)….

The Right of Individual Petition and the European Commission of Human Rights. The most radical innovation incorporated into the Convention was that individuals were to be allowed to petition the European Commission of Human Rights. The Convention was the first international instrument purporting to guarantee individual rights which also provided a means of enforcing them. Individuals were to have direct access to machinery of protection outside their own states, although under the compromise embodied in article 25, they could make application only against those signatory states that accepted the right of individual petition by lodging a separate declaration to that effect.

International legal historians probably will look back on the institution of this right as one of the greatest and most radical legal developments of the twentieth century. Even if the Convention is viewed as regional rather than international in a broader sense, the significance of the achievement is not diminished. The most startling aspect of the right of individual petition under article 25 is that by lodging declarations recognising the Commission's competence to receive such petitions, all but four signatory states have allowed their treatment of their own citizens to be subjected to review in an international forum as a matter of right….

The European Court of Human Rights—Its Jurisdiction and Judgments. One of the difficult issues that those who framed the European Convention on Human Rights had to address was whether there should be compulsory judicial review of claimed violations of the Convention. The High Contracting Parties agreed that each of them should have an opportunity to challenge another under the Convention, and that for such a purpose the Commission of Human Rights was a necessary forum. But there is a difference between a commission able to review the facts and perhaps steer the disputing parties towards a friendly settlement, on the one hand, and a court with compulsory jurisdiction and power to give binding judgment on the other. As with the right of individual petition, so too on the issue of the compulsory jurisdiction a compromise was reached. Under article 46 of the Convention, signatory states may make a special declaration accepting the compulsory jurisdiction of the European Court of Human Rights (the Court), but they are not subject to its jurisdiction unless they do so....

Cases may be referred to the Court only by the Commission or by one of the High Contracting Parties—individuals have no right to take their own cases to the Court. The Court's jurisdiction extends to "all cases concerning the interpretation and application of the...Convention" that are referred to it properly, and its judgments are final and not subject to appeal....

Enforcement of the Convention: The Incorporation Question. The rights created under the European Convention on Human Rights were intended to be real, but at the same time the primary obligation for enforcement was left to the signatory states within their own jurisdictions. Some states have incorporated the Convention into domestic law. For example, once the Belgian Parliament authorised ratification of the Convention and the government ratified it, the Convention's provisions were incorporated into Belgian domestic law under the terms of the Belgian Constitution. As a result, the status of the Convention in Belgium is comparable to that of Belgian domestic legislation, and individuals can pursue their rights under it in Belgian courts.... In Austria the Convention has secured a more privileged position. There it has the normative equivalency of constitutional law and its protections rank alongside the other guarantees of human rights contained in the Austrian Constitution of 1920 and other Basic Law.

Within the United Kingdom, the Republic of Ireland, Iceland, and the Scandinavian countries, however, there has been no domestic adoption of the European Convention on Human Rights.[1] The obligations of these states under the Convention remain essentially international treaty obligations. English courts are not bound by the provisions of the Convention, and the individual who feels that his rights have been violated in the United Kingdom must pursue his remedy before the European Commission. English courts do make a genuflection to the Convention, however, in that they are prepared to look at its content if there is doubt as to the scope and meaning of a provision of English law. It has been said that in such a case the courts should interpret the internal rule in a way that is consistent with the United Kingdom's obligations under the Convention....

Notes

1. The institutions and procedure under the Convention changed dramatically in 1998. The Commission was abolished, and individual appeals are now submitted directly to the Court, where they are screened by staff attor-

---

1. The United Kingdom has recently incorporated the Convention by statute.

neys. An official description of the organization of the Court can be found at <http://www.echr.coe.int/Eng/Edocs/HistoricalBackground.htm>, along with a detailed outline of procedures before the Court.

2. If someone in a country that has not incorporated the Convention into national law exhausts his domestic appeals, he may appeal to the ECHR. What if his state has incorporated the Convention into legislation? May he nevertheless skirt his country's courts and go directly to the ECHR? He must exhaust his national remedies first; but if he is still unsatisfied, he may go on to the European Court:

> It is not difficult to see the reason why applications still come to Strasbourg from those states in whose courts the Convention can be pleaded. In Germany the Convention does not prevail over Basic Law. It has the same status as any other federal law and is subject to the general rule *leges posteriores priores contrarias abrogant.* Similarly, although there is a presumption in Belgium that Acts of Parliament are intended to be in conformity with the Constitution and with treaty obligations, including obligations under the Convention, until recently the Belgian courts have hesitated to interfere with the doctrine of the supremacy of Parliament by reviewing the legality or constitutionality of Acts of Parliament.

J. A. Andrews, The European Jurisprudence of Human Rights, 43 Md. L. Rev. 463, 487 (1984).

3. If a state incorporates the Convention, must the interpretation the domestic courts give to provisions conform to those of the European Court? Are European judges going to be telling legislators what their statutes mean? This is a sensitive issue, and complicates the problems introduced by this sort of judicial review: Not only are unelected judges determining the fate of legislation; in these sorts of cases the unelected judges are not even, for the most part, citizens of the state whose law is in question. Does the signatory nation have any recourse, under the Convention? Should it?

* * *

2. The Text

THE EUROPEAN CONVENTION FOR THE PROTECTION OF HUMAN RIGHTS AND FUNDAMENTAL FREEDOMS
(1950)

Article 1 - Obligation to respect human rights. The High Contracting Parties shall secure to everyone within their jurisdiction the rights and freedoms defined in Section I of this Convention....

Article 8 - Right to respect for private and family life. 1. Everyone has the right to respect for his private and family life, his home and his correspondence.

2. There shall be no interference by a public authority with the exercise of this right except such as is in accordance with the law and is necessary in a democratic society in the interests of national security, public safety or the economic well-being of the country, for the prevention of disorder or crime, for the protection of health or morals, or for the protection of the rights and freedoms of others....

Notes

1. Article 8 permits interferences which are "in accordance with the law" and "necessary in a democratic society." Articles 9 (Freedom of thought, conscience and religion), 10 (Freedom of expression), and 11 (Freedom of assembly and association) contain the same wording. Within certain limits, something is *in accordance with the law* if it is provided for in national legislation, regulations, or common law rules. But what does it mean to be *necessary in a democratic society*? The Court has used the words *pluralism, tolerance,* and *broad-mindedness* in this connection,[2] and has said that freedom of debate is essential to the concept of democracy.[3] But to be necessary to democracy a restriction need not be indispensable; that would restrict the state's discretion within rather narrow bounds. The Court grants some leeway to a state in determining what is necessary in its circumstances. What it requires is that the State be pursuing a legitimate aim, and that the means be proportionate to the aim to be achieved.

2. The Court refers to the leeway it grants to the States as "the margin of appreciation." The Court is aware that one State's conception of a given right might differ to some acceptable degree from the conception of a different State, and variation within that margin is not something the Court will concern itself with. The Court has said that with respect to the extent it is necessary to curtail certain rights in deference to other rights, or to the public interest, "State authorities are in principle in a better position than the international judge to give an opinion on the exact content of these requirements."[4] Nevertheless the discretion granted to the States is not absolute, as a now-long history of cases under the Convention will attest.

3. What are the "legitimate aims" the State may pursue? Those enumerated in Article 8 are national security, public safety, and economic well-being of the community; prevention of disorder or crime; protection of health or morals;

---

2. Handyside v. U.K., 1 E.H.R.R. 757, Eur. Ct. H.R., Series A, no. 24, para. 49 (7 December 1976).
3. See Lingens v. Austria, July 8, 1986, A/103, para. 42.
4. Handyside, para. 48.

and the protection of the rights and freedoms of others. Should the State be permitted the same margin of appreciation with respect to each of these? Does the prevention of crime, for example, justify more extensive interference than the economic well-being of the community?

* * *

3. The Dudgeon Case

In the *Dudgeon* case, Northern Ireland appeals to the last two aims enumerated in Article 8, protection of health and morals and protection of the rights and freedoms of others, to justify the banning of certain sorts of behavior. What does "protection of morals" mean in this context? Does it mean protection of individuals from immorality? Does it mean protection of the community moral standard from individuals?

DUDGEON V. UNITED KINGDOM
4 E.H.R.R. 149 (1982)

Mr. Jeffrey Dudgeon, who is 35 years of age, is a shipping clerk resident in Belfast, Northern Ireland. Mr. Dudgeon is a homosexual and his complaints are directed primarily against the existence in Northern Ireland of laws which have the effect of making certain homosexual acts between consenting adult males criminal offences.

The relevant law in Northern Ireland. The relevant provisions currently in force in Northern Ireland are contained in the Offences against the Person Act 1861 ('the 1861 Act'), the Criminal Law Amendment Act 1885 ('the 1885 Act') and the common law....Acts of homosexuality between females are not, and have never been, criminal offences, although the offence of indecent assault may be committed by one woman on another under the age of 17.

As regards heterosexual relations, it is an offence, subject to certain exceptions, for a man to have sexual intercourse with a girl under the age of 17. Until 1950 the age of consent of a girl to sexual intercourse was 16 in both England and Wales and in Northern Ireland, but by legislation introduced in that year the age of consent was increased to 17 in Northern Ireland. While in relation to the corresponding offence in England and Wales it is a defence for a man under the age of 24 to show that he believed with reasonable cause the girl to be over 16 years of age, no such defence is available under Northern Ireland law....

Proposals for reform in Northern Ireland....On 27 July 1978, the Government published a proposal for a draft Homosexual Offences (Northern Ireland) Order 1978, the effect of which would have been to bring Northern Ireland law on the matter broadly into line with that of England and Wales. In particular, homosexual acts in private between two consenting male adults over the age of 21 would no longer have been punishable....On 2 July 1979, the then Secretary of State for Northern Ireland, in announcing to Parliament that the Government did not intend to pursue the proposed reform, stated:

> Consultation showed that strong views are held in Northern Ireland, both for and against change in the existing law....

The Alleged Breach of Article 8. The applicant complained that under the law in force in Northern Ireland he is liable to criminal prosecution on account of his homosexual conduct and that he has experienced fear, suffering and psychological distress directly caused by the very existence of the laws in question, including fear of harassment and blackmail. He further complained that, following the search of his house in January 1976, he was questioned by the police about certain homosexual activities and that personal papers belonging to him were seized during the search and not returned until more than a year later. He alleged that, in breach of Article 8 of the Convention, he has thereby suffered, and continues to suffer, an unjustified interference with his right to respect for his private life....

The Commission saw no reason to doubt the general truth of the applicant's allegations concerning the fear and distress that he has suffered in consequence of the existence of the laws in question. The Commission unanimously concluded that:

> the legislation complained of interferes with the applicant's right to respect for his private life guaranteed by Article 8 (1), in so far as it prohibits homosexual acts committed in private between consenting males....

The Court sees no reason to differ from the views of the Commission: the maintenance in force of the impugned legislation constitutes a continuing interference with the applicant's right to respect for his private life (which includes his sexual life) within the meaning of Article 8 (1). In the personal circumstances of the applicant, the very existence of this legislation continuously and directly affects his private life: either he respects the law and refrains from engaging (even in private with consenting male partners) in prohibited sexual acts to which he is disposed by reason of his homosexual tendencies, or he commits such acts and thereby becomes liable to criminal prosecution ....

In the Government's submission, the law in Northern Ireland relating to homosexual acts does not give rise to a breach of Article 8, in that it is justified by the terms of Article 8 (2). This contention was disputed by both the applicant and the Commission. An interference with the exercise of an Article 8 right will not be compatible with Article 8 (2) unless it is 'in accordance with the law', has an aim or aims that is or are legitimate under that paragraph and is 'necessary in a democratic society' for the aforesaid aim or aims.

["In accordance with the law":] It has not been contested that the first of these three conditions was met. As the Commission pointed out in paragraph 99 of its Report, the interference is plainly 'in accordance with the law' since it results from the existence of certain provisions in the 1861 and 1885 Acts and the common law....

["Legitimate aims":] It next falls to be determined whether the interference is aimed at 'the protection of...morals' or 'the protection of the rights and freedoms of others', the two purposes relied on by the Government.

The 1861 and 1885 Acts were passed in order to enforce the then prevailing conception of sexual morality. Originally they applied to England and Wales, to all Ireland, then unpartitioned, and also, in the case of the 1885 Act, to Scotland. In recent years the scope of the legislation has been restricted in England and Wales (with the 1967 Act) and subsequently in Scotland (with the 1980 Act): with certain exceptions it is no longer a criminal offence for two consenting males over 21 years of age to commit homosexual acts in private. In Northern Ireland, in contrast, the law has remained unchanged. The decision announced in July 1979 to take no further action in relation to the proposal to amend the existing law was, the Court accepts, prompted by what the United Kingdom Government judged to be the strength of feeling in Northern Ireland against the proposed change, and in particular the strength of the view that it would be seriously damaging to the moral fabric of Northern Irish society. This being so, the general aim pursued by the legislation remains the protection of morals in the sense of moral standards obtaining in Northern Ireland.

Both the Commission and the Government took the view that, in so far as the legislation seeks to safeguard young persons from undesirable and harmful pressures and attentions, it is also aimed at 'the protection of the rights and freedoms of others'. The Court recognises that one of the purposes of the legislation is to afford safeguards for vulnerable members of society, such as the young, against the consequences of homosexual practices. However, it is somewhat artificial in this context to draw a rigid distinction between 'protection of the rights and freedoms of others' and 'protection of...morals'. The latter may imply safeguarding the moral ethos or moral standards of a society as a whole, but may also, as the Government pointed out, cover protection of the moral interests and welfare of a particular section of society, for example schoolchildren. Thus, 'protection of the rights and freedoms of others', when meaning the safeguarding of the moral interests and welfare of certain individuals or classes of individuals who are in need of special protection for reasons such as lack of maturity, mental disability or state of dependence, amounts to one aspect of 'protection of...morals'. The Court will therefore take account of the two aims on this basis.

["Necessary in a democratic society":] As the Commission rightly observed in its Report, the cardinal issue arising under Article 8 in this case is to what extent, if at all, the maintenance in force of the legislation is 'necessary in a democratic society' for these aims. There can be no denial that some degree of regulation of male homosexual conduct, as indeed of other forms of sexual conduct, by means of the criminal law can be justified as 'necessary in a democratic society'. The overall function served by the criminal law in this field is, in the words of the Wolfenden report, 'to preserve public order and decency [and] to protect the citizen from what is offensive or injurious'. Furthermore, this necessity for some degree of control may even extend to consensual acts committed in private, notably where there is call (to quote the Wolfenden report once more),

> to provide sufficient safeguards against exploitation and corruption of others, particularly those who are specially vulnerable because they are young, weak in body or mind, inexperienced, or in a state of special physical, official or economic dependence.

In practice there is legislation on the matter in all the member States of the Council of Europe, but what distinguishes the law in Northern Ireland from that existing in the great majority of the member-States is that it prohibits generally gross indecency between males and buggery whatever the circumstances. It being accepted that some form of legislation is 'necessary' to protect particular sections of society as well as the moral ethos of society as a whole, the question in the present case is whether the contested provisions of the law of Northern Ireland and their enforcement remain within the bounds of what, in a democratic society, may be regarded as necessary in order to accomplish those aims.

A number of principles relevant to the assessment of the 'necessity', 'in a democratic society', of a measure taken in furtherance of an aim that is legitimate under the Convention have been stated by the Court in previous judgments. Firstly, 'necessary' in this context does not have the flexibility of such expressions as 'useful', 'reasonable', or 'desirable', but implies the existence of a 'pressing social need' for the interference in question. In the second place, it is for the national authorities to make the initial assessment of the pressing social need in each case; accordingly, a margin of appreciation is left to them. However, their decision remains subject to review by the Court.

As was illustrated by *The Sunday Times* judgment, the scope of the margin of appreciation is not identical in respect of each of the aims justifying restrictions on a right. The Government inferred from the *Handyside* judgment that the margin of appreciation will be more extensive where the protection of morals is in issue. It is an indisputable fact, as the Court stated in the *Handyside* judgment, that: 'the view taken...of the requirements of morals varies from time to time and from place to place, especially in our era,' and that

> By reason of their direct and continuous contact with the vital forces of their countries, State authorities are in principle in a better position

than the international judge to give an opinion on the exact content of those requirements.

However, not only the nature of the aim of the restriction but also the nature of the activities involved will affect the scope of the margin of appreciation. The present case concerns a most intimate aspect of private life. Accordingly, there must exist particularly serious reasons before interferences on the part of the public authorities can be legitimate for the purposes of Article 8 (2).

Finally, in Article 8 as in several other Articles of the Convention, the notion of 'necessity' is linked to that of a 'democratic society'. According to the Court's case-law, a restriction on a Convention right cannot be regarded as 'necessary in a democratic society' (two hallmarks of which are tolerance and broad-mindedness) unless, amongst other things, it is proportionate to the legitimate aim pursued.

The Court's task is to determine on the basis of the afore-stated principles whether the reasons purporting to justify the 'interference' in question are relevant and sufficient under Article 8 (2). The Court is not concerned with making any value-judgment as to the morality of homosexual relations between adult males....

[T]he reasons given by the Government, although relevant, are not sufficient to justify the maintenance in force of the impugned legislation in so far as it has the general effect of criminalising private homosexual relations between adult males capable of valid consent. In particular, the moral attitudes towards male homosexuality in Northern Ireland and the concern that any relaxation in the law would tend to erode existing moral standards cannot, without more, warrant interfering with the applicant's private life to such an extent. 'Decriminalisation' does not imply approval, and a fear that some sectors of the population might draw misguided conclusions in this respect from reform of the legislation does not afford a good ground for maintaining it in force with all its unjustifiable features.

To sum up, the restriction imposed on Mr. Dudgeon under Northern Ireland law, by reason of its breadth and absolute character, is, quite apart from the severity of the possible penalties provided for, disproportionate to the aims sought to be achieved.

In the opinion of the Commission, the interference complained of by the applicant can, in so far as he is prevented from having sexual relations with young males under 21 years of age, be justified as necessary for the protection of the rights of others.... This conclusion was accepted and adopted by the Government, but disputed by the applicant who submitted that the age of consent for male homosexual relations should be the same as that for heterosexual and female homosexual relations, that is, 17 years under current Northern Ireland law....

[handwritten margin note: The Court rejected Dudgeon argument about the age of consent]

The Court has already acknowledged the legitimate necessity in a democratic society for some degree of control over homosexual conduct notably in order to provide safeguards against the exploitation and corruption of those who are specially vulnerable by reason, for example, of their youth....However, it falls in the first instance to the national authorities to decide on the appropriate safeguards of this kind required for the defence of morals in their society and, in particular, to fix the age under which young people should have the protection of the criminal law....

Mr. Dudgeon has suffered and continues to suffer an unjustified interference with his right to respect for his private life. There is accordingly a breach of Article 8.

Note

1. In subsequent legislation, the law was changed in North Ireland. The Homosexual Offences (Northern Ireland) Order (1982), n1982 No. 1536 (N.I. 19), then read in part:

> (3) Subject to Article 4 (mental patients) and Article 5 (merchant seamen), and notwithstanding any other statutory provision or any rule of law, a homosexual act in private shall not be an offence if the parties consent thereto and have attained the age of 21 years.

Among additional changes made over the years, the age of consent has been lowered to 18.

* * *

C. The European Community and Review in the Ordinary Courts of Europe

STANLEY PAULSON, CONSTITUTIONAL REVIEW IN THE UNITED STATES AND AUSTRIA: NOTES ON THE BEGINNINGS
16 RATIO JURIS 223, 236 (2003)

Constitutional review, Kelsen writes, "acquires its greatest significance...in a *federal system*." Indeed, he argues, the political idea to which federalism gives expression is "only brought to completion with the institution of constitutional review."

* * *

In most of the world there is no long tradition, as there is in the United States, of ordinary courts examining legislation for validity. The recent developments in this area have almost all involved special constitutional courts. It is true, as we have just seen, that treaty provisions may prevail over conflicting legislation in the ordinary courts, but that is true only in some countries, and even in those countries ordinary courts tend to be hesitant about striking down legislation.

When we come to the European Union, we see a new sort of development, arising out of treaty law but well on the way toward a judicial federalism. As the cases that follow will show, there has been a gradual acceptance of a number of principles that support this federalism: in particular that European law prevails over the domestic law of the member-States (*supremacy*); that European law is law within the domestic legal order without the need for implementing legislation or regulation to become effective (*direct applicability*); and that private parties are among those who can invoke European law in cases before the ordinary courts (*invocability*, sometimes referred to as *direct effect*).

Thus the judges of the ordinary courts have the power, and the responsibility, to apply European law and to refuse to apply domestic law in cases in which the two conflict. That means that judges of the ordinary courts have the power to review and set aside legislation, a rather dramatic development in a Europe of traditional parliamentary supremacy and review limited to constitutional courts. And since the domestic courts must follow the European Court of Justice on the interpretation of European law, what we have in cases of conflict between European law and domestic law is the supremacy of European law as interpreted by European judges and enforced by the judges of the domestic courts.

It follows that the European Community is a great deal more than a treaty organization like NATO or the Council of Europe. Its members have yielded up sovereignty in certain areas to the new organization, and in some ways it is coming to resemble a federal state. Some parties favor that development; others favor the economic gains to be obtained through the Union but oppose any political development that suggests making a single federal state—resembling the United States, perhaps—out of these ancient sovereign nations. The struggle between these two sets of views accounts for many of the stops and starts we see in the evolution of the European Union.

1. European Institutions and European Law

The European Community is an organization created by certain European nations for their mutual economic benefit. The Community was created under three initial treaties: the 1951 European Coal and Steel Community Treaty, signed in Paris (ECSC); the 1957 European Atomic Energy Community Treaty, signed in Rome (Euratom); and the 1957 European Economic Community Treaty, also signed at Rome (EEC).[5] This came about, like many other things characteristic of Europe today, as part of the aftermath of the two devastating World Wars.

The first six members were France, Germany, Italy, and the Benelux countries: Belgium, the Netherlands, and Luxembourg. As of 2003 membership stands at fifteen.[6] The aim of the economic union was to promote the free movement of goods, services, and labor within the geographical area of the union. Under the original treaties and the Single Europe Act (1987), the Treaty on European Unification (1993), the Treaty of Amsterdam (1998), and the Treaty of Nice (2001), there has been an elimination of customs stops at the borders between these countries, and a gradual elimination of barriers to the movement of goods, like differential internal tariffs that would make goods manufactured in an EU member state cost more in one member state than in another, and like differential external tariffs, which would lead to the undermining of the higher tariffs established by some members by the lower tariffs charged by other members.

There has also been an effort to regularize product standards so that some members will not seem more attractive to industry than others. Workers are assured of free movement from one member state to another, and professionals like lawyers have more and more freedom to practice in neighboring member states. Monetary union was also a goal. A central European Bank has been created, and in 2002, after years of anticipation, the Euro was finally issued. All but a few of the member-States have adopted the new currency.

The primary institutions of the Community are the Commission, the Council, the Parliament, and the European Courts. Ministers from the member-States, representing the interests of their States, make up the Council. The

---

5. Strictly speaking the three treaties created three separate communities, but they were separate in name only, sharing most of their institutions, and they were referred to as one thing, the Common Market. The three communities have since been merged into a single entity, the European Community, under a subsequent treaty. "European Union" is sometimes used to refer to the same entity, but strictly speaking the Union exists within the Community as a somewhat closer alliance in respect of certain issues. The terms "European Union" and "European Community" are sometimes used interchangeably, and I will not make any effort to distinguish them in what follows.

6. In 1973 Denmark, Ireland and the U.K. were admitted; in 1981 Greece; in 1986 Portugal and Spain; and in 1995 Austria, Finland and Sweden. As of 2003, thirteen countries, including ten eastern European countries, Turkey, Malta and Cyprus are waiting to be admitted. Ten of these countries-Cyprus, Malta, Hungary, Poland, the Slovak Republic, Latvia, Estonia, Lithuania, the Czech Republic and Slovenia-have signed accession agreements with the EU, and are to be admitted in May, 2004, pending the outcome of national referenda in each of the applicant countries.

Foreign Minister of each State is the main representative to the Council; but different ministers will attend, depending on the subject matter to be discussed. For example, if the issue to be decided concerns agriculture, then the Council will consist of the Ministers of Agriculture. The Council is—up to now—the main legislative body, a function which it shares in greater and greater portion with the Parliament. The Parliament is directly elected. If the Council represents the governments that select its members, the Parliament represents (or should represent) a majority of the voters who elected them. The Council therefore shows the intergovernmental nature of the Community as an association of states; the Parliament increasingly shows what there is of a democratic nature to the community as an association of people.

The Commission serves as the executive arm of the Community, but also serves a policy-making function. It consists of members nominated by the member-States; depending on size, some States are represented by two Commission members, others by one. The Commission proposes legislation to the Council and the Parliament, and also has some modest lawmaking powers of its own.

The Courts of the European Community are the European Court of Justice (the "ECJ") and a lesser court, the Court of First Instance. The Court of Justice has several functions under the treaties, including hearing complaints raised by member-States or Community institutions (primarily the Commission) against a member-State (Articles 169/226[7] and 170/227), and complaints raised by member-States or Community institutions against a Community institution (Article 173/230). For our purposes here, however, the most important function is to take references from domestic courts seeking an interpretation of community law (Article 177/234)

TREATY OF ROME ESTABLISHING THE EUROPEAN ECONOMIC COMMUNITY
TITLE I, CHAPTER I, SECTION 4:
THE COURT OF JUSTICE (MARCH 25, 1957)[8]

Article 164 (Article 220): The Court of Justice shall ensure that in the interpretation and application of this Treaty the law is observed....

---

7. In the material that follows, Articles will be referred to by the original numbering in the E.E.C. Treaty, followed by the new numbering given to them in the Amsterdam Treaty. So, for example, Article 169 in the E.E.C. Treaty is Article 226 in the new numbering imposed by the later treaty.

8. *Available at* <www.europa.eu.int/eir-lex/en/treaties/dat/ec_cons_treaty_en.pdf>. Original Article numbers in italics; new numbering, post Amsterdam, in parentheses.

Article 169 (Article 226): If the Commission considers that a Member State has failed to fulfil an obligation under this Treaty, it shall deliver a reasoned opinion on the matter after giving the State concerned the opportunity to submit its observations. If the State concerned does not comply with the opinion within the period laid down by the Commission the latter may bring the matter before the Court of Justice.

Article 170 (Article 227): A Member State which considers that another Member State has failed to fulfill an obligation under this Treaty may bring the matter before the Court of Justice. Before a Member State brings an action against another Member State for an alleged infringement of an obligation under this Treaty, it shall bring the matter before the Commission. The Commission shall deliver a reasoned opinion after each of the States concerned has been given the opportunity to submit its own case and its observations on the other party's case both orally and in writing. If the Commission has not delivered an opinion within three months of the date on which the matter was brought before it, the absence of such opinion shall not prevent the matter from being brought before the Court of Justice....

Article 173 (Article 230): The Court of Justice shall review the legality of acts adopted jointly by the European Parliament and the Council, of acts of the Council, of the Commission, and of the ECB other than recommendations and opinions, and of acts of the European Parliament intended to produce legal effects vis-à-vis third parties.

It shall for this purpose have jurisdiction in actions brought by a Member State, the Council or the Commission on grounds of lack of competence, infringement of an essential procedural requirement, infringement of this Treaty or of any rule of law relating to its application, or misuse of powers.

The Court shall have jurisdiction under the same conditions in actions brought by the European Parliament and by the ECB for the purpose of protecting their prerogatives.

Article 177 (Article 234): The Court of Justice shall have jurisdiction to give preliminary rulings concerning:

(a) The interpretation of this Treaty;

(b) The validity and interpretation of acts of the institutions of the Community and of the ECB;

(c) The interpretation of the statutes of bodies established by an act of the Council, where those statutes so provide.

Where such a question is raised before any court or tribunal of a Member State, that court or tribunal may, if it considers that a decision on the question is necessary to enable it to give judgment, request the Court of Justice to give a ruling thereon. *Where any such question is raised in a case pending before a court or tribunal of a Member State against whose decisions there is no judicial remedy under national law, that court or tribunal shall bring the matter before the Court of Justice.* [Italics added.]

Notes

1. The procedure under Article 177 (234) resembles the procedure for obtaining preliminary rulings by the Council of State in France, and was based upon it. See Chapter One, Section B.1. above. In proceedings before the Court of Justice an Advocate General participates, who has more or less the same function as the Government Commissioner before the Council of State. And just as the briefs of the Government Commissioner help to understand the issues in a case before the Council, the briefs of the Advocate General help to understand the issues in a case before the Court of Justice. "For those who have studied European Community law and the proceedings before the European Court of Justice, the almost exactly parallel *rôle* of the Advocate-General should be noted. There is a statement of the facts of the case, the issues involved, considerable citation of previous decisions of the courts and a suggested solution. The conclusions of the *commissaire du gouvernement* are often published and these are important because of the very brief nature of the decision...." David Pollard, Sourcebook On French Law xvii (2nd ed., 1998).

2. No one seems to have expected Article 177 (234) to play the role it did in authorizing judicial review in the domestic courts. That is, no one seems to have expected that Article to be used as a way to introduce the possibility of questioning the validity of domestic laws under European law, much less as a way of permitting individual citizens to raise such questions. For what purpose was it intended, then? It envisions the Court of Justice answering the questions of domestic courts about the interpretation of European law. When was a question of European law expected to arise in domestic courts? While it seems clear that what was intended was to find a way for domestic courts to rely on an authoritative understanding of European law, no one seems to have been thinking about the possibility that conflicts with domestic law would arise in this context. Remember that when the Constitutional Council was created in France it seemed inconceivable that it could be used to enforce individual rights; its function was simply to be one of separation of powers. In both cases, the French and the European, it was the courts themselves that expanded their own powers.

3. In 2001 the European Council—that is, the meeting of the heads of state of the member-States—created a European Convention to which was assigned the task of drawing up a constitution for Europe. On June 27, 2003, a draft Constitution of Europe was presented to the European Council.

* * *

There are two types of subsidiary European legislation we should be aware of. There is, first of all, direct lawmaking, the enacting of rules that apply directly within the member-States without the intervention of any legislative act by the member-States themselves. These sorts of rules were called different things in each of the original three treaties, but they are now known simply as *regulations*. When the European Council, together with the Parliament, enacts a regulation, that rule is binding in all the member-States, and must be enforced in the domestic courts.

The second sort of rule is the *directive*. The directive is not itself a rule of law, but it is an order to the States to produce legislation conforming to the provisions of the directives. Directives are used instead of regulations when the subject of the law has to do with more sensitive matters, matters for which it would be better to leave the final wording of the law up to the member-States. For example, when a uniform products liability law was desired, a regulation could have been enacted to cover the matter. If that had been done, no action on the part of the states would have been required. Domestic courts would simply have enforced the provisions of the regulation. Instead what happened was that a directive was issued that set out the desired provisions of legislation to be adopted by the States. The individual states then passed legislation implementing the directive, some quickly, some after a long delay, some in the very words of the directive, others in different words meant to capture the essential features of the directive.

2. Development of Judicial Review in the Ordinary Courts

The *van Gend* case that follows was the case in which the Court of Justice first declared that the provisions of the treaties (in this case, Article 12) were directly applicable. From the argument of the Advocate General (the "AG") and the various parties before the Court of Justice we get some idea of the state of things early in the history of the EU.

TREATY OF ROME ESTABLISHING THE EUROPEAN ECONOMIC COMMUNITY (MARCH 25, 1957)

Article 12. Member States shall refrain from introducing between themselves any new customs duties on imports or exports or any charges having equivalent effect, and from increasing those which they already apply in their trade with each other.

* * *

VAN GEND EN LOOS V. NETHERLANDS
CASE 26/62 (EUROPEAN COURT OF JUSTICE,
5 FEBRUARY 1963)

1. Submissions of the Advocate General Before the European Court of Justice.

The present case originates in an action before the *Tariefcommissie*, a Dutch administrative tribunal. This latter is seised with a suit for annulment of a decision of the Dutch revenue authorities of 6 March 1961, concerning the application of a certain customs duty to the import of ureaformaldehyde from the Federal Republic of Germany. That decision was based on the new Dutch customs tariff which came into force on 1 March 1960 and which was formulated in the Brussels Protocol of 25 July 1958 by the Kingdom of Belgium, the Grand Duchy of Luxembourg and the Kingdom of The Netherlands; it was ratified in the latter country by the Law of 16 December 1959.

The parties to the proceedings are in agreement with the *Tariefcommissie* that at the date of import (9 September 1960) the imported goods were correctly classified in a particular tariff group of the customs tariff in force. But that tariff varied from the old tariff [which came into force in the three Benelux countries by virtue of the Customs Convention of 5 September 1944]. That tariff had enforced the Brussels nomenclature [fixed in the Agreement of 15 December 1950 on the Tariff Nomenclature for the Classification of Goods in Customs Tariffs], and this led to a change in the old tariff groups.

Whereas the product in question was before 1 March 1960 classified in a category subject to a duty of 3 per cent under the Dutch customs tariff (*Tariefbesluit* 1947), as is confirmed by two decisions of the *Tariefcommissie*, after the Brussels nomenclature was introduced, it became subject to a higher duty resulting from the rearrangement of the old tariff groups.

That is why the plaintiff considered that the modification of the customs tariff by the Brussels Protocol contravened Article 12 of the E.E.C. Treaty, and that the decision made by the customs authorities should be annulled in view of the provisions of the E.E.C. Treaty.

The *Tariefcommissie* has not adjudicated upon this issue but has submitted it to the Court on 16 August 1962 under Article 177 of the Treaty, asking the Court to settle two preliminary questions. It wished to know:

(1) Whether Article 12 of the E.E.C. Treaty has an internal effect, as the plaintiff claims; in other words, whether the nationals of member-States may, on the basis of the Article in question, enforce rights which the judge should protect.

(2) If the answer to that question is in the affirmative, whether there has been an illegal increase in the import duty, or whether it was only a reasonable modification of the duties applicable before 1 March

1960, a modification which, although an increase arithmetically, should nevertheless not be considered as prohibited under Article 12....

(Notice that the conflict in this case is not between a provision of the E.C. Treaty and national law, but between a provision of the E.C. Treaty and a provision of another treaty, the Brussels Protocol of 25 July, 1958, which provision was implemented in the Dutch customs tariff. The Protocol was evidently directly applicable, and so if the E.C. provision was also directly applicable there would be an apparent conflict to resolve. The Dutch Constitution provides that treaty provisions with appropriate features will be directly applicable in the Dutch courts. What the Dutch judge wanted to know, first of all, was whether Article 12 was directly applicable. This question would appear to be outside the ECJ's competence under Article 177, which was limited to *interpreting* the treaties. But the AG argued that in fact the question of direct applicability was a question of interpretation: "The effects of an international treaty depend in the first place on the legal significance which its authors intended to give to its different provisions ....If the examination is limited to this aspect, without passing judgment as to how the constitutional law of the member-State adopts the intended consequences of the treaty into its national legal system, it comes within the field of interpretation of the treaty. Even if the drafting of the first question is unfortunate, it is possible to see in it a request for an interpretation which is admissible and which the court can without difficulty pick out from the facts presented, and which it can examine under Article 177...." The Dutch government argued first that it was a question of domestic constitutional law whether a treaty provision had internal effect; and second that under the Dutch constitution Article 12 did not have internal effect. Violations of Article 12, according to the Dutch government, are to be resolved between the parties to the Treaty—the member-States—under Articles 169 and 170. The Commission, on the other hand, supported the plaintiff's argument, and denied both of those propositions: it argued that the European Court of Justice was the proper forum for questions about the interpretation and effect of Article 12; and it argued that Article 12 should in fact have internal effect. The Advocate General, as we will see, took a middle ground. He agreed with the plaintiff and the Commission that the question of direct applicability was properly one for the European court to answer; but he also argued that the European court should answer the question in the negative: Article 12 was not intended to have internal effect.)

2. Submissions of the Advocate General Before the European Court of Justice (continued).

...The opinions uttered in the course of the proceedings are not unanimous. The plaintiff in the Dutch action and the E.E.C. Commission maintain that Article 12 has a direct internal effect in that authorities and courts of member-States should respect it directly. According to this opinion, the first question should receive an affirmative answer. The Dutch, Belgian and German Governments, on the other hand, see in Article 12 only an obligation on the member-States.

In its written observations and during the oral proceedings, the Commission attempted to justify its contention by presenting a wide analysis of the structure of the Community. Very impressively, it showed that, by comparison with customary international law and general inter-State legal practice, the European Treaties constitute a profound innovation and that it would be false to examine them in the light only of the general principles of the law of nations.

It is appropriate that these statements should have been made during an action which raises the basic question of the relations between Community law and internal law.

He who is familiar with the law of the Community knows that in fact it is not restricted to the contractual relations between a number of States viewed as subjects of the law of nations. The Community has its own institutions, independent of the member-States, endowed with the power to take administrative action and to issue legal rules which directly create rights and obligations not only for the member-States and their administrative authorities but also for the nationals of the member-States. We can deduce this clearly from Articles 187, 189, 191 and 192 of the Treaty.

The E.E.C. Treaty also contains provisions which are certainly intended to act directly upon the national law and to modify or supplement it, e.g., Articles 85 and 86 relating to competition (prohibition of certain agreements, prohibition of the abusive use of a dominant position in the Common Market), the application of the rules on competition by the administrative authorities of the member-States (Article 88), and the duty of national courts to collaborate with the Community institutions as regards judgments and forced execution (Articles 177 and 192 of the Treaty; Articles 26 and 27 of the Statute of the Court). In this respect, one may also mention the provisions which are likely to have direct effects at a later stage, e.g., the provisions of the Title which is devoted to the free circulation of people, services and capital (Articles 48 and 60)....

It should...be noted that the wording of Article 12 does not use such terms as 'prohibition', 'prohibited', 'incompatible', 'without effect', ['interdiction', 'interdit', 'incompatible', 'sans effet'] which are found in other provisions of the Treaty. It is precisely when a provision is intended to be applied directly, i.e., by the administrative authorities of the member-States, that it is impossible to do without a precise indication of the legal effects intended.

But above all we must ask whether *by its contents* Article 12 appears of such a nature as to be applied directly. It should be emphasised that, at least at the present stage, the member-States still retain to a large degree their legislative powers as regards customs matters. In certain member-States these are contained in formal laws. The direct application of Article 12 would thus often take the form of supervision over legislative acts by the administrative authorities and the courts of the member-States, helped by the provisions of Article 12....

After all these examinations (which depend upon a general view of the treaty system) of the text, the substance and the context of the provision to be interpreted, I come to the conclusion that Article 12 should be legally classified in the same way as the other rules on customs union.... My conclusion therefore is that question No. 1 of the *Tariefcommissie* should receive a negative answer.....

I propose that the Court should restrict its judgment to the first question and should hold that Article 12 contains an obligation only for the member-States.

(The Advocate General pointed out one difficulty with accepting the argument of the plaintiff and the Commission. If the Court were to find that Article 12 was intended to have internal effect, then under the Dutch constitution the domestic courts would have to give it effect. But what about those member-States whose constitutions did not permit treaty provisions to have direct effect? Article 12 would not become part of internal law in those countries, no matter what the Court of Justice said about it. The Court's solution to this problem makes this case a landmark in European law.)

3. Judgment of the European Court of Justice.

JURISDICTION. The Government of The Netherlands and the Belgian Government dispute the Court's jurisdiction on the grounds that it was a request relating not to the interpretation of the Treaty but to its application within the framework of the constitutional law of The Netherlands. More particularly, [they argue that] the Court has no jurisdiction to give a decision on the question of the pre-eminence which should, in appropriate cases, be granted to the provisions of the E.E.C. Treaty over Dutch law...; the solution of such a problem falls within the exclusive jurisdiction of the national courts, subject to a reference to the Court in the circumstances set out in Articles 169 and 170 of the Treaty.

The Court is here not called upon to give a decision on the application of the Treaty according to the principles of Dutch internal law, which fall within the sphere of national jurisdiction, but is asked in accordance with Article 177 (1) (a) of the Treaty only to interpret the meaning of Article 12 of the said Treaty within the framework of Community law and in the light of its incidence on individuals.

The objection cannot therefore be sustained....

MERITS. The first question posed by the *Tariefcommissie* is whether Article 12 of the Treaty has an immediate effect in internal law, in that nationals of the member-States could, on the basis of the Article, enforce rights which the national court should protect.

To know whether the provisions of an international treaty have such an effect it is necessary to look at its spirit, its economic aspect and the terms used.

The purpose of the E.E.C. Treaty—to create a Common Market, the functioning of which directly affects the citizens of the Community—implies that this Treaty is more than an agreement creating only mutual obligations between the contracting parties. This interpretation is confirmed by the preamble to the Treaty which, in addition to mentioning governments, affects individuals. The creation of organs institutionalising certain sovereign rights, the exercise of which affects both member-States and citizens is a particular example. In addition, the nationals of the States, united into the Community, are required to collaborate in the functioning of that Community, by means of the European Parliament and the Economic and Social Council. Furthermore, the role of the Court of Justice in the framework of Article 177, the aim of which is to ensure uniformity of interpretation of the Treaty by the national courts, confirms that the States recognised in Community law have an authority capable of being invoked by their nationals before those courts. We must conclude from this that the Community constitutes a new legal order in international law, for whose benefit the States have limited their sovereign rights, albeit within limited fields, and the subjects of which comprise not only the member-States but also their nationals. Community law, therefore, apart from legislation by the member-States, not only imposes obligations on individuals but also confers on them legal rights. The latter arise not only when an explicit grant is made by the Treaty, but also through obligations imposed, in a clearly defined manner, by the Treaty on individuals as well as on member-States and the Community institutions....

The text of Article 12 sets out a clear and unconditional prohibition, which is not a duty to act but a duty not to act. This duty is imposed without any power in the States to subordinate its application to a positive act of internal law. The prohibition is perfectly suited by its nature to produce direct effects in the legal relations between the member-States and their citizens.

The carrying out of Article 12 does not require legislative intervention by the States. The fact that the Article designates the member-States as subject to the duty to abstain does not imply that their nationals may not be the beneficiaries of the duty.

The argument, invoked by the three Governments who presented memoranda to the Court containing their observations, based as it is upon Articles 169 and 170, must fail.

The fact that the Treaty, in the aforementioned Articles, allows the Commission and the member-States to bring before the Court a State which has not carried out its obligations, does not imply that individuals may not invoke these obligations, in appropriate cases, before a national court; and likewise, the fact that the Treaty puts at the disposal of the Commission means to ensure respect for the duties imposed on those subject to it does not exclude the possibility of invoking violation of these obligations in litigation between individuals before national courts....

For these reasons, according to the spirit, the economic aspect and the terms of the Treaty, Article 12 should be interpreted in such a sense as to produce direct effect and to create individual rights which internal courts should protect....

Notes

1. The important point is that the ECJ held that it had the jurisdiction to decide whether Article 12 had direct applicability. Why is that important? After all, the Dutch constitution recognized the possibility of direct applicability of treaty provisions, and subjected national law to directly applicable treaty provisions. The point is important because the Court was announcing that it was not up to the member states to decide, as a matter of national law, what effect E.C. treaty provisions were to have internally. Henceforward it would be a matter of European law, to be interpreted by the European court. This is to underscore the autonomous nature of European law; it is a separate and independent body of law.

2. What is important about Article 177 is not that it gives individuals access to the European court—it doesn't—but rather that it gives national courts access to the European court.

3. The Court said that the treaties created both rights and obligations for individuals—that is, that they had direct effect, or invocability. If it was not perceived at the outset, by the framers of the treaties, that national courts might be used to enforce those rights and obligations, what other function might Art. 177 have had? One argument is that it could have been intended to allow the ECJ to give guidance to national courts who are trying to interpret national acts implementing the treaties. Cf. A.M. Arnull, A.A. Dashwood, M.G. Ross, & D.A. Wyatt, European Union Law 74 (4th ed. 2000); also Trevor C. Hartley, The European Court, Judicial Objectivity and the Constitution of the European Union, 112 Law Quarterly Review. 95, 97 n.8 (1996).

4. Treaty provisions will have direct effect only if they satisfy certain criteria. The early version of the test can be seen in *van Gend*. To have direct effect, a provision must be a "clear and unconditional prohibition," and it must "not require legislative intervention by the States." See generally J.A. Winter, Direct Applicability and Direct Effect, (1972) Common Market Law Review 425; Pierre Pescatore, The Doctrine of Direct Effect, 8 European Law Review 155 (1983).

* * *

Granted that European law has direct applicability in domestic courts, and is invocable in those courts by private citizens, where does it stand in the hierarchy of law? Is it on a lower rung than legislation, so that any legislation whatever will trump it? Is it equal to legislation in effect, so that according to traditional rules of interpretation later statutes will prevail over it? The *Costa* case addresses that issue.

COSTA V. ENEL
CASE 6/64 (EUROPEAN COURT OF JUSTICE, 24 FEBRUARY 1964)

1. Facts, from the submission of the Advocate General to the Court of Justice.

....M. F. Costa, a lawyer practising in Milan, claims that he is not under an obligation to pay the amount of an invoice (1,925 Italian lire) which was demanded from him in respect of the supply of electricity by the Ente Nazionale Per L'Energia (ENEL). He objected to this payment before a Justice of the Peace [giudice conciliatore] (who was competent in first and last resort by virtue of the amount involved) claiming that the Law of 6 December 1962 nationalising the electrical industry in Italy was contrary to a certain number of Articles of the E.E.C. Treaty, and was unconstitutional. In this connection he demanded—and obtained—a preliminary reference of the whole matter on the one hand to the Italian Constitutional Court and on the other hand to this Court in pursuance of Article 177 of the Treaty.

[The Italian Constitutional Court, in its decision of 24 February/7 March 1964, had addressed various substantive constitutional questions, and then took on the question of the status under the Italian constitution of the lower court's appeal to the ECJ. The issue was raised by the Italian *giudice conciliatore*, who addressed to the Constitutional Court the question whether the law establishing ENEL conflicted with several provisions of the treaties, and thereby violated Article 11[9] of the Italian Constitution, which provided for the limitation of Italy's sovereignty under the treaties:

Article 11 is here prayed in aid in so far as it states that Italy agrees, under conditions of parity with other States, to such limitations of sovereignty as are necessary for the establishment of an order that will ensure peace and justice amongst nations; and it will promote and favour international organisations for this purpose. This means that, given certain circumstances, it is possible to stipulate treaties as a result of which we accept certain limitations to our sovereignty and it is

---

9. The Constitution of Italy, *Article 11*. Italy . . . will agree, on conditions of equality with other States, to the limitations of her sovereignty necessary to an organization for assuring peace and justice among nations; and will promote and favor international organizations constituted for this purpose.

quite lawful to give effect to such treaties by means of an ordinary Law; but this does not result in any deviation from the existing rule relating to the efficacy, within national law, of the obligations undertaken by the State in connection with its relations with other States, since Article 11 did not confer a greater effect upon the ordinary Law that gives effect to a treaty.... [W]ith regard to such Law, there must remain inviolate the prevalence of subsequent laws in accordance with the principles governing the succession of laws in time; it follows that any conflict between the one and the other cannot give rise to any constitutional matter. From the foregoing we reach the conclusion that for present purposes there is no point in dealing with the character of the E.E.C. and with the consequences that derive from the Law giving effect to the Treaty creating the E.E.C.; nor is it necessary to question whether the Law that is being attacked before us has violated the obligations undertaken by virtue of the Treaty aforesaid. It follows from this that the question regarding the remission of the file to the Court of Justice of the European Community, and the relevant question of jurisdiction, do not even arise.

The Constitutional Court then gave judgment for ENEL on all other constitutional issues. According to the Constitutional Court, E.C. Treaty provisions could be overridden by simple legislative act—at least in countries like Italy, where under the national constitution treaty provisions could not be enforced in the national courts until they had been transformed by the process of legislation into national law. While the case was being considered by the Constitutional Court, it was also being considered by the European Court of Justice. In its argument before the ECJ, the Italian government raised an argument we have seen before: that any claim that Italy was violating a provision of the Treaty could only be raised by member-States or by the Commission, not by private individuals, and only under Articles 169 or 170, and not by way of a request for a preliminary ruling under Article 177. In his submission, the European Advocate General made sure to stress to the Court that it had to draw the line between interpretation, which was its job, and application of European law, which was not. The Advocate General continues:]

2. The Advocate General's Argument.

What must be avoided—and this is a danger which begins to be noticed as cases under Article 177 multiply—is that this Court, under the guise of interpretation, more or less substitutes itself for the national judge who, let us not forget, retains jurisdiction to apply the Treaty and the regulations of the Community which internal legislation has incorporated by ratification: finding a clear cut division between application and interpretation is indeed one of the most delicate problems posed by Article 177, all the more so because this dividing line corresponds to that between Community and national jurisdiction and no judge has been entrusted with the duty of resolving such conflict. It must therefore be apparent that a conflict between this Court of Justice and the highest national court could be of such nature as seriously to prejudice the system of international control instituted by the Treaty which rests upon a necessary, and at the same time organic, co-operation between the two orders of jurisdiction.

We must firstly deal with the second objection, that is to say, with the allegation that a violation of the Treaty as a result of an internal Law subsequent and contrary to the Treaty itself can be dealt with only in the course of the proceedings relating to the failure of member-States envisaged in Articles 169, 170 and 171, a procedure which is not open to individuals and which leaves unaffected such contrast in law until such time as it is repealed in pursuance of the judgment of the Court that declares its incompatibility with the Treaty itself. We submit that that is not the problem: the real problem is that of the co-existence of two rules of law which (we shall assume) are incompatible but nevertheless both applicable within the internal order, the one derived from the Treaty or the institutions of the Community, the other from national laws: which one should prevail until such time as the conflict is resolved? This is the real problem....

[I]n what circumstances must such courts exercise their control and in particular apply the self-executing norms of the Treaty or the Community regulations duly passed, when there exists a national law to the contrary. The answer must be that if the national law came into force prior to the Treaty or to the publication of the Community regulations, the rules of implied repeal must suffice. Difficulties arise, however, when the internal law came into force subsequently to the Treaty and is contrary to a self-executing rule of it; alternatively, when the national law came into force subsequently to the lawful passing and publication of a Community regulation ....In [Italy], as you know, a judgment of the Constitutional Court dated 24 February/7 March 1964...decided that...since the Treaty was ratified by an ordinary Law, a later contradictory Law should have effect in accordance with the principles that govern the succession of laws in time, from which it followed that 'there was no need to inquire whether the Law in issue violated the obligations undertaken by virtue of the Treaty', and that, for the same reason, a reference of the matter to the Court of Justice of the European communities was entirely pointless (since it could only be useful in so far as it would bear upon a violation of the Treaty, bearing in mind the interpretation of the same already given by the Court).

It is patently not for us to criticise this judgment. We merely point out (although this is purely a formal remark) that the Italian Constitutional Court refers to the conflict between the Law in issue and the Law of ratification whereas the question relates to a conflict between a Law and a treaty (ratified by an ordinary Law).

But what we would insist upon are the disastrous consequences (and we do not think this expression is too strong) that such jurisprudence, if it is maintained, would risk having as regards the functioning of the system established by the Treaty and, as a consequence, the very future of the Common Market....

If we reach the stage where the constitutional judge of one of the member-States, in the fullness of his jurisdiction, feels bound to acknowledge that [immediate application of the self-executing regulations of the Treaty] cannot be achieved within the framework of the constitutional rules of his own country... such a decision would create an insoluble conflict between the two orders and would undermine the very foundations of the Treaty. For not only could the Treaty not receive application, on the conditions mentioned in it, within the country concerned but, as a consequence of a chain reaction, it could not even profitably apply within the other countries of the Community; certainly this would be so in those member-States of the Community (such as, for instance, France) where the precedence of international treaties is only granted 'on condition of reciprocity'....

These are the various reasons—and it may be that in certain ways they might be considered superfluous, but we have thought it necessary to express them in detail, by virtue of their extreme importance of principle—for which we submit that you must reject the demurrer of 'absolute inadmissibility' raised by the Italian Government in its submissions.

[The AG then went on to recommend that Articles 53 and 37(2), which do not impose obligations to take action but only obligations to refrain from taking action, produce direct effects and are enforceable in the national courts. See *van Gend*, wherein the Court in describing the features of Article 12 that permit it to have direct effect refers to the fact that it imposes a negative obligation—*i.e.*, an obligation to refrain from taking action. (Why should it make a difference whether a treaty provision imposes a negative obligation or an affirmative or positive obligation?) The Advocate General believed that the Court need not concern itself with the route a preliminary reference takes under Article 177. Whether the national court is free to refer an issue that raises the possibility of a conflict between national law and European law directly to the ECJ, as itself raising a question under European law, or must refer it to the Constitutional Court (which will then decide whether to refer it to the ECJ), thereby acknowledging the national constitution as final arbiter in such matters, is of no concern to him. Whether the Court shares his view of this matter is not clear from the judgment in the case. The issue lingers on, as we will see below.]

3. Opinion of the European Court of Justice.

[T]he Italian Government maintains that the request of the Milan judge is absolutely 'inadmissible' inasmuch as a national court, which is bound to apply a national law, cannot avail itself of Article 177. As opposed to other international treaties, the Treaty instituting the E.E.C. has created its own order which was integrated with the national order of the member-States the moment the Treaty came into force; as such, it is binding upon them. In fact, by creating a Community of unlimited duration, having its own institutions, its own personality and its own capacity in law, apart from having international standing and more particularly, real powers resulting from a limitation of competence or a transfer of powers from the States to the Community, the member-States, albeit within limited spheres, have restricted their sovereign rights and created a body of law applicable both to their nationals and to themselves. The reception, within the laws of each member-State, of provisions having a Community source, and more particularly of the terms and of the spirit of the Treaty, has as a corollary the impossibility, for the member-State, to give preference to a unilateral and subsequent measure against a legal order accepted by them on a basis of reciprocity.

In truth, the executive strength of Community laws cannot vary from one State to the other in favor of later internal laws without endangering the realization of the aims envisaged by the Treaty in Article 5 (2) and giving rise to a discrimination prohibited by Article 7. In any case, the obligations undertaken under the Treaty creating the European Community would not be unconditional, but merely potential if they could be affected by subsequent legislative acts of the signatories of the Treaty. Furthermore, whenever the right to legislate unilaterally is allowed to the member-States, it is under a precise and special provision (see for instance Articles 15, 93 (3), 223, 224 and 225).

It is also true that requests for derogation by member-States are subject to a special procedure of authorization....which would be meaningless if the member-States could exempt themselves from their obligations by means of an ordinary Law. The preeminence of Community law is confirmed by Article 189 which prescribes that Community regulations have an 'obligatory' value and are 'directly applicable within each member-State.' Such a provision which, it will be noticed, admits of no reservation, would be wholly ineffective if a member-State could unilaterally nullify its purpose by means of a Law contrary to Community dictates. It follows from all these observations that the rights created by the Treaty, by virtue of their specific original nature, cannot be judicially contradicted by an internal law, whatever it might be, without losing their Community character and without undermining the legal basis of the Community.

The transfer, by member-States, from their national order, in favour of the Community order of the rights and obligations arising from the Treaty, carries with it a clear limitation of their sovereign right upon which a subsequent unilateral law, incompatible with the aims of the Community, cannot prevail. As a consequence, Article 177 should be applied regardless of any national law in those cases where a question of interpretation of the Treaty arises.

[The Court then, following the recommendations of the Advocate General, declares that Articles 37 and 53 both create individual rights "which national courts are bound to safeguard"—contradicting the contention of the Italian Constitutional Court. Still unanswered, though, was the question raised by the Advocate General about which route—direct appeal to the ECJ or through the Constitutional Court—national judges may follow. The AG believed that this was an internal matter, to be decided by the courts of each member-State.]

Notes

1. Remember that Italy's way of dealing with treaty provisions is different from that of the Dutch. Does it make any difference here?

2. Early on The Netherlands objected that the issues being presented to the ECJ by the national courts raised constitutional questions and not questions of the interpretation of European law. What constitutional questions might those be? The first, in *van Gend*, was whether a provision of the treaty had internal effect. Under international law the question whether a provision of a treaty has internal effect is a constitutional question, to be decided under the constitution and law of the state that is called upon to apply the provision. The constitutional practice of some states permits treaty provisions to have internal effect; but that decision assuredly belongs to the state itself, under international law. In *van Gend*, the court not only decided that a certain provision had internal effect, but also that it was the proper authority for deciding that matter.

3. The second question, raised in *Costa*, is whether European law is to prevail over national legislation. Under international law, again, that question is a constitutional question, to be decided under the constitution and law of the state facing the conflict. In many states that question has been answered in the affirmative by the national constitution. Italy, however, was not one of those states. Not only did the outcome in *Costa* contradict Italian constitutional law; more importantly it decided that Italian constitutional law was irrelevant to the matter, and that the outcome was a question of European law.

* * *

3. The Response in the National Courts

a. Italy: *Frontini, Simmenthal, Granital*
THE ITALIAN CONSTITUTION

Article 23. No personal service or payment shall be forced on anyone, except as provided for by law.

＊ ＊ ＊

Costa declared the superiority of Community law, in those areas of law in which sovereignty had been transferred to the Community. This position, as we have seen, was at odds with the position taken by the Italian Constitutional Court in the same case. The Constitutional Court's position changed in 1973, in the *Frontini* case.[10]

In Italy, as in many countries in the world, the word 'law' ("*legge*") has the specific meaning of written law, and more specifically legislation. Article 23 of the Italian Constitution, therefore, is more definite than it might seem at first glance. Legislation is required before the state can impose a personal service or financial requirement on anyone. We see the import of this in the *Frontini* case.

The case concerned certain levies imposed under EEC regulations, and the question raised by the Turin court was this: If Community legislation trumped national legislation, as *Costa* claimed, then wasn't any provision of the treaty which provided for the imposition of tariffs in violation of Article 23 of the Italian Constitution, which reserved to the Italian Parliament the right to legislate concerning such things? The Turin court could not itself address a constitutional question, of course, and it was not within the jurisdiction of the Constitutional Court to address the constitutionality of a treaty provision or of a regulation promulgated under Article 189 of the EEC treaty. But the Turin judge (and judges in other Italian courts as well) wondered whether, if the Treaty deprived the Italian legislature (and the Italian people) of its monopoly over legislation over levies and personal service, the *statute ratifying the Treaty* was not unconstitutional. And that was a question that the Constitutional Court could indeed address.

And so, in 1973, the Italian Constitutional Court received and combined several references, including one from the Turin court, raising that question. The plaintiff in the case complained in the Turin court of an agricultural levy imposed by Italian authorities under EEC regulations. As the Constitutional Court paraphrased the Turin judge's concern.

> It appears…not unreasonable to wonder whether such limitation of national sovereignty, which introduces an instrument of supranational legislative activity capable of having a direct impact in every field and without precise limits on the rights of citizens, possibly affecting even the fundamental rights of the citizens and the fundamental principles of the structure of the state, can be held to have been permitted by Article 11 of the [Italian] constitution.[11]

---

10. Frontini v. Ministero delle Finanze, Case 183/73 (Italian Constitutional Court, 27 December 1973); English translation at 2 C.M.L.R. 372.
11. 2 C.M.L.R. at 382 (1974).

The issue, as the Court puts it, is the possibility of an "unauthorized removal of legislative power from the normal constitutionally authorized state organs." But why doesn't the mere existence of Article 11 in the Italian constitution, the article which approves of those limitations of sovereignty "necessary to international organizations for assuring peace and justice between nations," remove all doubt about the constitutionality of the statute ratifying the EEC treaty? Because although Article 11 permits the transfer of sovereignty under treaties, the statute transferring sovereignty must itself be constitutional. Certainly a statute ratifying a convention giving some international organization the right to deprive Italian citizens of fundamental rights would have some constitutional difficulties. And the question here was whether the EEC treaty was just such a convention.

The Court answered by dismissing the reference as unfounded. Article 11 permits such extra-national legislation. Italy profited from the deal, and the aims of the EEC treaty were fully consonant with the aims of Article 11. The European Community is a separate entity, the Court said, with its own laws, binding in national courts.

> Fundamental requirements of equality and legal certainty demand that the Community norms, which cannot be characterized as a source of international law, nor of foreign law, nor of internal law of the individual states, ought to have full compulsory efficacy and direct application in all the member states, without the necessity of reception and implementation statutes, as acts having the force and value of statute in every country of the Community, to the extent of entering into force everywhere simultaneously and receiving equal an uniform application in all their addresses.[12]

And the state should not even be permitted to incorporate the self-executing regulations into legislation, for that would subject them to possible variations from state to state, unacceptable in this multilateral context. The regulations are enforceable, as European legislation, in the national courts, without the intervention of national legislation.

Against the objection that European legislation was not subject to the limitations imposed by the Italian constitution, the Court replied that the European Community had safeguards of its own: the Council and the Commission are under the supervision of the Assembly (the Parliament), which aspires some day to be a democratic institution. Meanwhile they are also subject to direct supervision by the Italian government, and indirect supervision by the Italian Parliament.

Even so, why doesn't the Community's power to legislate conflict with Article 23 of the Italian Constitution, which reserves the power to legislate over

---

12. 2 C.M.L.R. at 386-387 (1974).

matters concerning the citizen's pocketbook to the Italian Parliament? Because Article 23 doesn't apply to Community law, "which comes out of an autonomous source, part of an order which is distinct from the internal order." But that doesn't ensure the subjection of that law to the fundamental rights of citizens. The Court points out various ways in which objections to European law may be brought before the ECJ, and adds that although EEC regulations must deal with economic matters—i.e., precisely the sorts of matters Article 23 reserves to the national legislature—"the precise and exact provisions of the Treaty provide a safe guarantee, so that it appears difficult to form even abstractly the hypothesis that a Community regulation can have an effect in civil, ethical-social, or political relations through which provisions conflict with the Italian constitution."[13]

The Court accepted the validity of European law as an independent body of law, and will not review individual regulations for conformity to the constitution. Nevertheless it reserves the right, should a regulation ever threaten fundamental principles, to review the Treaty's continuing validity under the constitution.

Note

1. Although the *Frontini* court recognized the independent validity of European law, the Italian Constitutional Court was not called upon to say whether earlier European legislation would prevail over subsequent Italian legislation—a question answered in the affirmative (from the European point of view) in *Costa*. Would that answer be accepted by the Constitutional Court? If European legislation has the same force in the national courts as national legislation then when there is a conflict between a European law and a subsequent national law the subsequent law should prevail. The same would be true if the Italian legislature enacted a law intended to reproduce a European regulation: insofar as it varied from the regulation, the regulation would be repealed. Clearly this would not do, and European legislation had to prevail, when there was a conflict, even over subsequent national legislation. That issue was settled (from the Italian point of view) in *Industrie Chimiche*, Italian Constitutional Court, Case No. 232/75, in which the Constitutional Court held that under Article 11 of the Italian constitution European legislation prevails even over subsequent legislation. There was a hitch, however. If European law should ever conflict with fundamental rights, the Court still reserved the authority to intervene. The German Constitutional Court expressed similar reservations in *Internationale Handelsgesellschaft mbH v. Einfuhr- & Vorratsstelle fuer Getreide & Futtermittel*, German Constitutional Court, May 29, 1974.

---

13. 2 C.M.L.R. at 389 (1974).

* * *

Although the Italian Constitutional Court had accepted the supremacy of European law, it held out against judicial review in the ordinary courts. *Frontini* had accepted the legitimacy of European law, putting it on the same level as Italian law. That meant that when European law conflicted with earlier Italian legislation then under normal principles of statutory interpretation the later of the two—the European law—was to be given effect. Thus there was no need for the national judge to refer the issue to the Constitutional Court; he could simply disregard the earlier Italian statute.

But the priority of *subsequent* Italian legislation was not handled the same way; by the same interpretive principle later Italian legislation should prevail over earlier European law. The only reason it did not is Article 11 of the Constitution, which (as we have seen in the notes above) the Court interpreted as granting precedence to all European law, whether prior or subsequent to Italian law. And thus the later conflicting Italian statute must be seen as violating Article 11, and thus as unconstitutional. And that would seem to make it an issue for the Constitutional Court: it would be up to that Court to strike down the national provision as unconstitutional.

And so, according to *Industrie Chimiche*, the local judge cannot simply refuse to apply the Italian law; he must refer the case to the Constitutional Court for a declaration of unconstitutionality. If an interpretation of European law is required, only the Constitutional Court can refer the matter to the ECJ for an interpretation. But if that is to be so, then the ordinary courts really do not have the power of judicial review of legislation. That was the status of the law in Italy when the *Simmenthal*[14] case was decided by the ECJ.

The Italian *pretore*, a judge in a first instance court, was faced with a conflict between "certain rules of Community law and subsequent national law." The subsequent national law should therefore have been invalid under the principle of the supremacy of Community law. But under *Frontini* the proper way to proceed would have been to refer the matter to the Constitutional Court for a ruling of unconstitutionality under Article 11. The *pretore* put the question before the European Court: If a subsequent national law conflicts with European law, should that national law be disregarded without waiting for a ruling from the constitutional court? Does the domestic judge have the right and duty to set the national law aside for inconsistency with European law? The European Court responded:

---

14. Amministrazione delle Finanze dello Stato v. Simmenthal Sp.A., Case 106/77 (European Court of Justice, 9 March 1978); English at [1978] E.C.R. 629.

The effectiveness of [Article 177] would be impaired if the national court were prevented from forthwith applying Community law in accordance with the Decision or the case-law of the [European Court of Justice]. It follows from the foregoing that every national court must, in a case within its jurisdiction, apply Community law in its entirety and protect rights which the latter confers on individuals and must accordingly set aside any provision of national law which may conflict with it, whether prior or subsequent to the Community rule.

Accordingly any provision of a national legal system and any legislative, administrative or judicial practice which might impair the effectiveness of Community law by withholding from the national court having jurisdiction to apply such law the power to do everything necessary at the moment of its application to set aside national legislative provisions which might prevent Community rules from having full force and effect are incompatible with those requirements which are the very essence of Community law.

The...question should therefore be answered to the effect that a national court which is called upon, within the limits of its jurisdiction, to apply provisions of Community law is under a duty to give full effect to those provisions, if necessary refusing of its own motion to apply any conflicting provision of national legislation, even if adopted subsequently, and it is not necessary for the court to request or await the prior setting aside of such provision by legislative or other constitutional means.[15]

In *Granital*[16] the Constitutional Court eventually accepted the principle that the ordinary courts are entitled to measure Italian legislation against European law. It abandoned the earlier position of *Industrie Chimiche*, and held that while the national law is not repealed by the conflict with European law, it should not be applied in national courts. But the Court cautioned that Community law must not infringe on basic constitutional principles. Subsequently in *Fragd*[17] the Court elaborated upon this last point: If the domestic court suspects that Community law is exceeding reasonable bounds, reference must be made to the Constitutional Court.

---

15. [1978] E.C.R. at 644.

16. S.p.A. Granital v. Amministrazione finanziaria, Case 170/84 (Italian Constitutional Court, 8 June 1984).

17. Fragd v. Amministrazione delle Finanze, Case 232/89 (Italian Constitutional Court, 1989).

b. France: Jacques Vabre
THE FRENCH CONSTITUTION

Article 55. Treaties or agreements duly ratified or approved shall, upon publication, prevail over Acts of Parliament, subject, in regard to each agreement or treaty, to its application by the other party.

* * *

The French Constitutional Council denied that it had jurisdiction over questions involving treaties early on.[18] France is considered monist with respect to treaties. In the French abortion case (see section III.C.3, above), the Constitutional Council was presented with two objections to the abortion bill: that it conflicted with the Declaration of the Rights of Man (and thus with the Preamble to the 1958 Constitution), and that it conflicted with the European Convention on Human Rights. The Council ruled that the bill did not violate the Constitution. But as to the European Convention, it held that it had no jurisdiction over treaties: for one thing, whether a treaty was in effect would depend upon the mutual compliance of the parties, and the Constitutional Council was in no position to determine whether there was compliance. The Constitutional Council thus effectively took itself out of the picture with respect to all treaties, and in particular with respect to European law. It was left to the ordinary and administrative courts—the Court of Cassation and the Council of State—to decide whether and how to apply that body of law.

The French Court of Cassation was the first to take up the challenge, in *Jacques Vabre*.[19] Lower courts had already accepted supremacy, though not quite completely; the supremacy of European law was based on the French constitutional provision, rather than on the character of European law. In the *Jacques Vabre* case the Court of Appeal had accepted a dispute that arose under European law—whether the plaintiffs were entitled to recover taxes levied against them in violation of the European treaties—and had found in favor of the plaintiffs. The Court of Cassation upheld the judgment of the Court of Appeal:

> It is…complained against the judgment that…whereas…it is for the fiscal court to judge the legality of regulations laying down a tax which is challenged, but it could not without exceeding its powers discard the application of an internal statute on the pretext that it is unconsti-

---

18. In the abortion decision (Decision 74-44DC (15 January 1975)) reproduced above in Chapter Three.

19. Administration des Douanes v. Societe des Cafes Jacques Vabre, [1975] Dall. Jur. 497 (French Court of Cassation,14 May 1975); English translation at 2 C.M.L.R. 336 (1974).

tutional....But the Treaty of 25 March 1957, which by virtue of the above-mentioned Article of the Constitution has an authority greater than that of statutes, institutes a separate legal order integrated with that of the member-States. Because of that separateness, the legal order which it has created is directly applicable to the nationals of those States and is binding on their courts. Therefore the Cour d'Appel was correct and did not exceed its powers in deciding that Article 95 of the Treaty was to be applied in the instant case, and not section 265 of the Customs Code, even though the latter was later in date.[20]

The appellants also raised the excuse that the Constitutional Council had given for its lack of jurisdiction over treaty matters, that the courts could not know whether the treaty was mutually complied with. But the Court of Cassation brushed that issue aside.

[I]n the Community legal order the failings of a member-State of the European Economic Community to comply with the obligations falling on it by virtue of the Treaty of 25 March 1957 are subject to the procedure laid down by Article 170 of that Treaty and so the plea of lack of reciprocity cannot be made before the national courts. Whence it follows that this ground must be dismissed.[21]

The Court of Cassation dismissed the appeal, thereby accepting for the ordinary courts of France the role of conducting review of domestic legislation under European law. The authority for that review, however, appears to remain in the constitutional provision—Article 55—and not in the nature of European law.

The Council of State took longer to come around. It rejected the supremacy of European law in *Semoules*,[22] holding that subsequent legislation took precedence over treaties. In the 1990 *Nicolo*[23] case the Council changed its mind. The case involved a contested election to the European Parliament, challenged under a provision of the E.E.C. Treaty. There was no great fanfare; the Council simply found that the election code did not violate the Treaty—thereby accepting responsibility for reviewing regulations under European law.

c. Germany: The European Union and Human Rights

The French courts recognized the supremacy of European law, founded on a domestic constitutional provision. Other national courts have been more willing to recognize in European law an autonomous source of law. There is,

---

20. 2 C.M.L.R. at 369 (1974).
21. 2 C.M.L.R. at 369 (1974).
22. Semoules (Council of State, 1 March 1968).
23. Nicolo (Council of State, 20 October 1989).

however, a general reluctance to give up all control. In Germany the Constitutional Court has for a long time insisted that the supremacy of European law depends upon its recognition of the fundamental rights of German citizens.

GERHARD WEGEN AND CHRISTOPHER KUNER, GERMANY: FEDERAL CONSTITUTIONAL COURT DECISION CONCERNING THE MAASTRICHT TREATY

33 INTERNATIONAL LEGAL MATERIALS 388 (1994)

Introduction. On October 12, 1993 the German Federal Constitutional Court rejected constitutional challenges to Germany's participation in the European Union (formerly the European Communities) under the German Basic Law, and made possible the entry into force of the Treaty on European Union (Maastricht Treaty) on November 1, 1993. The Court's decision is of fundamental importance for understanding the legal status of Germany's participation in the European Union, both now and in years ahead.

Background of the Decision. The case was brought as a result of constitutional complaints filed by two classes of complainants, the first being a group of politicians and professors, including a prominent former official of the EEC, and the second being several German members of the European Parliament belonging to the "Green" Party. The complaints challenged the constitutionality of the Maastricht Treaty, which was signed at Maastricht on February 7, 1992....Under Article 59(2) of the German Basic Law, parliamentary ratification is required for most treaties entered into by the Federal Republic of Germany. On December 2, 1992, the Federal Parliament adopted a law approving the Maastricht Treaty by a vote of 543 to 25, and on December 18, 1992, the Federal Council approved this law unanimously. The law was then promulgated on December 30, 1992, and entered into force on December 31, 1992. However, it was still necessary for the Federal President to sign the Instrument of Ratification, and before this happened constitutional complaints were filed as mentioned above with the Federal Constitutional Court. The Federal President then stated that he would not sign the Instrument of Ratification until the Federal Constitutional Court had reached a decision in the case....

The Decision of the Federal Constitutional Court. The complainants alleged that the German Act of Accession to the Maastricht Treaty and the Act Amending the Basic Law, which had been adopted earlier, would violate their constitutional rights as follows:

(1) Article F, paragraph 3 of the Treaty grants the European Union an exclusive competence for jurisdictional conflicts which it can use to assume any further responsibilities it may require, thereby violating the German peoples' right of representation by their elected representatives;

(2) The European Union evidences a lack of democracy, in that real decisions are reached by the heads of government, rather than the ostensibly-democratic institutions such as the European Parliament;...

(4) The Maastricht Treaty reduces the protection of basic rights by the Federal Constitutional Court by transferring some of the responsibility for their protection to the institutions of the European Union;...

(7) The expansion of the powers of the European Union will mean that in many cases laws will be adopted not by the legislator, but by the executive that has the responsibility for enforcing them;...

In ruling on constitutional complaints, the Federal Constitutional Court first determines if they are admissible (*zulassig*), and if so, whether they are well-founded (*begrundet*). In this case, the Court found that one of the complaints regarding a diminution of democracy in the European Union was admissible, but that none of them were well-founded. Its decision on the one admissible constitutional complaint was based on the fact that, under the principle of democracy which underlies the Basic Law, the Federal Government may not assign the duties and rights of the Federal Parliament to the European Union to such an extent that the minimum requirements of democratic legitimation would be violated. That is, while the principle of democracy does not prevent Germany from becoming a member of an "inter-governmental community" such as the European Union, there must be some minimum amount of democracy which remains vested with the national authorities of the Member States. However, after examining both German constitutional law and the structure and history of the Maastricht Treaty, the Court found that no such violation had occurred in this case, since the German constitutional order evidences a favorable attitude toward European integration, and the institutions of the European Union are sufficiently democratic to survive constitutional challenge.

The Court rejected all the other constitutional complaints....With regard to basic rights, the Federal Constitutional Court found that it would continue to oversee the protection of basic rights sufficiently, and that such rights would also be protected by the European Court of Justice and other institutions of the European Union.

Analysis of the Decision. The Court's emphasis on protecting basic rights under the national laws of the Member States, rather than under the international law of human rights applicable within the European Union, leaves the reader with the distinct impression that it has less than total confidence in the ability of the Union to protect basic rights. The Court is also determined to ensure that any interpretation of the Union's powers is kept within strict limits, even stating that an interpretation which exceeds such powers would have no binding effect in Germany. This conclusion could introduce a good deal of uncertainty into the German legal system, since there is no central authority for determining when the entities of the Communities have exceeded their powers....

The decision holds important implications for the separation of powers in Germany. Under German constitutional law executive authority rests with the Federal President and the Federal Government (i.e., the Federal Chancellor and his cabinet), and legislative authority with the Federal Parliament and Federal Council. One of the complaints brought against the Maastricht Treaty was that it allows the executive to allocate powers to the European Union which properly belong to the legislative branch. While the Court did not fully accept this argument, the limits the Court set on the transfer of sovereignty from the Federal Republic of Germany may lead to strains in Germany's constitutional structure in the future if the German parliament is faced with approving a further expansion of the Union's powers.

Notes

1. Apparently, then, the supremacy of European law in German Courts depends upon the willingness of the ECJ to enforce fundamental rights. What is the position of the European Union on human rights? A specific policy has been slow to develop, but in recent years the Union has made some dramatic moves. In 1977 the Council, the Commission, and the Parliament issued a joint declaration[24] in which they asserted that:

> 1. The European Parliament, the Council and the Commission stress the prime importance they attach to the protection of fundamental rights, as derived in particular from the constitutions of the Member States and the European Convention for the Protection of Human Rights and Fundamental Freedoms.
>
> 2. In the exercise of their powers and in pursuance of the aims of the European Communities they respect and will continue to respect these rights.

2. In a 1979 case[25] the ECJ acknowledged the Convention and its own duty to recognize rights from a number of sources. And in 1992 the significance of both the Convention and national rights traditions was written into the Maastricht Treaty.

---

24. Joint Declaration by the European Parliament, the Council and the Commission Concerning the Protection of Fundamental Rights and the European Convention for the Protection of Human Rights and Fundamental Freedoms, April 5, 1977, 1977 O.J. (C103) 1.

25. Hauer v Land Rheinland-Pfalz, 13 December 1979, Case 44/79, [1980] 3 C.M.L.R. 42, European Court of Justice.

Article F (Article 6). 1. The Union shall respect the national identities of its Member States, whose systems of government are founded on the principles of democracy.

2. The Union shall respect fundamental rights, as guaranteed by the European Convention for the Protection of Human Rights and Fundamental Freedoms signed in Rome on 4 November 1950 and as they result from the constitutional traditions common to the Member States, as general principles of Community law....[26]

3. In an effort to move even further toward bringing the Union under the Convention, the Council of Ministers considered the possibility of making the Union itself (in addition to the individual member-States, all of which had ratified the European Convention on Human Rights) a signatory to the Convention. To that end, the Council asked the ECJ for an opinion on the question, whether accession to the Convention was possible for the Union. The Court replied: "As Community law now stands, the Community has no competence to accede to the European Convention for the Protection of Human Rights and Fundamental Freedoms because no provision of the Treaty confers on the Community institutions in a general way the power to enact rules concerning human rights or to conclude international agreements in this field...."[27]

4. In 1999 the European Council entrusted a special Convention with the task of drawing up a draft of a Charter of Fundamental Rights. The Convention presented its draft on October 2, 2000, and on December 7, 2000, the Presidents of the European Parliament, the Council, and the Commission signed the Charter. The reach of the rights incorporated into the document is apparently rather limited. According to Article 55, "The provisions of this Charter are addressed to the institutions and bodies of the Union with due regard for the principle of subsidiarity and to the Member States only when they are implementing Union law." According to the Principle of Subsidiarity, outside the areas entrusted exclusively to the European Union by the treaties the Union may act only where the matter could not be better dealt with by the Member States; it is a principle of deference. European action under the Charter is limited by such deference. The member-States, on the other hand, are bound by the Charter only when they are implementing Union law. As to purely domestic law, in other words, the Charter does not apply.

---

26. Treaty on European Union (Maastrict Treaty), February 7, 1992, 1992 O.J. (C 224) 1, 1 C.M.L.R. 573, *online at* <http://www.europa.eu.int/ en/record/mt/top.html>. (Original article numbers in bold, new numbering [after the Amsterdam treaty] in parentheses.)

27. Opinion 2/94 (Accession by the Communities to the Convention for the Protection of Human Rights and Fundamental Freedoms)(European Court of Justice, 28 March 1996).

5. In the draft Constitution of Europe submitted on June 27, 2003, the Charter was incorporated and provision was made for accession to the European Convention on Human Rights.

THE CONSTITUTION OF EUROPE
(DRAFT, 27 JUNE 2003)

Article 7: Fundamental rights. 1. The Union shall recognize the rights, freedoms and principles set out in the Charter of Fundamental Rights which constitutes Part II of this Constitution.

2. The Union shall seek accession to the European Convention for the Protection of Human Rights and Fundamental Freedoms. Accession to that Convention shall not affect the Union's competence as defined in this Constitution.

3. Fundamental rights, as guaranteed by the European Convention for the Protection of Human Rights and Fundamental Freedoms, and as they result from the constitutional traditions common to the Member States, shall constitute general principles of the Union's law.

INDEX OF CASES

Listed here are only those cases that are discussed at some length in the text.
All citations are to chapter sections.

Britain

Bonham's Case	II.B.

European Court of Human Rights

Dudgeon v. United Kingdom	IV.A.3.

European Court of Justice

Decision of 5 February 1963 (van Gend en Loos)	IV.C.2.
Decision of 24 February 1964 (Costa v. ENEL)	IV.C.2.
Decision of 9 March 1978 (Simmenthal)	IV.C.3.a.

French Constitutional Council

Decision of 16 January 1962	III.D.3.a.
Decision of 16 July 1971 (Simone de Beauvoir)	III.D.3.b.
Decision of 15 January 1975 (Abortion)	III.D.3.c.

French Council of State

Decision of 5 May 1944	I.B.2.
Decision of 26 June 1959 (Syndicat-General)	III.D.2.
Decision of 1 March 1968 (Semoules)	IV.C.3.b.
Decision of 20 October 1989 (Nicolo)	IV.C.3.b.

French Court of Cassation

Decision of 14 May 1975 (Jacques Vabre)	IV.C.3.b.

French Tribunal of Cassation

Decision of 3 September 1797	I.B.2.

German Constitutional Court

Decision of 25 February 1975 (Abortion I)	III.C.2.
Decision of 12 October 1993 (Maastricht Treaty)	IV.C.3.c.

INDEX OF CONSTITUTIONAL PROVISIONS

* * *

INDEX OF TREATY PROVISIONS

INDEX OF STATUTORY PROVISIONS

GENERAL INDEX